How to
Master Skills for the

Second Edition

TOEFL® iBT

SPEAKING Advanced

DARAKWON

How to
Master Skills for the   Second Edition

TOEFL® iBT
SPEAKING Advanced

Publisher Kyudo Chung
Editor Sangik Cho
Authors Michael A. Putlack, Stephen Poirier, E2K
Proofreader Michael A. Putlack
Designers Minji Kim, Hyeonju Yoon

First Published in December 2007 By Darakwon, Inc.
Second edition first published in March 2025 by Darakwon, Inc.
Darakwon Bldg., 211, Munbal-ro, Paju-si, Gyeonggi-do 10881
Republic of Korea
Tel: 02-736-2031 (Ext. 250)
Fax: 02-732-2037

ISBN 978-89-277-8095-3 14740
       978-89-277-8084-7 14740 (set)

www.darakwon.co.kr

Photo Credits
Shutterstock.com

Components Main Book / Answer Key / Free MP3 Downloads
7 6 5 4 3 2 1   25 26 27 28 29

Table of **Contents**

INTRODUCTION

1 Information on the TOEFL® iBT

A The Format of the TOEFL® iBT

Section	Number of Questions or Tasks	Timing	Score

Reading	**20 Questions**
	
	• **2 reading passages**
	  – with 10 questions per passage
	  – approximately 700 words long each
		35 Minutes	30 Points

Listening	**28 Questions**
	
	• **2 conversations**
	  – 5 questions per conversation
	  – 3 minutes each
	• **3 lectures**
	  – 6 questions per lecture
	  – 3-5 minutes each
		36 Minutes	30 Points

Speaking	**4 Tasks**
	
	• **1 independent speaking task**
	  – 1 personal choice/opinion/experience
	  – preparation: 15 sec. / response: 45 sec.
	• **2 integrated speaking tasks: Read-Listen-Speak**
	  – 1 campus situation topic
	    reading: 75-100 words (45 sec.)
	    conversation: 150-180 words (60-80 sec.)
	  – 1 academic course topic
	    reading: 75-100 words (50 sec.)
	    lecture: 150-220 words (60-120 sec.)
	  – preparation: 30 sec. / response: 60 sec.
	• **1 integrated speaking task: Listen-Speak**
	  – 1 academic course topic
	    lecture: 230-280 words (90-120 sec.)
	  – preparation: 20 sec. / response: 60 sec.
		17 Minutes	30 Points

Writing	**2 Tasks**
	
	• **1 integrated writing task: Read-Listen-Write**
	  – reading: 230-300 words (3 min.)
	  – lecture: 230-300 words (2 min.)
	  – a summary of 150-225 words (20 min.)
	• **1 academic discussion task**
	  – a minimum 100-word essay (10 min.)
		30 Minutes	30 Points

B What Is New about the TOEFL® iBT?

- The TOEFL® iBT is delivered through the Internet in secure test centers around the world at the same time.
- It tests all four language skills and is taken in the order of Reading, Listening, Speaking, and Writing.
- The test is about 2 hours long, and all of the four test sections will be completed in one day.
- Note taking is allowed throughout the entire test, including the Reading section. At the end of the test, all notes are collected and destroyed at the test center.
- In the Listening section, one lecture may be spoken with a British or Australian accent.
- There are integrated tasks requiring test takers to combine more than one language skill in the Speaking and Writing sections.
- In the Speaking section, test takers wear headphones and speak into a microphone when they respond. The responses are recorded and transmitted to ETS's Online Scoring Network.
- In the Writing section, test takers must type their responses. Handwriting is not possible.
- Test scores will be reported online. Test takers can see their scores online 4-8 business days after the test and can also receive a copy of their score report by mail.

2 Information on the Speaking Section

The Speaking section of the TOEFL® iBT measures test takers' English speaking proficiency. This section takes approximately 17 minutes and has four questions. The first question is called Independent Speaking Task, and you will be asked to speak about a familiar topic based on your personal preference. The remaining three questions are Integrated Speaking Tasks, and you will be required to integrate different language skills—listening and speaking or listening, reading, and speaking.

A Types of Speaking Tasks

- **Task 1** Independent Speaking Task: Personal Preference
  - This task will ask you to make and defend a personal choice between two possible opinions, actions, or situations. You should justify your choice with reasons and details.
  - You will be given 15 seconds to prepare your answer and 45 seconds to say which of the two options you think is preferable.

- **Task 2** Integrated Speaking Task: Reading & Conversation
  - This task will ask you to respond to a question based on what you have read and heard. You will first read a short passage presenting a campus-related issue and will then listen to a dialogue on the same topic. Then, you will be asked to summarize one speaker's opinion within the context of the reading passage.
  - You will be given 30 seconds to prepare your answer and 60 seconds to speak on the question. You should be careful not to express your own opinion in your response.

- **Task 3** Integrated Speaking Task: Reading & Lecture
  - This task also asks you to respond to a question based on what you have read and heard. You will first read a short passage about an academic subject and will then listen to an excerpt from a lecture

on that subject. Then, you will be asked to combine and convey important information from both the reading passage and the lecture.

– You will be given 30 seconds to prepare your answer and 60 seconds to speak on the question.

• **Task 4** Integrated Speaking Task: Lecture

– In this task, you will first listen to an excerpt from a lecture that explains a term or concept and gives some examples to illustrate it. Then, you will be asked to summarize the lecture and explain how the examples are connected with the overall topic.

– You will be given 20 seconds to prepare your answer and 60 seconds to respond to the question.

B Types of Speaking Topics

• Personal Experience and Preference

– The question in Task 1 will be about everyday issues of general interest to test takers. For example, a question may ask about a preference between studying at home and at the library, a preference between living in a dormitory and an off-campus apartment, or a preference between a class with a lot of discussion and one without discussion.

• Campus Situations

– The question in Task 2 will be about campus-related issues. For example, a question may ask about a university policy, rule, or procedure, future university plans, campus facilities, or the quality of life on campus.

• Academic Course Content

– The question in Task 3 will be about academic subjects. For example, a question may ask about a life science, a social science, a physical science, or a topic in the humanities like animal domestication or economics.

– The question in Task 4 will also be about academic-related topics. For example, a question may ask about a process, a method, a theory, an idea, or a phenomenon of any type in fields like natural science, social science, or psychology.

C Important Features of Evaluation

• Delivery

Delivery means how clear your speech is. In order to get good grades on the speaking tasks, you should speak smoothly and clearly, have good pronunciation, pace yourself naturally, and have natural-sounding intonation patterns.

• Language Use

Language use is about the effectiveness of your use of grammar and vocabulary to express your ideas. In order to get good grades on the speaking tasks, you should be able to use both basic and more complex language structures and choose the appropriate words.

• Topic Development

Topic development is related to how fully you respond to the question and how coherently you give your ideas. In order to get good grades on the speaking test, you should make sure that the relationship between your ideas and your progression from one idea to the next is clear and easy to follow.

HOW TO USE THIS BOOK

How to Master Skills for the TOEFL® iBT Speaking Advanced is designed to be used either as a textbook for a TOEFL® iBT speaking preparation course or as a tool for individual learners who are preparing for the TOEFL® test on their own. With a total of sixty units, this book is organized to prepare you for the test by providing you with a comprehensive understanding of the test and a thorough analysis of every question type. Each unit provides a step-by-step program that helps develop your test-taking abilities. At the back of the book are two actual tests of the Speaking section of the TOEFL® iBT.

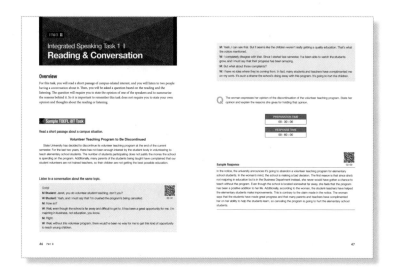

❶ Overview

This section is designed to prepare you for the type of task the part covers. You will be given a full sample question and a model answer in an illustrative structure. You will also be given information on time allotments.

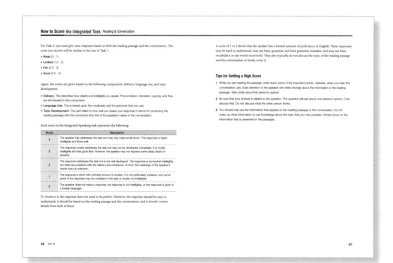

❷ How to Score the Task

This section provides the grading criteria for the task, so you can understand how responses are graded in the actual TOEFL® iBT test. Also you can use the grading table in the section to evaluate your response to each question yourself.

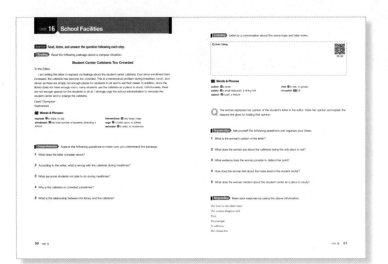

❸ Exercise

In this part of the unit, you will actually do a lot of exercises that the unit covers. The topics in the questions will be various and will reflect actual TOEFL® questions. You will be given an example to refer to and a sample response to compare with yours at the end.

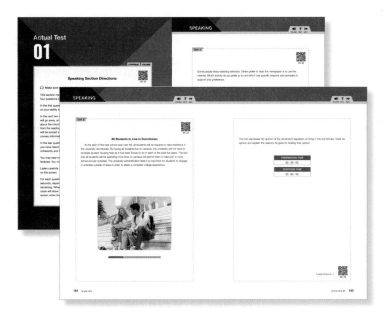

❹ Actual Test

This part will give you a chance to experience an actual TOEFL® iBT test. You will be given two sets of tests that are modeled on the Speaking section of the TOEFL® iBT. The topics are similar to those on the real test, as are the questions. This similarity will allow you to develop a sense of your test-taking ability.

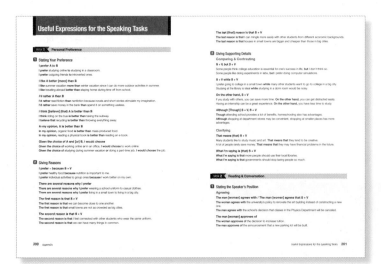

❺ Useful Expressions for the Speaking Tasks

There are a number of expressions and collocations that are typically used in every task and topic. This supplementary part will provide you with a chance to review the expressions and collocations you need to remember while working on each unit.

PART I

Independent Speaking Task
Personal Preference

The independent speaking section consists of one task. You will be presented with a question or a situation. Then, you will provide a response based upon your own ideas, opinions, and experiences. In this section, you will not read or listen to any other material. You will be given 15 seconds to prepare your answer after the question is presented, and you will have 45 seconds to respond to the question.

Independent Speaking Task **I**
Personal Preference

Overview

This task is about personal preference. It asks you to express your preference from a given pair of choices. In this task, the questions mostly ask you to express an opinion and to support it. Some other questions let you take a position and defend it. When responding to this question, you are to give some details and examples as well as reasons to rationalize your answer.

▶ Sample TOEFL iBT Task

 Some people prefer to make many friends. Others prefer to have a small number of close friends. Which approach do you think is better and why? Use specific reasons and examples to support your preference.

PREPARATION TIME
00 : 15 : 00

RESPONSE TIME
00 : 45 : 00

Sample Response

01-01

My preference is to have many different friends. For starters, I have many different interests. By maintaining a large group of friends, I can maintain all of them. For example, I can watch movies with some friends, visit museums with others, and hang out at home with even more friends. If I only had a small circle of friends, I probably wouldn't be able to engage in as many activities as I do now. Another important thing is that I love meeting all kinds of people. My friends all have different personalities. This means I get to associate with people who are completely different from one another. So depending upon my mood, I can choose which of my friends I'll talk to or go out with that day.

How to Score the Independent Task

The following scores are given for the Speaking test:

- ◆ **Weak** (0 - 1)
- ◆ **Limited** (1.5 - 2)
- ◆ **Fair** (2.5 - 3)
- ◆ **Good** (3.5 - 4)

The scores are given based on the following components: delivery, language use, and topic development.

- ◇ **Delivery**: This describes how clearly and intelligibly you speak. Pronunciation, intonation, pacing, and flow are all included in this component.
- ◇ **Language Use**: This is based upon the vocabulary and the grammar that you use.
- ◇ **Topic Development**: This part refers to how well you create your response in terms of connecting various ideas and then elaborating on them.

There is a general description of what each score indicates about the speaker's English ability. Each score on the Independent Speaking task represents the following:

Score	Description
4	The speaker fully addresses the task and may only make small errors. The response is highly intelligible and flows well.
3	The response mostly addresses the task but may not be developed completely. It is mostly intelligible and has good flow. However, the speaker may not express some ideas clearly or properly.
2	The response addresses the task but it not well developed. The response is somewhat intelligible, but there are problems with the delivery and coherence. At time, the meanings of the speaker's words may be unknown.
1	The response is short with a limited amount of contact. It is not particularly coherent, and some parts of the response may be unrelated to the task or mostly not intelligible.
0	The speaker does not make a response, the response is not intelligible, or the response is given in a foreign language.

To receive a 4, the response does not need to be perfect. However, the response should be easy to understand, it should make a good argument, and it should contain details.

A score of 1 or 2 shows that the speaker has a limited amount of proficiency in English. These responses may be hard to understand, may use basic grammar and have grammar mistakes, and may use basic vocabulary or use words incorrectly. They also typically do not discuss the topic or barely cover it.

Each score is also based on specific criteria such as the following:

Score	Delivery	Language Use	Topic Development
4	The response flows well, and the speaker's voice is clear and understandable. There could be minor pronunciation or intonation mistakes, but they do not affect how intelligible the response is.	The response uses good grammar and a high level of vocabulary. The response is spoken naturally, and the speaker uses both basic and complex grammar structures well. There may be some errors, but they do not detract from the response.	The response is well developed and is related to the task. There are clear relationships between the ideas mentioned in the response.
3	The response is mostly clear and fairly fluid. There may be some pronunciation, intonation, or pacing issues, so the listener may have to make an effort to understand the response at times.	The response uses effective grammar and vocabulary, and the ideas are mostly coherent. There may be some vocabulary that is imprecise or used improperly. The grammar structures used may be limited in range. These issues do not interfere with the understanding of the response.	The response is mostly understandable and provides ideas and information that are relevant. The response is limited in its development. It may not be specific, or the speaker may not elaborate on certain ideas. The relationships between different ideas may not always be easy to understand.
2	The response is intelligible, but the listener must make an effort to understand due to unclear speech, awkward intonation, or poor rhythm and pacing. It may not be possible to understand the meanings of some parts.	The response is limited in its grammar and vocabulary usage. This prevents the ideas in the response from being explained well. The response mostly only uses basic grammar and vocabulary well. The connections made between sentences and ideas are unclear.	The response is related to the task, but there are a limited number of ideas presented. The response does not elaborate on the ideas presented. Some ideas or sentences may be repeated, and the connections between ideas may be unclear.
1	There are many problems with pronunciation, intonation, and pacing that make understanding the response difficult or impossible. The delivery is choppy and fragmented. The speaker pauses and hesitates frequently.	The response has a limited range of grammar and vocabulary that prevents ideas from being expressed and connected to one another. Some responses may rely upon memorized expressions or those that have been practiced regularly.	There is a limited amount of related content. There are only general ideas related. The speaker may not be able to go into detail and may often repeat the prompt or other words.

Tips for Getting a High Score

1 Use the preparation time to write down a couple of the points that you want to make. It is easy to forget what you want to say when you are speaking. So write down your points to ensure that you remember everything.

2 Be sure that your answer is related to the question. Follow the instructions precisely. For instance, if the question asks which of two choices you prefer, only discuss one of them. Do not say that you prefer both.

3 You do not have to tell the truth in your response. You can make up information to make your argument. The graders are only interested in knowing how well you can speak English. So feel free to make up something about a family member or your personal life that is a good argument but may not be true.

4 Try to give two examples for your response. Do not simply develop one example. Give two and show how they are connected to each other and to the question.

5 Be sure to use a wide variety of grammar structures in your response. Try to use complex sentences— sentences with subordinating conjunctions such as *because*, *since*, *as*, and *although*—when you give your response. That will increase the quality of your response.

6 Be sure to use advanced vocabulary. That will show that you have a high level of English.

7 Do not repeat yourself when you give a response. Make a point and then move on to something else. Repeating yourself is a time waster, and you will lose points for doing it.

Unit 01 Cell Phones

Exercise Read and answer the question following each step.

Q Do you agree or disagree with the following statement?
The use of cell phones should be prohibited in public.
Give specific reasons and examples to support your opinion.

Organization Ask yourself the following questions and organize your ideas.

1 Do you believe cell phone usage should be prohibited in public or not?

2 Why do you feel that way about cell phones?

3 What reasons can you provide to back up your opinion?

Choice A	Choice B
Agree I am the kind of person who believes cell phones should definitely be prohibited in public places.	Disagree In my opinion, people should not be prohibited from using their cell phones in public.
First reason	First reason
Details	Details
Second reason	Second reason
Details	Details

Responding Make your response by using the above information.

I'm the kind of person who

For starters,

In other words,

Additionally,

Speaking Now say your response out loud and record your time. While you are speaking, do not look at the written response.

Response time: 45 seconds	Your speaking time: _____ seconds

Comparing Listen to a sample response and compare it with yours.

Choice A   Choice B

01-02   01-03

📋 **Self-Rating** Rate your response based on the following criteria.

Delivery		Score			
How clearly did you speak your response?		1	2	3	4
Language Use		**Score**			
How well did you control language structures to convey your ideas?		1	2	3	4
How appropriately did you use vocabulary to convey your ideas?		1	2	3	4
Topic Development		**Score**			
How fully did you answer the question?		1	2	3	4
How coherently did you present your ideas?		1	2	3	4

Exercise Read and answer the question following each step.

Q Some schools have all of their first-year students live together in dormitories. Other schools have first-year students live together with students from other years. Which housing arrangement do you think is better and why? Use specific reasons and examples to support your preference.

Organization Ask yourself the following questions and organize your ideas.

1 Should freshmen live with one another or be matched with students from other years?

2 What makes you feel that is the best solution?

3 What are the possible benefits to this living situation?

Choice A	Choice B
Live together with one another Personally, I prefer a situation in which all first-year students live together in dormitories.	**Live together with students from other years** I would rather attend a school that had first-year students living with upperclassmen than one where freshmen lived with other freshmen.
First reason	First reason
Details	Details
Second reason	Second reason
Details	Details

Responding ▷ Make your response by using the above information.

Personally, I prefer

First off,

Simply put,

Another important thing is

Speaking ▷ Now say your response out loud and record your time. While you are speaking, do not look at the written response.

Response time: 45 seconds	Your speaking time: _____ seconds

Comparing ▷ Listen to a sample response and compare it with yours.

Choice A   Choice B

01-04   01-05

📝 Self-Rating ▷ Rate your response based on the following criteria.

Delivery	Score			
How clearly did you speak your response?	1	2	3	4

Language Use	Score			
How well did you control language structures to convey your ideas?	1	2	3	4
How appropriately did you use vocabulary to convey your ideas?	1	2	3	4

Topic Development	Score			
How fully did you answer the question?	1	2	3	4
How coherently did you present your ideas?	1	2	3	4

Unit 03 Part-Time Jobs

Exercise Read and answer the question following each step.

Q Do you agree or disagree with the following statement?

Students should take classes during the day and work part-time jobs at night or on the weekend.

Give specific reasons and examples to support your opinion.

Organization Ask yourself the following questions and organize your ideas.

1 Do you believe that students should study during the day and work part time or not?

2 Why should students either work or not work while also studying?

3 What benefits would this have for students?

Choice A	Choice B
Agree I support the idea of having students take classes during the day and work part time either at night or on the weekend.	**Disagree** I believe college students should not be expected to study during the day and then find part-time jobs at night or on the weekend.
First reason	First reason
Details	Details
Second reason	Second reason
Details	Details

Responding Make your response by using the above information.

I believe
The first reason is
Second of all,
That way,

Speaking Now say your response out loud and record your time. While you are speaking, do not look at the written response.

Response time: 45 seconds   Your speaking time: _____ seconds

Comparing Listen to a sample response and compare it with yours.

Choice A	Choice B
01-06	01-07

Self-Rating Rate your response based on the following criteria.

Delivery	Score			
How clearly did you speak your response?	1	2	3	4
Language Use	**Score**			
How well did you control language structures to convey your ideas?	1	2	3	4
How appropriately did you use vocabulary to convey your ideas?	1	2	3	4
Topic Development	**Score**			
How fully did you answer the question?	1	2	3	4
How coherently did you present your ideas?	1	2	3	4

Exercise Read and answer the question following each step.

Q Some people believe it is better to go to university or college right after graduating from high school. Other people believe it is better to take a year off between high school and university or college. Which do you prefer and why? Give specific reasons and examples to support your opinion.

Organization > Ask yourself the following questions and organize your ideas.

1 Should a person go to college or university immediately after high school or take a year off?

2 Why do you feel that this is the better solution for a high school graduate?

3 What are the benefits of attending college or university in this manner?

Choice A	Choice B
Go to college or university immediately In my opinion, a person should attend college or university immediately after graduating from high school.	**Take a year off** I believe it is better for people to take a year off between high school and college.
First reason	First reason
Details	Details
Second reason	Second reason
Details	Details

Responding Make your response by using the above information.

I believe

For one,

Another thing is

For example,

Speaking Now say your response out loud and record your time. While you are speaking, do not look at the written response.

Response time: 45 seconds	Your speaking time: _____ seconds

Comparing Listen to a sample response and compare it with yours.

Choice A   Choice B

01-08   01-09

Self-Rating Rate your response based on the following criteria.

Delivery	Score			
How clearly did you speak your response?	1	2	3	4

Language Use	Score			
How well did you control language structures to convey your ideas?	1	2	3	4
How appropriately did you use vocabulary to convey your ideas?	1	2	3	4

Topic Development	Score			
How fully did you answer the question?	1	2	3	4
How coherently did you present your ideas?	1	2	3	4

Unit 05 Measures of Success

Exercise Read and answer the question following each step.

Q
Do you agree or disagree with the following statement?
Having money and power is the best way to measure success.
Give specific reasons and examples to support your opinion.

Organization Ask yourself the following questions and organize your ideas.

1 Do you agree or disagree that money and power are the best measures of success?

2 Why do you believe these are the best measures of success?

3 What reasons can you give to defend your opinion?

Choice A	Choice B
Agree I would agree that money and power are the two best measures of a person's success.	**Disagree** I could not disagree more that money and power are the most important indicators of success.
First reason	First reason
Details	Details
Second reason	Second reason
Details	Details

Responding ▶ Make your response by using the above information.

Personally, I think

The first reason is

Another good point is

In other words,

Speaking ▶ Now say your response out loud and record your time. While you are speaking, do not look at the written response.

Response time: 45 seconds   Your speaking time: _____ seconds

Comparing ▶ Listen to a sample response and compare it with yours.

Choice A   Choice B

01-10   01-11

Self-Rating ▶ Rate your response based on the following criteria.

Delivery	Score			
How clearly did you speak your response?	1	2	3	4

Language Use	Score			
How well did you control language structures to convey your ideas?	1	2	3	4
How appropriately did you use vocabulary to convey your ideas?	1	2	3	4

Topic Development	Score			
How fully did you answer the question?	1	2	3	4
How coherently did you present your ideas?	1	2	3	4

Exercise Read and answer the question following each step.

Q Some people like to read nonfiction books. Others like reading fiction books. Which kind of books do you like to read and why? Use specific reasons and examples to support your preference.

Organization Ask yourself the following questions and organize your ideas.

1 Do you prefer to read either nonfiction or fiction books?

2 Why do you enjoy reading books in this genre?

3 What is it about this genre that attracts you?

Choice A	Choice B
Reading nonfiction books I prefer to read nonfiction books much more than fiction books.	**Reading fiction books** I love reading books, and most of all, I prefer to read works of fiction instead of nonfiction.
First reason	First reason
Details	Details
Second reason	Second reason
Details	Details

Responding Make your response by using the above information.

Of the two options, I prefer to

One reason I prefer this is

On the other hand,

Another good point is

Speaking Now say your response out loud and record your time. While you are speaking, do not look at the written response.

Response time: 45 seconds   Your speaking time: _____ seconds

Comparing Listen to a sample response and compare it with yours.

Choice A   Choice B

01-12   01-13

Self-Rating Rate your response based on the following criteria.

Delivery	Score			
How clearly did you speak your response?	1	2	3	4
Language Use	**Score**			
How well did you control language structures to convey your ideas?	1	2	3	4
How appropriately did you use vocabulary to convey your ideas?	1	2	3	4
Topic Development	**Score**			
How fully did you answer the question?	1	2	3	4
How coherently did you present your ideas?	1	2	3	4

Exercise Read and answer the question following each step.

Q Some people like to watch films. Others like to attend concerts. Which activity do you prefer to do? Give specific reasons and examples to support your opinion.

Organization Ask yourself the following questions and organize your ideas.

1 Do you prefer to watch films or to attend concerts?

2 Why do you enjoy doing this activity?

3 What features of films or concerts are so attractive to you?

Choice A	Choice B
Watching films As for me, I prefer watching films to attending concerts.	**Attending concerts** I would say I prefer attending concerts rather than watching films.
First reason	First reason
Details	Details
Second reason	Second reason
Details	Details

▌Responding Make your response by using the above information.

As for me, I prefer

One of the main reasons is

For example,

Another important thing is

▌Speaking Now say your response out loud and record your time. While you are speaking, do not look at the written response.

Response time: 45 seconds	Your speaking time: _____ seconds

▌Comparing Listen to a sample response and compare it with yours.

Choice A   Choice B

01-14   01-15

▌Self-Rating Rate your response based on the following criteria.

Delivery	Score			
How clearly did you speak your response?	1	2	3	4
Language Use	**Score**			
How well did you control language structures to convey your ideas?	1	2	3	4
How appropriately did you use vocabulary to convey your ideas?	1	2	3	4
Topic Development	**Score**			
How fully did you answer the question?	1	2	3	4
How coherently did you present your ideas?	1	2	3	4

Unit **08** | Summer Vacation Activities

Exercise Read and answer the question following each step.

Q Some students like to stay on campus and attend school during summer vacation. Other students prefer to get jobs and to work off campus. Which activity do you think is better and why? Use specific reasons and examples to support your preference.

Organization Ask yourself the following questions and organize your ideas.

1 Do you think it is better for students to take classes or to work off campus during summer?

2 Why do you feel that way about your choice?

3 How could a student benefit by doing this activity during summer?

Choice A	Choice B
Take classes In my opinion, it is better for students to remain on campus and to take classes during summer.	**Work off campus** I truly believe college students would be wise to get jobs and to work off campus during their summer vacations.
First reason	First reason
Details	Details
Second reason	Second reason
Details	Details

28 Part I

Responding Make your response by using the above information.

In my opinion,

For starters,

In addition,

Another reason is

Speaking Now say your response out loud and record your time. While you are speaking, do not look at the written response.

Response time: 45 seconds	Your speaking time: _____ seconds

Comparing Listen to a sample response and compare it with yours.

Choice A   Choice B

01-16   01-17

Self-Rating Rate your response based on the following criteria.

Delivery	Score			
How clearly did you speak your response?	1	2	3	4

Language Use	Score			
How well did you control language structures to convey your ideas?	1	2	3	4
How appropriately did you use vocabulary to convey your ideas?	1	2	3	4

Topic Development	Score			
How fully did you answer the question?	1	2	3	4
How coherently did you present your ideas?	1	2	3	4

Exercise Read and answer the question following each step.

Q Do you agree or disagree with the following statement?

People in modern society live more comfortable lives than their grandparents' generation did.

Give specific reasons and examples to support your opinion.

Organization Ask yourself the following questions and organize your ideas.

1 Do you agree that people in modern times live more comfortably than their grandparents?

2 Why do you believe this to be correct?

3 What particular aspects now or in the past make or made life more comfortable?

Choice A	Choice B
Agree I must agree that people in modern society have lives vastly more comfortable than the lives which my grandparents' generation lived.	Disagree I actually disagree with the statement and feel that my grandparents' generation led more comfortable lives.
First reason	First reason
Details	Details
Second reason	Second reason
Details	Details

Responding Make your response by using the above information.

I must agree that

One reason I feel like this is

Second,

Therefore

Speaking Now say your response out loud and record your time. While you are speaking, do not look at the written response.

| Response time: 45 seconds | Your speaking time: _____ seconds |

Comparing Listen to a sample response and compare it with yours.

Choice A   Choice B

01-18   01-19

Self-Rating Rate your response based on the following criteria.

Delivery	Score			
How clearly did you speak your response?	1	2	3	4

Language Use	Score			
How well did you control language structures to convey your ideas?	1	2	3	4
How appropriately did you use vocabulary to convey your ideas?	1	2	3	4

Topic Development	Score			
How fully did you answer the question?	1	2	3	4
How coherently did you present your ideas?	1	2	3	4

Exercise Read and answer the question following each step.

Q Do you agree or disagree with the following statement?
People cannot learn important lessons about life in classrooms.
Give specific reasons and examples to support your opinion.

Organization Ask yourself the following questions and organize your ideas.

1 Do you think people can or cannot learn important lessons about life in classrooms?

2 Why do you think that this is the case?

3 What examples do you know that prove or disprove this statement?

Choice A	Choice B
Agree I agree that people cannot learn important lessons about life in the classroom.	Disagree I could not disagree more with the statement that students cannot learn about life in the classroom.
First reason	First reason
Details	Details
Second reason	Second reason
Details	Details

▶ Responding Make your response by using the above information.

I think it is right to say that

First of all,

For example,

Secondly,

▶ Speaking Now say your response out loud and record your time. While you are speaking, do not look at the written response.

Response time: 45 seconds	Your speaking time: _____ seconds

▶ Comparing Listen to a sample response and compare it with yours.

Choice A   Choice B

01-20   01-21

📝 Self-Rating Rate your response based on the following criteria.

Delivery	Score			
How clearly did you speak your response?	1	2	3	4

Language Use	Score			
How well did you control language structures to convey your ideas?	1	2	3	4
How appropriately did you use vocabulary to convey your ideas?	1	2	3	4

Topic Development	Score			
How fully did you answer the question?	1	2	3	4
How coherently did you present your ideas?	1	2	3	4

Exercise Read and answer the question following each step.

Q Some people prefer to take classes in the morning. Other people prefer taking classes in the afternoon. When do you like taking classes and why? Use specific reasons and examples to support your preference.

Organization Ask yourself the following questions and organize your ideas.

1 Do you prefer to take classes in the morning or in the afternoon?

2 Why do you feel that way?

3 What are the benefits to having classes at that time?

Choice A	Choice B
Taking classes in the morning I would much rather take classes in the morning.	Taking classes in the afternoon Of the two choices, taking classes in the afternoon is more appealing to me than taking classes in the morning.
First reason	First reason
Details	Details
Second reason	Second reason
Details	Details

Responding ▶ Make your response by using the above information.

For one thing,

Another reason I prefer

Of the two choices,

One of the reasons is

Speaking ▶ Now say your response out loud and record your time. While you are speaking, do not look at the written response.

Response time: 45 seconds	Your speaking time: _____ seconds

Comparing ▶ Listen to a sample response and compare it with yours.

Choice A 01-22   Choice B 01-23

Self-Rating ▶ Rate your response based on the following criteria.

Delivery		Score		
How clearly did you speak your response?	1	2	3	4
Language Use		**Score**		
How well did you control language structures to convey your ideas?	1	2	3	4
How appropriately did you use vocabulary to convey your ideas?	1	2	3	4
Topic Development		**Score**		
How fully did you answer the question?	1	2	3	4
How coherently did you present your ideas?	1	2	3	4

Exercise Read and answer the question following each step.

Q Do you agree or disagree with the following statement?
All students should do volunteer work on weekends.
Give specific reasons and examples to support your opinion.

Organization Ask yourself the following questions and organize your ideas.

1 Do you believe that all students should do volunteer work on weekends or not?

2 What makes you support your belief?

3 What are some benefits and drawbacks to volunteering on weekends?

Choice A	Choice B
Agree I strongly agree that all students should do volunteer work on weekends.	**Disagree** I disagree that all students should do volunteer work on weekends.
First reason	First reason
Details	Details
Second reason	Second reason
Details	Details

Responding Make your response by using the above information.

I strongly agree that

As for me,

The primary reason is that

As an example,

Speaking Now say your response out loud and record your time. While you are speaking, do not look at the written response.

Response time: 45 seconds	Your speaking time: _____ seconds

Comparing Listen to a sample response and compare it with yours.

Choice A   Choice B

01-24   01-25

Self-Rating Rate your response based on the following criteria.

Delivery	Score			
How clearly did you speak your response?	1	2	3	4
Language Use	**Score**			
How well did you control language structures to convey your ideas?	1	2	3	4
How appropriately did you use vocabulary to convey your ideas?	1	2	3	4
Topic Development	**Score**			
How fully did you answer the question?	1	2	3	4
How coherently did you present your ideas?	1	2	3	4

Exercise Read and answer the question following each step.

Q Do you agree or disagree with the following statement?
Everyone should be required to recycle.
Give specific reasons and examples to support your opinion.

Organization Ask yourself the following questions and organize your ideas.

1 Do you believe that everyone should be required to recycle or not?

2 Why do you have that opinion?

3 What are some of the benefits and drawbacks to recycling?

Choice A	Choice B
Agree I believe that everyone should be required to recycle, so I agree with the statement.	**Disagree** I do not agree with the statement that everyone should have to recycle.
First reason	First reason
Details	Details
Second reason	Second reason
Details	Details

Make your response by using the above information.

One thing to remember is

Something else to consider is

Secondly,

In other words,

Speaking Now say your response out loud and record your time. While you are speaking, do not look at the written response.

Response time: 45 seconds   Your speaking time: _____ seconds

Comparing Listen to a sample response and compare it with yours.

Choice A   Choice B

01- 26   01- 27

Self-Rating Rate your response based on the following criteria.

Delivery	Score			
How clearly did you speak your response?	1	2	3	4
Language Use	**Score**			
How well did you control language structures to convey your ideas?	1	2	3	4
How appropriately did you use vocabulary to convey your ideas?	1	2	3	4
Topic Development	**Score**			
How fully did you answer the question?	1	2	3	4
How coherently did you present your ideas?	1	2	3	4

Unit 14 Sleeping Arrangements on Trips

Exercise Read and answer the question following each step.

Q Some people enjoy going camping and sleeping outdoors on trips. Other people enjoy staying at hotels on trips. Which type of trip do you think is better and why? Use specific reasons and examples to support your preference.

Organization Ask yourself the following questions and organize your ideas.

1 Do you like camping and sleeping outdoors or staying at hotels on trips?

2 Why do you prefer that type of sleeping arrangement?

3 How do you feel when you sleep that way?

Choice A	Choice B
Camping and sleeping outdoors I absolutely love to spend time outdoors, so given the two choices, I would prefer to go camping and to sleep outdoors.	**Staying at hotels** Of the two choices I was given, I would take the latter one, so I prefer to sleep at hotels on my trips.
First reason	First reason
Details	Details
Second reason	Second reason
Details	Details

Responding Make your response by using the above information.

I would prefer to

Firstly,

A second reason is

Instead,

Speaking Now say your response out loud and record your time. While you are speaking, do not look at the written response.

Response time: 45 seconds	Your speaking time: _____ seconds

Comparing Listen to a sample response and compare it with yours.

Choice A   Choice B

01- 28   01- 29

Self-Rating Rate your response based on the following criteria.

Delivery	Score			
How clearly did you speak your response?	1	2	3	4

Language Use	Score			
How well did you control language structures to convey your ideas?	1	2	3	4
How appropriately did you use vocabulary to convey your ideas?	1	2	3	4

Topic Development	Score			
How fully did you answer the question?	1	2	3	4
How coherently did you present your ideas?	1	2	3	4

Exercise Read and answer the question following each step.

Q Some people prefer to read printed books. Other people prefer reading e-books. Which type of book do you prefer to read and why? Use specific reasons and examples to support your preference.

Organization Ask yourself the following questions and organize your ideas.

1 When you read, do you prefer printed books or e-books?

2 Why do you like reading that type of book?

3 What are some advantages of each type of book?

Choice A	Choice B
Reading printed books I would much rather read printed books than e-books for a couple of reasons.	Reading e-books I know that many people prefer printed books, but I love technology, so I would much rather read e-books.
First reason	First reason
Details	Details
Second reason	Second reason
Details	Details

Responding Make your response by using the above information.

I would much rather

One of them is

For one thing,

Another important thing is

Speaking Now say your response out loud and record your time. While you are speaking, do not look at the written response.

Response time: 45 seconds   Your speaking time: _____ seconds

Comparing Listen to a sample response and compare it with yours.

Choice A   Choice B

01-30   01-31

Self-Rating Rate your response based on the following criteria.

Delivery	Score			
How clearly did you speak your response?	1	2	3	4

Language Use	Score			
How well did you control language structures to convey your ideas?	1	2	3	4
How appropriately did you use vocabulary to convey your ideas?	1	2	3	4

Topic Development	Score			
How fully did you answer the question?	1	2	3	4
How coherently did you present your ideas?	1	2	3	4

PART II

Reading & Conversation

....

The integrated speaking section consists of three tasks. These tasks will present you with a reading passage and a listening conversation or lecture or merely a listening lecture. Topics will come from a variety of fields, but they are normally based on campus situations or are academic topics.

In this task, you will be presented with a short reading passage about a campus situation topic. Next, you will listen to a short conversation between two students about the same topic. Then, you will provide a response based upon what you read and heard. You will be asked to describe one student's opinion about the topic in the reading passage. You will be given 30 seconds to prepare your answer after the question is presented, and you will have 60 seconds to respond to the question.

Integrated Speaking Task 1 | Reading & Conversation

Overview

For this task, you will read a short passage of campus-related interest, and you will listen to two people having a conversation about it. Then, you will be asked a question based on the reading and the listening. The question will require you to state the opinion of one of the speakers and to summarize the reasons behind it. So it is important to remember this task does not require you to state your own opinion and thoughts about the reading or listening.

Sample TOEFL iBT Task

Read a short passage about a campus situation.

Volunteer Teaching Program to Be Discontinued

State University has decided to discontinue its volunteer teaching program at the end of the current semester. For the last two years, there has not been enough interest by the student body in volunteering to teach elementary school students. The number of students participating does not justify the money the school is spending on the program. Additionally, many parents of the students being taught have complained that our student volunteers are not trained teachers, so their children are not getting the best possible education.

Listen to a conversation about the same topic.

> **Script**
>
> **M Student**: Janet, you do volunteer student teaching, don't you?
>
> **W Student**: Yeah, and I must say that I'm crushed the program's being canceled.
>
> **M**: How so?
>
> **W**: Well, even though the school is far away and difficult to get to, it has been a great opportunity for me. I'm majoring in business, not education, you know.
>
> **M**: Right.
>
> **W**: Well, without this volunteer program, there would've been no way for me to get this kind of opportunity to teach young children.

02-01

M: Yeah, I can see that. But it seems like the children weren't really getting a quality education. That's what the notice mentioned.

W: I completely disagree with that. Since I started last semester, I've been able to watch the students grow, and I must say that their progress has been amazing.

M: But what about those complaints?

W: I have no idea where they're coming from. In fact, many students and teachers have complimented me on my work. It's such a shame the school's doing away with this program. It's going to hurt the children.

Q The woman expresses her opinion of the discontinuation of the volunteer teaching program. State her opinion and explain the reasons she gives for holding that opinion.

PREPARATION TIME
00 : 30 : 00

RESPONSE TIME
00 : 60 : 00

Sample Response
02-02

In the notice, the university announces it's going to abandon a volunteer teaching program for elementary school students. In the woman's mind, the school is making a bad decision. The first reason is that since she's not majoring in education but is in the Business Department instead, she never would have gotten a chance to teach without the program. Even though the school is located somewhat far away, she feels that the program has been a positive addition to her life. Additionally, according to the woman, the student-teachers have helped the elementary students make improvements. This is contrary to the claim made in the notice. The woman says that the students have made great progress and that many parents and teachers have complimented her on her ability to help the students learn, so canceling the program is going to hurt the elementary school students.

For Task 2, you must give your response based on both the reading passage and the conversation. The score you receive will be similar to the one in Task 1:

◆ **Weak** (0 - 1)

◆ **Limited** (1.5 - 2)

◆ **Fair** (2.5 - 3)

◆ **Good** (3.5 - 4)

Again, the scores are given based on the following components: delivery, language use, and topic development.

◇ **Delivery**: This describes how clearly and intelligibly you speak. Pronunciation, intonation, pacing, and flow are all included in this component.

◇ **Language Use**: This is based upon the vocabulary and the grammar that you use.

◇ **Topic Development**: This part refers to how well you create your response in terms of connecting the reading passage with the comments that one of the speakers makes in the conversation.

Each score on the Integrated Speaking task represents the following:

Score	Description
4	The speaker fully addresses the task and may only make small errors. The response is highly intelligible and flows well.
3	The response mostly addresses the task but may not be developed completely. It is mostly intelligible and has good flow. However, the speaker may not express some ideas clearly or properly.
2	The response addresses the task but is not well developed. The response is somewhat intelligible, but there are problems with the delivery and coherence. At time, the meanings of the speaker's words may be unknown.
1	The response is short with a limited amount of contact. It is not particularly coherent, and some parts of the response may be unrelated to the task or mostly not intelligible.
0	The speaker does not make a response, the response is not intelligible, or the response is given in a foreign language.

To receive a 4, the response does not need to be perfect. However, the response should be easy to understand, it should be based on the reading passage and the conversation, and it should contain details from both of them.

A score of 1 or 2 shows that the speaker has a limited amount of proficiency in English. These responses may be hard to understand, may use basic grammar and have grammar mistakes, and may use basic vocabulary or use words incorrectly. They also typically do not discuss the topic of the reading passage and the conversation or barely cover it.

Tips for Getting a High Score

1 While you are reading the passage, write down some of the important points. Likewise, when you hear the conversation, pay close attention to the speaker who feels strongly about the information in the reading passage. Take notes about that person's opinion.

2 Be sure that your answer is related to the question. The question will ask about one person's opinion. Only discuss that. Do not discuss what the other person thinks.

3 You should only use the information that appears in the reading passage or the conversation. Do not make up other information or use knowledge about the topic that you may possess. Simply focus on the information that is presented in the passages.

Exercise Read, listen, and answer the question following each step.

Reading Read the following passage about a campus situation.

Student Center Cafeteria Too Crowded

To the Editor,

I am writing this letter to express my feelings about the student center cafeteria. Ever since enrollment here increased, the cafeteria has become too crowded. This is a tremendous problem during breakfast, lunch, and dinner as there are simply not enough places for students to sit and to eat their meals. In addition, since the library does not have enough room, many students use the cafeteria as a place to study. Unfortunately, there are not enough spaces for the students to sit at. I strongly urge the school administration to renovate the student center and to enlarge the cafeteria.

David Thompson
Sophomore

📖 Words & Phrases

express v to state; to say
enrollment n the total number of students attending a school

tremendous a very large; huge
urge v to insist upon; to advise
renovate v to redo; to modernize

Comprehension Answer the following questions to make sure you understand the passage.

1 What does the letter complain about?

2 According to the writer, what is wrong with the cafeteria during mealtimes?

3 What are some students not able to do during mealtimes?

4 Why is the cafeteria so crowded sometimes?

5 What is the relationship between the library and the cafeteria?

Listen to a conversation about the same topic and take notes.

Note Taking

02-03

📖 Words & Phrases

author n a writer
eatery n a small restaurant; a dining hall
aspect n a part; a feature

chat v to talk; to gossip
occupied adj full

Q The woman expresses her opinion of the student's letter to the editor. State her opinion and explain the reasons she gives for holding that opinion.

Organization Ask yourself the following questions and organize your ideas.

1 What is the woman's opinion of the letter?

2 What does the woman say about the cafeteria being the only place to eat?

3 What evidence does the woman provide to defend her point?

4 How does the woman feel about the noise level in the student center?

5 What does the woman mention about the student center as a place to study?

Responding Make your response by using the above information.

The letter to the editor states

The woman disagrees with

First,

For example,

In addition,

She claims that

Speaking ▷ Now say your response out loud and record your time. While you are speaking, do not look at the written response.

Response time: 60 seconds	Your speaking time: _____ seconds

Comparing ▷ Listen to a sample response and compare it with yours.

02-04

📋 Self-Rating Rate your response based on the following criteria.

Delivery	Score			
How clearly did you speak your response?	1	2	3	4

Language Use	Score			
How well did you control language structures to convey your ideas?	1	2	3	4
How appropriately did you use vocabulary to convey your ideas?	1	2	3	4

Topic Development	Score			
How fully did you answer the question?	1	2	3	4
How coherently did you present your ideas?	1	2	3	4

Exercise Read, listen, and answer the question following each step.

Reading Read the following passage about a campus situation.

All Freshmen May Live on Campus

Beginning next semester, all freshmen will be eligible to live in student dormitories on campus. The previous rule not guaranteeing on-campus housing for freshmen has been changed due to numerous complaints by both students and parents. This new regulation will permit first-year students more easily to form study groups with their peers on campus. This should enable them to improve their overall grade point averages. Additionally, the university has determined there is enough space in school parking lots to accommodate the extra cars that will be parked there by freshmen, so parking will not be an issue to consider.

📖 Words & Phrases

eligible (adj) entitled to something
regulation (n) a rule; a law
peer (n) an equal; someone the same age as another

grade point average (n) the total average of a student's grades
accommodate (v) to fit; to have room for

Comprehension Answer the following questions to make sure you understand the passage.

1 What is mentioned in the announcement?

2 What should freshmen now be able to do more easily?

3 How should students benefit from this?

4 What should all first year students be able to do next semester?

5 How was this decision reached?

Listening — Listen to a conversation about the same topic and take notes.

📝 Note Taking

02-05

📖 Words & Phrases

illogical adj unreasonable; lacking in logic or reason
atmosphere n a mood; a feeling
conducive adj helpful to; favorable

incidentally adv by the way
jam packed adj completely full; very crowded

Q The woman expresses her opinion of the university's change in policy. State her opinion and explain the reasons she gives for holding that opinion.

Organization — Ask yourself the following questions and organize your ideas.

1 What is the woman's opinion of the university's change in policy?

2 How does the woman feel about the student environment in the dormitories?

3 When did the woman actually join a study group?

4 What does the woman think will happen to the campus parking situation?

5 What will the result of not building new parking lots be?

Responding — Make your response by using the above information.

The announcement mentions that

However, the woman opposes

One reason she gives is

In fact,

The second reason the woman mentions

She clearly believes

Speaking Now say your response out loud and record your time. While you are speaking, do not look at the written response.

Response time: 60 seconds　　Your speaking time: _____ seconds

Comparing Listen to a sample response and compare it with yours.

02-06

Self-Rating Rate your response based on the following criteria.

Delivery	Score			
How clearly did you speak your response?	1	2	3	4

Language Use	Score			
How well did you control language structures to convey your ideas?	1	2	3	4
How appropriately did you use vocabulary to convey your ideas?	1	2	3	4

Topic Development	Score			
How fully did you answer the question?	1	2	3	4
How coherently did you present your ideas?	1	2	3	4

Exercise Read, listen, and answer the question following each step.

Reading Read the following passage about a campus situation.

Summertime Dormitory Policy

On account of severe space restrictions, returning students will not be able to leave all of their possessions in their dormitory rooms as usual during summer school. Because of the expansion of special summer programs, more dormitory rooms than normal will be used this summer. Therefore, students will be restricted to three boxes apiece for the duration of summer. While this may not seem like much, this policy is being implemented to ensure that all students are treated in the fairest, most equitable possible manner. The housing office has more information concerning this policy.

Words & Phrases

severe adj strict; harsh
expansion n development; growth
duration n a period of time; an extent

implement v to employ; to practice
equitable adj fair; even

Comprehension Answer the following questions to make sure you understand the passage.

1 What change in school policy is covered by the announcement?

2 Why can students no longer leave all of their possessions at school during summer?

3 What will be a result of the increase in special summer programs?

4 Why has the school decided to implement this regulation?

5 What will the school be able to guarantee by limiting students to three boxes each?

Listening ▶ Listen to a conversation about the same topic and take notes.

⊘ Note Taking

02-07

📖 Words & Phrases

aggravated adj irritated; annoyed

unfortunate adj regrettable; unlucky

mover n a person who moves someone's property from one place to another

not add up phr not to make sense

serve one's needs phr to assist someone

Q The woman expresses her opinion of the change in the university's policy. State her opinion and explain the reasons she gives for holding that opinion.

Organization ▶ Ask yourself the following questions and organize your ideas.

1 What opinion of the change in the university's policy does the woman hold?

2 Why is the woman unable to take her possessions with her?

3 What would the woman have to do to get all of her possessions home?

4 How does the woman respond to the school's claim that there is not enough room on campus?

5 What does the woman mention about the new dormitory?

Responding ▶ Make your response by using the above information.

The announcement declares that

The woman speaks out against

To begin with,

She states that

Her next point of contention is that

She says that

Speaking Now say your response out loud and record your time. While you are speaking, do not look at the written response.

Response time: 60 seconds   Your speaking time: _____ seconds

Comparing Listen to a sample response and compare it with yours.

02-08

Self-Rating Rate your response based on the following criteria.

Delivery	Score			
How clearly did you speak your response?	1	2	3	4
Language Use	**Score**			
How well did you control language structures to convey your ideas?	1	2	3	4
How appropriately did you use vocabulary to convey your ideas?	1	2	3	4
Topic Development	**Score**			
How fully did you answer the question?	1	2	3	4
How coherently did you present your ideas?	1	2	3	4

Exercise Read, listen, and answer the question following each step.

Reading Read the following passage about a campus situation.

Student Numbers to Increase in Seminars

Seminar classes will no longer be restricted to fifteen students per class. Instead, the number of students permitted to take each seminar has increased to twenty-five. Not enough students have been able to enroll in these discussion-based seminars despite their popularity because of a lack of instructors. This change will ensure students will be able to register in the seminar of their choice. Since our freshman and sophomore classes are much bigger than we had anticipated, this will guarantee that all students can fulfill their graduation requirement of taking at least one seminar class.

📖 Words & Phrases

restrict v to limit
enroll v to sign up for; to register for
lack n an absence; a deficiency of

anticipate v to expect; to await
fulfill v to complete; to satisfy

Comprehension Answer the following questions to make sure you understand the passage.

1 What change does the notice describe?

2 What is the first reason as to why the change is being made?

3 Why are students not always able to take the seminars they want to?

4 What is the second reason mentioned for making the change?

5 In what way will this change help students graduate?

Listening Listen to a conversation about the same topic and take notes.

✏ Note Taking

02-09

📖 **Words & Phrases**

slight adj small; minor

suffer v to experience something unpleasant

disturbed adj bothered; annoyed

insufficient adj lacking; not enough; inadequate

misguided adj foolish; erroneous

Q The man expresses his opinion of the new regulation on seminars. State his opinion and explain the reasons he gives for holding that opinion.

Organization Ask yourself the following questions and organize your ideas.

1 How does the man feel about the new regulation on seminars?

2 How does the style of the seminars influence the man's opinion?

3 Why does the man feel the larger class numbers will negatively affect the seminars?

4 What does the man say about hiring more part-time professors at the school?

5 Why does the man believe it is a mistake to hire part-time professors?

Responding Make your response by using the above information.

The topic of the notice is

The male student opposes

He claims

Furthermore,

Overall,

Speaking Now say your response out loud and record your time. While you are speaking, do not look at the written response.

Response time: 60 seconds	Your speaking time: _____ seconds

Comparing Listen to a sample response and compare it with yours.

02-10

Self-Rating Rate your response based on the following criteria.

Delivery	Score			
How clearly did you speak your response?	1	2	3	4

Language Use	Score			
How well did you control language structures to convey your ideas?	1	2	3	4
How appropriately did you use vocabulary to convey your ideas?	1	2	3	4

Topic Development	Score			
How fully did you answer the question?	1	2	3	4
How coherently did you present your ideas?	1	2	3	4

Exercise Read, listen, and answer the question following each step.

Reading Read the following passage about a campus situation.

Seniors Eligible to Teach Freshman Classes

Central University is beginning a new program in the fall semester. Eligible seniors may now co-teach certain classes alongside a professor in their department. Students must have a 3.50 GPA both overall and in their major to qualify as teachers. This program should be of particular interest to students considering pursuing teaching careers although that is not a requisite to become an instructor. Student-teachers will need to prepare lesson plans and make themselves available for office hours for their students as well. Inquire at the student services office for more information.

📖 Words & Phrases

co-teach v to teach together with another person
alongside prep beside; next to
pursue v to chase; to follow

requisite n a requirement
lesson plan n a detailed plan for a class

Comprehension Answer the following questions to make sure you understand the passage.

1 What is the topic of the notice?

2 How can a student become eligible for this program?

3 What kind of GPA do students need to participate in the program?

4 Which students in particular may be interested in this program?

5 What will students accepted to the program have to do?

Listening Listen to a conversation about the same topic and take notes.

⌧ Note Taking

02-11

📖 **Words & Phrases**

entertain the notion phr to consider; to think about an idea
intriguing adj interesting; fascinating
prospect n the potential

terribly adv very; extremely
upperclassman n a college junior or senior

Q The man expresses his opinion of the co-teaching program the university is creating. State his opinion and explain the reasons he gives for holding that opinion.

Organization Ask yourself the following questions and organize your ideas.

1 What is the man's opinion of the new co-teaching program?

2 What does the man think a result of the program will be?

3 In what way will that help students in the future?

4 What does the man feel about student-teachers having to keep office hours?

5 How does the man compare the time professors have to the time students have?

Responding Make your response by using the above information.

The topic of the notice is

In the man's mind,

First, he thinks that

He feels

Another reason is that

He mentions

Speaking ▸ Now say your response out loud and record your time. While you are speaking, do not look at the written response.

Response time: 60 seconds	Your speaking time: _____ seconds

Comparing ▸ Listen to a sample response and compare it with yours.

02-12

Self-Rating Rate your response based on the following criteria.

Delivery	Score			
How clearly did you speak your response?	1	2	3	4

Language Use	Score			
How well did you control language structures to convey your ideas?	1	2	3	4
How appropriately did you use vocabulary to convey your ideas?	1	2	3	4

Topic Development	Score			
How fully did you answer the question?	1	2	3	4
How coherently did you present your ideas?	1	2	3	4

Unit 21 Night Classes

Exercise Read, listen, and answer the question following each step.

Reading Read the following passage about a campus situation.

Night Classes to Be Offered

Due to overwhelming demand, the school will offer night classes on a limited basis this spring semester starting in January. Night school classes will be taught between the hours of six and ten in the evening. These classes, however, will be open only to students currently employed full time. Students must provide proof of employment to be able to register. Night school classes will be held in every department and should enable those students with jobs to facilitate their studies while not interrupting their work schedules.

📖 Words & Phrases

overwhelming [adj] enormous; tremendous
limited [adj] restricted
proof [n] verification; evidence

facilitate [v] to simplify; to make easier
interrupt [v] to disrupt

Comprehension Answer the following questions to make sure you understand the passage.

1 What has the university decided to do?

2 Why is the school making this change?

3 How many students have requested the change to be made?

4 Which students will be able to benefit from the program?

5 Why will these students be able to benefit from the program?

🖊 **Note Taking**

02-13

📖 **Words & Phrases**

confess v to admit; to declare

coursework n the work one does in a class during the entire semester

tailor v to adapt; to modify

be denied an opportunity phr not to be given a chance to do something

wreak havoc phr to damage; to destroy

Q The man expresses his opinion of the new night school program. State his opinion and explain the reasons he gives for holding that opinion.

Organization Ask yourself the following questions and organize your ideas.

1 What opinion does the man give of the new night school program?

2 What is the main reason the man feels the program is unfair?

3 How is the man affected by the school's decision to restrict student participation?

4 What is another reason the man gives for opposing the new program?

5 How will the number of professors teaching night school affect the student body?

Responding Make your response by using the above information.

According to the notice,

The man's opinion is that

More than anything else, the reason is

He claims

Another reason he gives is

Therefore,

Speaking Now say your response out loud and record your time. While you are speaking, do not look at the written response.

Response time: 60 seconds	Your speaking time: _____ seconds

Comparing Listen to a sample response and compare it with yours.

02-14

Self-Rating Rate your response based on the following criteria.

Delivery	Score			
How clearly did you speak your response?	1	2	3	4

Language Use	Score			
How well did you control language structures to convey your ideas?	1	2	3	4
How appropriately did you use vocabulary to convey your ideas?	1	2	3	4

Topic Development	Score			
How fully did you answer the question?	1	2	3	4
How coherently did you present your ideas?	1	2	3	4

Exercise Read, listen, and answer the question following each step.

Reading Read the following passage about a campus situation.

Undergraduates Eligible for Graduate Courses

Juniors and seniors are now permitted to enroll in classes being offered in their departments' graduate programs. All graduate classes are those in the 500s and 600s. Students must have their advisors' written permission to register for these classes and are restricted to one per semester. This should enable the most advanced students to have access to a quality graduate-level education while they are still undergraduates. Not only that, but it should also help students determine if they are both interested in and qualified to attend a graduate program upon graduation.

📖 Words & Phrases

permit v to allow; to let
written permission phr a letter that allows someone to do something
per prep each; every

access n admission
determine v to conclude; to decide

Comprehension Answer the following questions to make sure you understand the passage.

1 What new policy is discussed in the announcement?

2 According to the notice, what kind of classes may students now attend?

3 What restriction has been placed on the students?

4 Why is this regulation being implemented?

5 How will this new regulation be able to help students?

📝 Note Taking

02-15

📖 Words & Phrases

anthropology n the study of ancient humans and their cultures

comprehensive adj all-encompassing; inclusive

overloaded adj having too much work to do

flooded adj inundated; swamped

unqualified adj not capable of doing something

Q The man expresses his opinion of the new policy on graduate school classes. State his opinion and explain the reasons he gives for holding that opinion.

Organization ▸ Ask yourself the following questions and organize your ideas.

1 What opinion does the man have about the new policy on graduate school classes?

2 How does the man think undergraduates will perform in graduate classes?

3 What point does the man bring up in mentioning his sister's coursework?

4 What does the man say is true of students in graduate school?

5 What does the man think will happen to the graduate students' educations?

Responding ▸ Make your response by using the above information.

The notice mentions that

The man is skeptical about

First, the man thinks

He mentions that

Second of all,

According to him,

Speaking ▸ Now say your response out loud and record your time. While you are speaking, do not look at the written response.

Response time: 60 seconds	Your speaking time: _____ seconds

Comparing ▸ Listen to a sample response and compare it with yours.

02-16

Self-Rating ▸ Rate your response based on the following criteria.

Delivery	Score			
How clearly did you speak your response?	1	2	3	4
Language Use	**Score**			
How well did you control language structures to convey your ideas?	1	2	3	4
How appropriately did you use vocabulary to convey your ideas?	1	2	3	4
Topic Development	**Score**			
How fully did you answer the question?	1	2	3	4
How coherently did you present your ideas?	1	2	3	4

Exercise Read, listen, and answer the question following each step.

Reading Read the following passage about a campus situation.

Library to Be Renovated

Thanks to a generous grant from the Sadowski Foundation, Lufkin Library will undergo renovations this summer, completely changing the library's facade. This facelift will give the library a more updated and modern appearance. Of the many changes to be made, two stand out. First, wooden floors are going to be added to the library, replacing the current concrete floors. And the entire library—both inside and outside—is going to be painted. There will be some times when various sections of the library will be unavailable to patrons. We hope you understand and bear with us.

📖 Words & Phrases

renovation 🔵 repair; renewal
facade 🔵 an appearance; the front
facelift 🔵 a reconstruction

patron 🔵 a user, typically of some kind of service
bear with 🔵 to abide by; to be patient with

Comprehension Answer the following questions to make sure you understand the passage.

1 What is the purpose of the announcement?

2 How is the school able to renovate the library?

3 How will these renovations affect the library's appearance?

4 What are the two major changes to be made to the library?

5 What will happen to the patrons once the renovations begin?

┌───┐
│ ✐ Note Taking   │
│   │
│   │
│   02-17   │
│   │
│   │
│   │
└───┘

📖 Words & Phrases

dingy adj dark and dirty

trifle n something small

stellar adj outstanding; excellent

periodical n a magazine or journal published regularly

woefully adv sadly

Q The woman expresses her opinion of the renovations to the library. State her opinion and explain the reasons she gives for holding that opinion.

■ **Organization** ▶ Ask yourself the following questions and organize your ideas.

1 What is the woman's opinion of the future renovations to the library?

2 How does the woman feel about the proposal to install wooden floors?

3 What does the woman think the wooden floor will do?

4 What does the woman think about the proposal to paint the library?

5 What does the woman say about the library's collection of materials?

■ **Responding** ▶ Make your response by using the above information.

The purpose of the announcement is to

In the woman's mind,

During the conversation, she states

She's also against the idea of

She notes that

Speaking Now say your response out loud and record your time. While you are speaking, do not look at the written response.

Response time: 60 seconds   Your speaking time: _____ seconds

Comparing Listen to a sample response and compare it with yours.

02-18

Self-Rating Rate your response based on the following criteria.

Delivery	Score			
How clearly did you speak your response?	1	2	3	4

Language Use	Score			
How well did you control language structures to convey your ideas?	1	2	3	4
How appropriately did you use vocabulary to convey your ideas?	1	2	3	4

Topic Development	Score			
How fully did you answer the question?	1	2	3	4
How coherently did you present your ideas?	1	2	3	4

Exercise Read, listen, and answer the question following each step.

Reading Read the following passage about a campus situation.

Library to Purchase Online Reference Materials

In order to maximize space in the main library, Head Librarian John Hanlin has announced that, from now on, the majority of the library's reference budget will be spent on purchasing online materials. "These materials take up much less space than reference books, which tend to be large," said Hanlin. "This will let us purchase more materials while using less room." Hanlin also stressed that many publishers give discounts to customers purchasing online materials as opposed to those buying actual books, thereby saving money. This transition likely will stay in effect after the new library is constructed in three years.

📖 Words & Phrases

maximize v to make the most of

space n room; area

tend v to be inclined to

stress v to emphasize

transition n a change; a conversion

Comprehension Answer the following questions to make sure you understand the passage.

1 What topic does the article cover?

2 Why is the change in the library's policy being made?

3 What effect will purchasing online materials have?

4 How is it better to purchase online materials than printed materials?

5 Why will the library be able to save money on these purchases?

■ Listening ▶ Listen to a conversation about the same topic and take notes.

Note Taking	
	02-19

📖 Words & Phrases

in print `phr` a paper version; on paper
up and running `phr` active; functioning; operational
bother `n` an annoyance; an inconvenience

access `v` to use; to make contact with
version `n` a type; a kind

Q The man expresses his opinion of the library's policy on purchasing reference materials. State his opinion and explain the reasons he gives for holding that opinion.

■ Organization ▶ Ask yourself the following questions and organize your ideas.

1 What does the man say about the policy on purchasing reference materials?

2 How does the man feel this will benefit the library?

3 What will be the result of the school spending less money on online materials?

4 What is another way the man feels students will benefit from this policy change?

5 How will students be able to access the new materials now?

■ Responding ▶ Make your response by using the above information.

The newspaper article covers

The man fully supports

For one, he thinks that

He feels this is important because

Another reason is

He mentions that

Speaking Now say your response out loud and record your time. While you are speaking, do not look at the written response.

Response time: 60 seconds	Your speaking time: _____ seconds

Comparing Listen to a sample response and compare it with yours.

02-20

Self-Rating Rate your response based on the following criteria.

Delivery	Score			
How clearly did you speak your response?	1	2	3	4

Language Use	Score			
How well did you control language structures to convey your ideas?	1	2	3	4
How appropriately did you use vocabulary to convey your ideas?	1	2	3	4

Topic Development	Score			
How fully did you answer the question?	1	2	3	4
How coherently did you present your ideas?	1	2	3	4

Exercise Read, listen, and answer the question following each step.

Reading Read the following passage about a campus situation.

Parking Policy to Change

In light of the fact that students, staff, and faculty members had difficulty finding parking spaces last semester, the following change is being implemented for the fall semester: Freshmen are not allowed to park on campus any longer. No parking permits will be issued to any first-year students. This move is also being made in an effort to cut down on the traffic problems that are plaguing campus. Reducing the number of cars should take care of this problem. Hopefully, this move should ease both the parking and traffic issues. Contact the dean of students for more information.

📖 Words & Phrases

in light of phr with regards to; in consideration of
implement v to put into practice
issue v to give out

cut down on phr to reduce
plague v to cause problems

Comprehension Answer the following questions to make sure you understand the passage.

1 What is the purpose of the notice?

2 Why is the school making this change in its parking policy?

3 What problem did people at the university have the previous semester?

4 How is the decision related to traffic on campus?

5 What does the school believe can be done to solve the problem?

Listening Listen to a conversation about the same topic and take notes.

📎 Note Taking

02-21

📖 **Words & Phrases**

thrilled adj pleased; excited
atrocious adj horrible; awful
a drop in the bucket phr a very small amount; miniscule

ban v to prohibit
alleviate v to ease; to make lighter

The man expresses his opinion of the university's new freshman parking policy. State his opinion and explain the reasons he gives for holding that opinion.

Organization Ask yourself the following questions and organize your ideas.

1 What opinion does the man give on the university's new freshman parking policy?

2 What is the first reason the man opposes the change in the parking policy?

3 What does the man say about the number of freshmen who applied for parking permits?

4 What does the man suggest the school do to help with the parking problem?

5 Where does the man propose that the school construct a new parking lot?

Responding Make your response by using the above information.

The purpose of the announcement is to

The man expresses

One reason he gives is that

According to him,

Additionally, he suggests that

He points out that

Speaking ▸ Now say your response out loud and record your time. While you are speaking, do not look at the written response.

Response time: 60 seconds	Your speaking time: _____ seconds

Comparing ▸ Listen to a sample response and compare it with yours.

02-22

Self-Rating Rate your response based on the following criteria.

Delivery	Score			
How clearly did you speak your response?	1	2	3	4

Language Use	Score			
How well did you control language structures to convey your ideas?	1	2	3	4
How appropriately did you use vocabulary to convey your ideas?	1	2	3	4

Topic Development	Score			
How fully did you answer the question?	1	2	3	4
How coherently did you present your ideas?	1	2	3	4

Exercise Read, listen, and answer the question following each step.

Reading Read the following passage about a campus situation.

Madison Hall for Seniors Only

Madison Hall, a dormitory with room for 350 students, will be undergoing a change starting in the fall semester. Only seniors will be allowed to live in the dormitory. This change is being made due to constant requests by upperclassman to be separated from freshmen and sophomores. By having their own dormitory, seniors will be able to focus on completing their studies during their final year as well as applying for jobs and to graduate schools. Interested seniors can apply for a room in Madison Hall by visiting the student housing office at 45 Anderson Avenue.

📖 Words & Phrases

dormitory n a building in which students live, often on a school campus

constant adj continual

upperclassman n a junior or a senior

separate v to put apart from something else

interested adj wanting to do something; curious about

Comprehension Answer the following questions to make sure you understand the passage.

1 What is mentioned in the announcement?

2 Who can live in the dormitory?

3 Why is this change being made?

4 What are the expected benefits of the change?

5 What should interested students do?

Listening Listen to a conversation about the same topic and take notes.

Note Taking

02-23

Words & Phrases

noisy adj very loud

concentrate v to focus

frustrating adj making one feel angry or annoyed

appeal v to be attractive to

annoying adj bothersome

Q The woman expresses her opinion of the rule for the dormitory. State her opinion and explain the reasons she gives for holding that opinion.

Organization Ask yourself the following questions and organize your ideas.

1 What is the woman's opinion of the rule for the dormitory?

2 What does the woman say about the dormitories?

3 Why does the woman feel frustrated?

4 What appeals to the woman?

5 How does the woman think some seniors will feel?

Responding Make your response by using the above information.

The announcement reads that

The reason stated

The woman supports

First, she

She says that

In addition, she points out

Speaking Now say your response out loud and record your time. While you are speaking, do not look at the written response.

Response time: 60 seconds   Your speaking time: _____ seconds

Comparing Listen to a sample response and compare it with yours.

02-24

Self-Rating Rate your response based on the following criteria.

Delivery	Score			
How clearly did you speak your response?	1	2	3	4

Language Use	Score			
How well did you control language structures to convey your ideas?	1	2	3	4
How appropriately did you use vocabulary to convey your ideas?	1	2	3	4

Topic Development	Score			
How fully did you answer the question?	1	2	3	4
How coherently did you present your ideas?	1	2	3	4

Exercise Read, listen, and answer the question following each step.

Reading Read the following passage about a campus situation.

No More Intramural Sports

Effective immediately, all intramural sports are canceled. This includes intramural football, soccer, volleyball, and baseball. The school is undergoing a funding crisis and does not have enough money to pay for these events. In addition, participation in intramural sports has been declining for the past five years. As such, the school is spending too much money on activities that few students participate in. Students are still welcome to play sports on the school's fields and courts. However, they will have to organize their own teams and determine playing times by themselves.

📖 Words & Phrases

immediately adv at once
intramural adj involving only the members of a student body

crisis n a big problem
decline v to go down; to decrease
organize v to set up; to arrange

Comprehension Answer the following questions to make sure you understand the passage.

1 What does the announcement mention?

2 What events are included in the announcement?

3 What is the first reason given?

4 What is the second reason given?

5 What does the announcement mention that students can do?

Listen to a conversation about the same topic and take notes.

📝 Note Taking

02-25

📖 Words & Phrases

big deal phr something important
point out v to mention
simply adv clearly

get in shape phr to be fit; to be in good condition
administration n management; a group of people who run an organization

Q The woman expresses her opinion of the university's decision. State her opinion and explain the reasons she gives for holding that opinion.

Organization Ask yourself the following questions and organize your ideas.

1 What is the woman's opinion of the university's decision?

2 What does the woman say about herself?

3 According to the woman, how is the announcement incorrect?

4 Why the woman surprised?

5 How has the woman improved thanks to doing a certain activity?

Responding Make your response by using the above information.

According to the announcement,

The announcement states that

The woman expresses

First of all,

She claims

Next,

Speaking ▶ Now say your response out loud and record your time. While you are speaking, do not look at the written response.

Response time: 60 seconds	Your speaking time: _____ seconds

Comparing ▶ Listen to a sample response and compare it with yours.

02-26

Self-Rating Rate your response based on the following criteria.

Delivery	Score			
How clearly did you speak your response?	1	2	3	4

Language Use	Score			
How well did you control language structures to convey your ideas?	1	2	3	4
How appropriately did you use vocabulary to convey your ideas?	1	2	3	4

Topic Development	Score			
How fully did you answer the question?	1	2	3	4
How coherently did you present your ideas?	1	2	3	4

Exercise Read, listen, and answer the question following each step.

Reading Read the following passage about a campus situation.

New Course Requirement

There is a new course requirement for students. All freshmen and sophomores must take one course in the Physical Education Department in order to graduate. In addition, all incoming students will be required to take one course. Juniors and seniors are exempt from this requirement. The university must not only train the minds of students but also their bodies, which is the primary reason for this requirement. There are numerous courses for students to choose from in the department, and they are offered at various times throughout the day. Call 594-2938 extension 42 for more information.

📖 Words & Phrases

requirement n something a person must do
incoming adj arriving
exempt adj not having to do something

train v to teach; to instruct
numerous adj very many

Comprehension Answer the following questions to make sure you understand the passage.

1 What does the announcement mention?

2 According to the announcement, who is exempt?

3 What is the primary reason for the requirement?

4 What does the announcement state about the courses?

5 How can students get more information?

Listening Listen to a conversation about the same topic and take notes.

🖊 Note Taking

02-27

📖 Words & Phrases

extra adj additional; more than necessary
work out v to exercise
jog v to run at a slow pace

outstanding adv excellent; very good
make an exception phr to exclude someone or something from a rule

---

Q The man expresses his opinion of the new course requirement. State his opinion and explain the reasons he gives for holding that opinion.

Organization Ask yourself the following questions and organize your ideas.

1 What is the man's opinion of the new course requirement?

2 What is the first reason the man gives for his opinion?

3 What would the man rather do?

4 What is the second reason the man gives for his opinion?

5 What does the woman suggest the man do?

Responding Make your response by using the above information.

The announcement declares that

The man is upset about

First, he remarks that

He was hoping to

He also notes that

As a result,

Speaking ▶ Now say your response out loud and record your time. While you are speaking, do not look at the written response.

Response time: 60 seconds	Your speaking time: _____ seconds

Comparing ▶ Listen to a sample response and compare it with yours.

02-28

Self-Rating Rate your response based on the following criteria.

Delivery	Score			
How clearly did you speak your response?	1	2	3	4

Language Use	Score			
How well did you control language structures to convey your ideas?	1	2	3	4
How appropriately did you use vocabulary to convey your ideas?	1	2	3	4

Topic Development	Score			
How fully did you answer the question?	1	2	3	4
How coherently did you present your ideas?	1	2	3	4

Exercise Read, listen, and answer the question following each step.

Reading Read the following passage about a campus situation.

Engineering School to Expand

The School of Engineering, which includes the Chemical, Civil, Electrical, and Mechanical Engineering departments, will be expanding this year. There are plans to hire up to twenty full-time professors for these departments. The school is eager to increase the sizes of the engineering departments. In recent years, the number of students in the School of Engineering has risen by thirty percent, so more professors are needed. The school is also interested in stressing classes in the fields of science and technology. The first professors to be hired will begin teaching in the spring semester.

📖 Words & Phrases

expand v to become larger
eager adj enthusiastic; wanting to do something
recent adj relating to a time not long past

stress v to emphasize
technology n the practical application of knowledge

Comprehension Answer the following questions to make sure you understand the passage.

1 What is the announcement about?

2 What specifically will the school do?

3 How does the school feel about this plan?

4 What has happened in recent years?

5 What does the school want to stress?

⊘ Note Taking

02-29

📖 **Words & Phrases**

roommate 🔵 a person with whom one lives
individual adj relating to one person
employ v to hire

specialized adj designed or trained for one purpose
make sense phr to be logical

Q The woman expresses her opinion of the university's plan. State her opinion and explain the reasons she gives for holding that opinion.

Organization Ask yourself the following questions and organize your ideas.

1 What is the woman's opinion of the university's plan?

2 What is the woman's first reason for her opinion?

3 What is a possible result of the woman's first reason?

4 What is the woman's second reason for her opinion?

5 What is a possible result of the woman's second reason?

Responding Make your response by using the above information.

The announcement concerns

Additionally,

The woman supports this decision

She says that

The woman believes that

This, in turn,

Speaking Now say your response out loud and record your time. While you are speaking, do not look at the written response.

Response time: 60 seconds   Your speaking time: _____ seconds

Comparing Listen to a sample response and compare it with yours.

02-30

Self-Rating Rate your response based on the following criteria.

Delivery	Score			
How clearly did you speak your response?	1	2	3	4

Language Use	Score			
How well did you control language structures to convey your ideas?	1	2	3	4
How appropriately did you use vocabulary to convey your ideas?	1	2	3	4

Topic Development	Score			
How fully did you answer the question?	1	2	3	4
How coherently did you present your ideas?	1	2	3	4

Exercise Read, listen, and answer the question following each step.

Reading Read the following passage about a campus situation.

New Cafeteria Payment Rules

Effective starting on August 29, the university's four cafeterias will no longer accept cash payments from students, faculty, and staff members. Instead, all payments must be made by student ID card, debit card, or credit card. Many students have complained about long lines to get into the cafeteria recently. Cash transactions can take up to three or four times as long as card transactions, so banning cash should speed up the process. In addition, eliminating cash transactions will ensure that there are no imbalances in transactions and that cash does not go missing at times.

📖 Words & Phrases

cafeteria [n] a restaurant in which diners serve themselves and take their food to their tables

complain [v] to express unhappiness about something

transaction [n] an exchange of goods or services, often for money

ban [v] to prohibit a certain activity

eliminate [v] to get rid of; to remove

Comprehension Answer the following questions to make sure you understand the passage.

1 What is mentioned in the notice?

2 How will students have to make payments?

3 What have students complained about?

4 How will the change benefit students?

5 What is another benefit mentioned in the notice?

Listen to a conversation about the same topic and take notes.

📝 Note Taking

02-31

📖 **Words & Phrases**

cash n money such as bills and coins

meal plan n a prepaid account for students to buy meals at a school

convenient adj being related to personal comfort

discriminate v to make a difference in how people are treated

cash register n a machine with a money drawer that is used to make sales

Q The man expresses his opinion of the announcement about the cafeterias. State his opinion and explain the reasons he gives for holding that opinion.

Organization Ask yourself the following questions and organize your ideas.

1 What is the man's opinion of the announcement about the cafeterias?

2 What type of payment method does the man always use?

3 What does the man say about that payment method?

4 What is the second reason the man gives for his opinion?

5 What does the man suggest that the school do?

Responding Make your response by using the above information.

The notice mentions that

According to the notice,

The man disagrees with

The first reason he gives is that

The next point he makes is that

He states that

Speaking ▶ Now say your response out loud and record your time. While you are speaking, do not look at the written response.

Response time: 60 seconds	Your speaking time: _____ seconds

Comparing ▶ Listen to a sample response and compare it with yours.

02-32

Self-Rating Rate your response based on the following criteria.

Delivery	Score			
How clearly did you speak your response?	1	2	3	4
Language Use	**Score**			
How well did you control language structures to convey your ideas?	1	2	3	4
How appropriately did you use vocabulary to convey your ideas?	1	2	3	4
Topic Development	**Score**			
How fully did you answer the question?	1	2	3	4
How coherently did you present your ideas?	1	2	3	4

PART III

Integrated Speaking Task 2
Reading & Lecture

In this task, you will be presented with a short reading passage about an academic topic. Next, you will listen to a short lecture by a professor about the same topic. Then, you will provide a response based upon what you read and heard. You will be asked to explain how the professor's lecture relates to the reading passage. You will be given 30 seconds to prepare your answer after the question is presented, and you will have 60 seconds to respond to the question.

PART III

Integrated Speaking Task 2 I
Reading & Lecture

Overview

For this task, you will read a short passage about an academic subject and listen to a professor give a brief excerpt from a lecture on that subject. Then, you will be asked a question based on the passage and lecture. Although the topics are academic in nature, none of the passages or lectures requires you to have prior knowledge of any academic field in particular. You only need to integrate and convey the key information from both sources.

Sample TOEFL iBT Task

Read a short passage about an academic subject.

Creative Destruction

Many companies, particularly in the twentieth century, have introduced new products or inventions that revolutionized their industries. When this occurs, an existing industry is often either completely destroyed or is reduced greatly in stature and ability to turn a profit. This is referred to as creative destruction. While the invention wipes out one field in the industry, it creates another new one, which, in turn, often spurs dramatic economic growth. One example of creative destruction is the invention of the automobile. While sales of automobiles dramatically rose, the horse and buggy disappeared as an industry.

Listen to a lecture about the same topic.

Script

W Professor: I need to speak for a bit about creative destruction. Now, we live in a time where radical technological innovations change our world or, at least, a part of it with stunning regularity. Oftentimes, when something comes up that causes creative destruction, it sparks an entire new industry while simultaneously killing off another.

I'm sure some of you remember computer discs. There were five-and-a-quarter-inch floppy discs and then the smaller three-point-five-inch hard discs. Remember them? Well, what happened to them? Anyone? You don't see them anymore, do you? Why not? Well, people began using CD-ROMs to record and save information on, so no one needed computer discs anymore. The invention and use of CD-ROMs caused creative destruction in the computer industry. They literally killed the computer disc market, but they started an entire new one of their own.

Okay, how about another? Let's think about digital cameras. Do you know of anyone lately who's purchased a camera that uses film? I sure don't. Digital cameras are cheaper and better than regular cameras, and you can manipulate your pictures with a computer to a much greater extent than you can with film in the darkroom. The film camera industry isn't dead yet, but it's certainly on its way to being replaced completely by digital cameras.

 Q The professor describes two advances in technology. Explain how these advances are related to creative destruction.

PREPARATION TIME
00 : 30 : 00

RESPONSE TIME
00 : 60 : 00

03-02

Sample Response

The subject of the talk is how dramatic changes in technology can cause existing technology to disappear or become unpopular. The professor provides a couple of different examples. The first concerns the computer industry. While people once used computer discs, as soon as CR-ROMs were invented, people began using them since they had more storage space than computer discs. This caused the computer disc industry to die while creating the CD-ROM industry. The second example is about cameras. The professor mentions that since digital cameras are better and cheaper than regular film-using cameras, no one buys regular cameras nowadays. The result is that the camera industry is dying while the digital camera industry is growing. Both of the professor's examples relate to creative destruction, which occurs when a radical development causes an existing technology to disappear while creating a different new one.

How to Score the Integrated Task Reading & Lecture

For Task 3, you must give your response based on both the reading passage and the lecture. The score you receive will be similar to the ones in Tasks 1 and 2:

◆ **Weak** (0 - 1)

◆ **Limited** (1.5 - 2)

◆ **Fair** (2.5 - 3)

◆ **Good** (3.5 - 4)

Again, the scores are given based on the following components: delivery, language use, and topic development.

◇ **Delivery**: This describes how clearly and intelligibly you speak. Pronunciation, intonation, pacing, and flow are all included in this component.

◇ **Language Use**: This is based upon the vocabulary and the grammar that you use.

◇ **Topic Development**: This part refers to how well you create your response in terms of connecting the reading passage with the comments that the professor makes in the lecture.

Each score is based on specific criteria such as the following:

Score	Delivery	Language Use	Topic Development
4	The response flows well, and the speaker's voice is clear and understandable. There could be minor pronunciation or intonation mistakes, but they do not affect how intelligible the response is. The pace may vary as the speaker attempts to recall information that was provided.	The response uses good grammar and a high level of vocabulary. The response is spoken natural, and the speaker uses both basic and complex grammar structures well. There may be some errors, but they do not detract from the response.	The response is well developed and contains information that is relevant to the question. It provides details from both the reading passage and the lecture, but some minor mistakes may be made.
3	The response is mostly clear and is fairly fluid. There may be some pronunciation, intonation, or pacing issues, so the listener may have to make an effort to understand the response at times.	The response uses effective grammar and vocabulary, and the ideas are mostly coherent. There may be some vocabulary that is imprecise or used improperly. The grammar structures used may be limited in range. These issues do not interfere with the understanding of the response.	The response is mostly understandable and provides information that is relevant to the task. There may be some missing information, mistakes, a lack of specificity, or choppiness in how the passages are described.

2	The response is intelligible, but the listener must make an effort to understand due to unclear speech, awkward intonation, or poor rhythm and pacing. It may not be possible to understand the meanings of some parts.	The response is limited in its grammar and vocabulary usage. This prevents the ideas in the response from being explained well. The response mostly only uses basic grammar and vocabulary well. The connections between sentences and points made in the passages are unclear.	The response is related to the task, but some information is either incomplete or incorrect. It may omit key points or fail to develop important points. It may also contain a misunderstanding of the information in one of the passages. The ideas may not be well connected, so the listener may not understand the points being made.
1	There are many problems with pronunciation, intonation, and pacing that make understanding the response difficult or impossible. The delivery is choppy and fragmented. The speaker pauses and hesitates frequently.	The response has a limited range of grammar and vocabulary that prevents ideas from being expressed and connected to one another. Some responses may rely upon memorized expressions or those that have been practiced regularly.	There is a limited amount of related content. Most ideas discussed are incorrect, are only covered vaguely, or are repeated. The speaker may also repeat the prompt.

Tips for Getting a High Score

1   The professor may give one or two examples. If two examples are used, be sure to include both of them in your response.

2   Be sure to use a wide variety of grammar structures in your response. Try to use complex sentences—sentences with subordinating conjunctions such as *because*, *since*, *as*, and *although*—when you give your response. That will increase the quality of your response.

3   Be sure to use advanced vocabulary. That will show that you have a high level of English. But also try to paraphrase the information in the reading passage rather than stating it word for word.

4   Do not repeat yourself when you give a response. Discuss the first point the professor makes and then move on to the next point. Repeating yourself is a time waster, and you will lose points for doing it.

Exercise Read, listen, and answer the question following each step.

Reading Read the following passage about an academic subject.

Shaping

Parents normally desire to have their children act in a positive manner. To do so, parents often rely upon shaping to help manage their children's behavior. In using shaping, a parent sets goals for a child. As the child completes a goal—typically a fairly small step—the parent praises the child and then encourages the child to continue to the next goal. Should the child not be successful, the parent does not praise the child. Since children are typically eager to be praised, they are often willing to have their behavior shaped by their parents to receive more compliments.

📖 Words & Phrases

goal n an objective; an aim
step n a stage
praise v to compliment

encourage v to support; to cheer
eager adj enthusiastic; keen

Comprehension Answer the following questions to make sure you understand the passage.

1 Why do parents use shaping?

2 What must a parent do to use shaping?

3 What does the parent do when the child is successful at something?

4 What does the parent do if the child fails at something?

5 Why does shaping often work well on children?

Listening Listen to a lecture about the same topic and take notes.

> ✎ Note Taking
>
>
>
> 03-03

📖 **Words & Phrases**

raise v to bring up; to rear
mold v to shape; to alter
mark n a spot

pay one a compliment phr to praise someone
realize v to recognize; to become aware

Q The professor describes how she helped improve her daughter's drawing skills. Explain how the professor's actions relate to shaping.

Organization Ask yourself the following questions and organize your ideas.

1 What was the professor's daughter trying to do?

2 How did the professor encourage her daughter?

3 What did the professor do when her daughter did not color something in the proper place?

4 What was the second step the professor had her daughter move on to?

5 How did the professor react to her daughter in this step?

Responding Make your response by using the above information.

The professor lectures on

She states that at first,

However,

The professor was using shaping,

For example,

Speaking Now say your response out loud and record your time. While you are speaking, do not look at the written response.

> Response time: 60 seconds   Your speaking time: _____ seconds

Comparing Listen to a sample response and compare it with yours.

03-04

Self-Rating Rate your response based on the following criteria.

Delivery	Score			
How clearly did you speak your response?	1	2	3	4

Language Use	Score			
How well did you control language structures to convey your ideas?	1	2	3	4
How appropriately did you use vocabulary to convey your ideas?	1	2	3	4

Topic Development	Score			
How fully did you answer the question?	1	2	3	4
How coherently did you present your ideas?	1	2	3	4

Read, listen, and answer the question following each step.

Reading Read the following passage about an academic subject.

Memorization

Scientists have conducted countless studies on what makes people memorize better. They have determined that people's environments have dramatic effects on their memorization skills. In fact, researchers have come to the realization that several factors affect people's abilities to memorize facts. Among these factors are the physical setting, the people situated nearby, and even the time of day. When conducting long-term studies on groups of people, they have discovered that when people are put into similar or familiar circumstances, their memorization skills vastly improve. Simply put, being in a comfortable environment helps tremendously.

📖 Words & Phrases

conduct v to carry out; to implement
come to the realization phr to understand; to realize
physical setting phr a place; a location

circumstance n a situation
vastly adv greatly; very much

Comprehension Answer the following questions to make sure you understand the passage.

1 What have researchers conducted studies on?

2 What conclusion did the researchers arrive at?

3 What factors affect people's abilities at memorizing?

4 What was learned from the long-term studies?

5 What does the passage read about comfortable environments?

Listening Listen to a lecture about the same topic and take notes.

✎ Note Taking

03-05

📖 **Words & Phrases**

quiz v to test; to ask
hinder v to obstruct; to bother
split up v to divide

ignore v not to pay attention to
at hand phr nearby

Q The professor describes an experiment that he conducted with students in two separate classes. Explain how the professor's experiment relates to memorization.

Organization Ask yourself the following questions and organize your ideas.

1 What kind of experiment did the professor conduct?

2 What did the professor make the first group of students do?

3 How did the students feel after having taken the test?

4 What did the professor have the second group of students do?

5 What did these students claim to have felt about their environment?

Responding Make your response by using the above information.

During his lecture, the professor mentions

According to the lecturer,

In both cases,

This research noted that

Speaking Now say your response out loud and record your time. While you are speaking, do not look at the written response.

Response time: 60 seconds	Your speaking time: _____ seconds

Comparing Listen to a sample response and compare it with yours.

03-06

Self-Rating Rate your response based on the following criteria.

Delivery		Score		
How clearly did you speak your response?	1	2	3	4

Language Use		Score		
How well did you control language structures to convey your ideas?	1	2	3	4
How appropriately did you use vocabulary to convey your ideas?	1	2	3	4

Topic Development		Score		
How fully did you answer the question?	1	2	3	4
How coherently did you present your ideas?	1	2	3	4

Exercise Read, listen, and answer the question following each step.

Reading Read the following passage about an academic subject.

Cyclic Population Change

Contrary to popular belief, ecosystems are not static environments but are constantly changing. Some of the biggest changes occur in the populations of the species inhabiting them. Species' populations are constantly in states of imbalance. For example, some years, there are large numbers of prey. This causes the numbers of predators to increase since the ecosystem can support more of them. However, eventually, there will be too many predators but not enough prey. This results in large numbers of predators dying since they lack food to eat. This population change occurs in regular cycles in virtually every ecosystem.

📖 **Words & Phrases**

static adj unchanging; stable
state n a condition
imbalance n inequality; unevenness

eventually adv finally; at last
virtually adv practically; almost

Comprehension Answer the following questions to make sure you understand the passage.

1 What do most people erroneously believe about ecosystems?

2 What is one way that ecosystems often change?

3 What is true about the populations of species in an ecosystem?

4 What will make the number of predators increase?

5 Why will the number of predators suddenly decrease?

Listening Listen to a lecture about the same topic and take notes.

> Note Taking
>
>
>
> 03-07

Words & Phrases

record number (n) the greatest amount of something
feast on (phr) to devour; to eat entirely
miniscule (adj) very small; tiny

overfeed (v) to eat too much
look behind one's back (phr) to check for danger

 Q The professor describes the changing numbers of mice and wolves in the forest. Explain how this is related to cyclic population change.

Organization Ask yourself the following questions and organize your ideas.

1 What does the professor say is true of cyclic population change?

2 What is the first phase of cyclic population change?

3 What happens during the second phase of cyclic population change?

4 What occurs in the third phase of cyclic population change?

5 What does the professor say happens after the mice's numbers recover?

Responding Make your response by using the above information.

In the lecture, the professor focuses on

First, the professor sets up a scenario where

The professor notes that

It notes that

Speaking ▶ Now say your response out loud and record your time. While you are speaking, do not look at the written response.

Response time: 60 seconds	Your speaking time: _____ seconds

Comparing ▶ Listen to a sample response and compare it with yours.

03-08

Self-Rating ▶ Rate your response based on the following criteria.

Delivery	Score			
How clearly did you speak your response?	1	2	3	4

Language Use	Score			
How well did you control language structures to convey your ideas?	1	2	3	4
How appropriately did you use vocabulary to convey your ideas?	1	2	3	4

Topic Development	Score			
How fully did you answer the question?	1	2	3	4
How coherently did you present your ideas?	1	2	3	4

Exercise Read, listen, and answer the question following each step.

Reading Read the following passage about an academic subject.

Short-Term Memories

Every day, people commit thousands of bits of information to their short-term memories. Unfortunately, many memories remain only for a short time and are quickly forgotten. Psychologists have determined two reasons as to why people lose their short-term memories. The first is decay. A memory decays, or fades away, when it is not used by the person. The second reason is interference. This happens when a new memory enters the brain and simply causes the other memory to depart. Because of these two factors, people are unable to retain every short-term memory they have.

📖 Words & Phrases

commit v to entrust
psychologist n a person who studies the mind and how it works

decay n the process of disappearance
fade away v to disappear slowly
retain v to keep; to hold on to

Comprehension Answer the following questions to make sure you understand the passage.

1 How many memories do people have each day?

2 What happens to many of people's memories?

3 What is the first reason why short-term memories disappear?

4 What is the second reason that short-term memories disappear?

5 What is the end result of decay and interference?

Listening Listen to a lecture about the same topic and take notes.

Note Taking

03-09

Words & Phrases

chagrin n regret; embarrassment
digit n a number
disuse n neglect

old friend phr someone who has been a friend for a long time
converse v to talk about; to discuss

Q The professor describes two different examples related to remembering facts. Explain how these examples relate to short-term memory.

Organization Ask yourself the following questions and organize your ideas.

1   What does the professor imply about why people lose certain memories?

2   What example does the professor give about a phone number?

3   According to the professor, why does the person forget the number?

4   What is the personal example about memory that the professor gives?

5   In the professor's opinion, why did he forget the titles of the books?

Responding Make your response by using the above information.

The professor notes

His first example is

The professor's second example is

This represents the idea of

Speaking Now say your response out loud and record your time. While you are speaking, do not look at the written response.

Response time: 60 seconds   Your speaking time: _____ seconds

Comparing Listen to a sample response and compare it with yours.

03-10

Self-Rating Rate your response based on the following criteria.

Delivery	Score			
How clearly did you speak your response?	1	2	3	4

Language Use	Score			
How well did you control language structures to convey your ideas?	1	2	3	4
How appropriately did you use vocabulary to convey your ideas?	1	2	3	4

Topic Development	Score			
How fully did you answer the question?	1	2	3	4
How coherently did you present your ideas?	1	2	3	4

Exercise Read, listen, and answer the question following each step.

Reading Read the following passage about an academic subject.

Scent Marketing

Stores commonly search for ways to entice shoppers to purchase more products when they visit. One effective method they have discovered is scent marketing. Sellers have discovered that shoppers often associate scents with certain memories or even feelings. Studies have determined that depending upon the scent, people can be made to feel comfortable, relaxed, tense, or many other feelings. Scents that evoke pleasant memories are particularly effective. By ensuring that these scents are in various sections of their stores, owners can subconsciously encourage shoppers to purchase more products than they normally would.

📖 Words & Phrases

entice v to lure; to attract
effective adj successful
associate v to connect; to relate

evoke v to call up; to bring forth
subconsciously adv unknowingly; without knowing

Comprehension Answer the following questions to make sure you understand the passage.

1 What does the passage mention that stores often search for?

2 What is one effective method of getting shoppers to buy more items?

3 What is the importance of scents to shoppers?

4 How can people be made to feel by different scents?

5 How does scent marketing work?

Listening Listen to a lecture about the same topic and take notes.

> **Note Taking**
>
>
>
> 03-11

Words & Phrases

besiege (v) to assault; to overwhelm

fragrance (n) an aroma; a pleasant smell

appealing (adj) attractive

in a nutshell (phr) in short; briefly

more often than not (phr) usually; typically

 Q The professor explains how fragrances affect people's shopping habits. Explain how this is related to scent marketing.

Organization Ask yourself the following questions and organize your ideas.

1 What does the professor say about department stores and scents?

2 What happened in the study conducted at the department store?

3 What was the result of this study?

4 What is the association between running shoes and fragrances?

5 According to the professor, what was the second result of the survey on running shoes?

Responding Make your response by using the above information.

The lecturer mentions that

According to the reading,

In the first example,

The second example concerned

This once again shows

Speaking Now say your response out loud and record your time. While you are speaking, do not look at the written response.

Response time: 60 seconds	Your speaking time: _____ seconds

Comparing Listen to a sample response and compare it with yours.

03-12

Self-Rating Rate your response based on the following criteria.

Delivery	Score			
How clearly did you speak your response?	1	2	3	4

Language Use	Score			
How well did you control language structures to convey your ideas?	1	2	3	4
How appropriately did you use vocabulary to convey your ideas?	1	2	3	4

Topic Development	Score			
How fully did you answer the question?	1	2	3	4
How coherently did you present your ideas?	1	2	3	4

Read, listen, and answer the question following each step.

Read the following passage about an academic subject.

Fixed Action Patterns

Animals and humans sometimes engage in actions that are virtually impossible to stop once initiated. For example, an animal may receive a stimulus that will cause it, consciously and automatically, to respond with a predictable response. These responses are fixed action patterns. Mating dances are an example of this. Oftentimes, the mere presence of a female triggers the onset of the male's mating dance, which it must then complete in its entirety. While fixed action patterns are more common in animals, humans engage in some. For example, the sight of a person yawning often also causes others nearby to yawn.

📖 Words & Phrases

engage in phr to do; to participate in
stimulus n something that provokes a response or action
predictable adj expected; unsurprising

mating dance phr a series of movements designed to attract a mate
trigger v to cause; to set off

Answer the following questions to make sure you understand the passage.

1 What does the passage read about some actions animals engage in?

2 What is a fixed action pattern?

3 What is an example of a fixed action pattern?

4 According to the passage, how common are fixed action patterns in humans?

5 What is an example of a human fixed action pattern?

✏ Note Taking

03-13

📖 Words & Phrases

illustrate [v] to provide an example; to demonstrate

belly [n] a stomach

breeding season [n] the time when an animal species mates and reproduces

hatch [v] to break open, as in an egg

imaginary [adj] make-believe; made-up

Q The professor describes the automatic behavior of two different species. Explain how these behavioral responses relate to fixed action patterns.

Organization Ask yourself the following questions and organize your ideas.

1 What does the professor say about fixed action responses?

2 What does the male stickleback fish do during its mating season?

3 What will the male stickleback fish do if it sees the color red?

4 How do graylag geese get their eggs back into their nests?

5 In what way does the graylag goose engage in a fixed action pattern?

Responding Make your response by using the above information.

The professor begins her lecture by mentioning that

She states that

However,

Also,

These are both examples of

Speaking ▸ Now say your response out loud and record your time. While you are speaking, do not look at the written response.

Response time: 60 seconds	Your speaking time: _____ seconds

Comparing ▸ Listen to a sample response and compare it with yours.

03-14

Self-Rating Rate your response based on the following criteria.

Delivery	Score			
How clearly did you speak your response?	1	2	3	4

Language Use	Score			
How well did you control language structures to convey your ideas?	1	2	3	4
How appropriately did you use vocabulary to convey your ideas?	1	2	3	4

Topic Development	Score			
How fully did you answer the question?	1	2	3	4
How coherently did you present your ideas?	1	2	3	4

Exercise Read, listen, and answer the question following each step.

Reading Read the following passage about an academic subject.

Creative Categorization

Marketing experts do their utmost to induce customers to purchase their products. Often, when faced with a product that, for whatever reason, does not appeal to a large segment of the population, marketers merely change the category it is in. This process is called creative categorization. By doing this, marketers can increase the appeal of a product. The two most common methods of creative categorization are to change the cost or design of a product. By doing so, products may go from being ones purchased by a small number of people to ones with mass appeal.

📖 Words & Phrases

utmost n the best of one's abilities

induce v to persuade

segment n a section

categorization n a classification

mass appeal phr attraction to a large number of people

Comprehension Answer the following questions to make sure you understand the passage.

1 What do marketers attempt to do?

2 What do some marketers do when their products do not appeal to many people?

3 What is creative categorization?

4 What are the two most common ways marketers use creative categorization?

5 According to the passage, what is often the end result of creative categorization?

Listening Listen to a lecture about the same topic and take notes.

> **Note Taking**
>
>
>
> 03-15

Words & Phrases

executive n a manager; a high-ranking employee
break into phr to enter
timepiece n a watch; a clock

tout v to promote
the masses phr the great majority of people

Q The professor describes how two different products began to appeal to a greater number of people. Explain how they are related to creative categorization.

Organization Ask yourself the following questions and organize your ideas.

1 What does the professor say about a problem marketing executives may have?

2 According to the professor, what used to be true about watches?

3 How have people's perceptions of watches changed today?

4 At first, who used to use mobile phones?

5 What is true about mobile phone usage today?

Responding Make your response by using the above information.

The subject of the talk is

The professor states that

The second example given is

As described in the reading,

Speaking Now say your response out loud and record your time. While you are speaking, do not look at the written response.

| Response time: 60 seconds | Your speaking time: _____ seconds |

Comparing Listen to a sample response and compare it with yours.

03-16

Self-Rating Rate your response based on the following criteria.

Delivery	Score			
How clearly did you speak your response?	1	2	3	4
Language Use	**Score**			
How well did you control language structures to convey your ideas?	1	2	3	4
How appropriately did you use vocabulary to convey your ideas?	1	2	3	4
Topic Development	**Score**			
How fully did you answer the question?	1	2	3	4
How coherently did you present your ideas?	1	2	3	4

Exercise Read, listen, and answer the question following each step.

Reading Read the following passage about an academic subject.

Process Explanation

Telling a person how something works or runs is referred to as process explanation. There are two separate ways in which this may be accomplished. The first of the two is called directive process explanation. When a person employs this method, that individual explains how to do something step by step. This may often be accomplished through the use of either oral or written directions. The second method is called information process explanation. Explanations of this sort typically just provide information about a topic and do not actually explain how to do something.

📖 **Words & Phrases**

refer to phr to call
directive n instruction
employ v to use; to utilize

step by step phr one thing at a time
oral adj spoken

Comprehension Answer the following questions to make sure you understand the passage.

1 What is process explanation?

2 According to the passage, what is directive process explanation?

3 How may a person accomplish directive process explanation?

4 What is the second kind of process explanation mentioned?

5 What is true about this kind of process explanation?

Listening ▶ Listen to a lecture about the same topic and take notes.

> 📝 Note Taking
>
>
>
> 03-17

📖 Words & Phrases

comprehend Ⓥ to understand
technologically challenged phr unable to use new technology well

have no clue phr not to know; to have no idea
take off Ⓥ to leave; to depart
impart Ⓥ to provide; to pass on

Q The professor explains two different ways to learn about smartphones. Explain how these ways relate to process explanation.

Organization ▶ Ask yourself the following questions and organize your ideas.

1 What does the professor say that people need when they do not understand something?

2 What problem did the professor have with his smartphone?

3 How did the professor's friend help him with his problem?

4 What does the professor say about the program he watched on television?

5 What was the end result of the professor watching the program?

Responding ▶ Make your response by using the above information.

During the lecture, the professor talks about

The professor's first example is

The second example concerns

This relates to the reading in that

Speaking Now say your response out loud and record your time. While you are speaking, do not look at the written response.

Response time: 60 seconds   Your speaking time: _____ seconds

Comparing Listen to a sample response and compare it with yours.

03-18

Self-Rating Rate your response based on the following criteria.

Delivery	Score			
How clearly did you speak your response?	1	2	3	4

Language Use	Score			
How well did you control language structures to convey your ideas?	1	2	3	4
How appropriately did you use vocabulary to convey your ideas?	1	2	3	4

Topic Development	Score			
How fully did you answer the question?	1	2	3	4
How coherently did you present your ideas?	1	2	3	4

Exercise Read, listen, and answer the question following each step.

Reading Read the following passage about an academic subject.

Competence Stages

People possess various levels of competence for doing different skills. A person's skill level may often be divided into two stages: conscious competence and unconscious competence. At the conscious competence level, a person knows how to do something or at least understands the theory. However, people must concentrate very much when doing this action lest they make a mistake. At the unconscious competence level, people are typically very adept at doing some activity. In fact, people often do not even need to think or concentrate on this action when doing it.

📖 Words & Phrases

competence Ⓝ an ability; a capability
level Ⓝ a rank
unconscious adj unknowing; unaware

concentrate Ⓥ to focus
adept adj skilled; proficient

Comprehension Answer the following questions to make sure you understand the passage.

1 What is true about people's abilities at doing different skills?

2 What are the two stages of skill levels?

3 What is conscious competence?

4 What is unconscious competence?

5 How are these two levels different from one another?

Listen to a lecture about the same topic and take notes.

📎 Note Taking

📖 Words & Phrases

manuscript Ⓝ a paper; a book

deadline Ⓝ a date or time by which something must be finished

typist Ⓝ a person who is typing

swerve Ⓥ to veer suddenly; to make a sudden move to the side

slam Ⓥ to press down suddenly

Q The professor describes two different events from the previous day. Explain how these events are related to competence stages.

Organization Ask yourself the following questions and organize your ideas.

1 What was the professor doing in her office yesterday?

2 What did the professor try to do at the same time?

3 What was the result of the professor's actions?

4 What incidents occurred while the professor was driving?

5 Why did the professor not have an accident?

Responding Make your response by using the above information.

The topic of the lecture is

The professor tells the class

She next describes

Both of the professor's examples

Now say your response out loud and record your time. While you are speaking, do not look at the written response.

Response time: 60 seconds   Your speaking time: _____ seconds

Comparing Listen to a sample response and compare it with yours.

03-20

Self-Rating Rate your response based on the following criteria.

Delivery	Score			
How clearly did you speak your response?	1	2	3	4

Language Use	Score			
How well did you control language structures to convey your ideas?	1	2	3	4
How appropriately did you use vocabulary to convey your ideas?	1	2	3	4

Topic Development	Score			
How fully did you answer the question?	1	2	3	4
How coherently did you present your ideas?	1	2	3	4

Exercise Read, listen, and answer the question following each step.

Reading Read the following passage about an academic subject.

Paradoxes of Choice

A paradox is a statement that seems true yet has an apparent contradiction in it. There are many kinds of paradoxes. One is the paradox of choice. In this paradox, while people have many options from which to choose, the actual process of making a choice is not liberating but is often, in fact, stressful. While people often claim to be pleased to have so many choices, actually having to make a decision typically leads to complaints about not being able to choose something. In this case, having so many choices becomes burdensome rather than liberating.

📖 Words & Phrases

apparent adj obvious
contradiction n a disagreement
option n a choice

liberating adj freeing
burdensome adj oppressive; troublesome

Comprehension Answer the following questions to make sure you understand the passage.

1 What is a paradox?

2 What is a paradox of choice?

3 What do people often state about having choices?

4 What do people often do when they must make a choice?

5 What is often the result of having to make a choice?

Listening Listen to a lecture about the same topic and take notes.

Note Taking

03-21

Words & Phrases

wide range phr a big selection

mall n a large building with many stores in it

brand n the name of a company that sells products

make up one's mind phr to decide; to choose

at times phr sometimes; occasionally

Q The professor explains how his family members were forced to make two separate decisions. Explain how these decisions are related to paradoxes of choice.

Organization Ask yourself the following questions and organize your ideas.

1 What does the professor say people often believe about having so many choices?

2 What did the professor and his daughter do the previous night?

3 What happened to the professor's daughter?

4 What were the professor and his wife trying to do last night?

5 What did the professor and his wife finally decide to do?

Responding Make your response by using the above information.

The professor gives a talk on

The professor says

The second story related is

Both instances are examples of

Speaking Now say your response out loud and record your time. While you are speaking, do not look at the written response.

Response time: 60 seconds   Your speaking time: _____ seconds

Comparing Listen to a sample response and compare it with yours.

03-22

Self-Rating Rate your response based on the following criteria.

Delivery	Score			
How clearly did you speak your response?	1	2	3	4

Language Use	Score			
How well did you control language structures to convey your ideas?	1	2	3	4
How appropriately did you use vocabulary to convey your ideas?	1	2	3	4

Topic Development	Score			
How fully did you answer the question?	1	2	3	4
How coherently did you present your ideas?	1	2	3	4

Read, listen, and answer the question following each step.

Read the following passage about an academic subject.

The Principle of Allocation

Every organism on the Earth has a limited number of resources it can utilize for various purposes. Among these purposes are acquiring food through either foraging or hunting, avoiding being caught and killed by predators, finding a mate, reproducing, growing larger, and finding or building shelter. When organisms utilize resources, such as food, to doing one of these tasks, they cannot use those resources for other tasks. This means the organisms will never achieve their maximum potential in all aspects. Organisms therefore engage in trade-offs, such as by allocating resources to finding food at the expense of acquiring shelter.

📖 Words & Phrases

acquire v to get; to obtain
forage v to search for food
task n a job; a chore

trade-off n the act of giving up one thing in return for another
allocate v to set apart; to designate

Comprehension Answer the following questions to make sure you understand the passage.

1 What do organisms have a limited number of?

2 How can organisms use these things?

3 What happens when organisms use resources to do a task?

4 What is a result of using these resources?

5 What is an example of a trade-off organisms engage in?

Listening Listen to a lecture about the same topic and take notes.

📝 Note Taking

03-23

📖 Words & Phrases

daily adj each day; every day
basis n a fixed pattern; a fixed system
poorly adj badly

neglect v to ignore
wise up v to become smarter; to act in a better way

Q The professor describes his behavior in the past. Explain how the professor's behavior is related to the principle of allocation.

Organization Ask yourself the following questions and organize your ideas.

1 According to the professor, what do the students do every day?

2 How do people decide which activities to do and which ones not to do?

3 What did the professor do when he was younger?

4 What was a result of the professor's actions?

5 How did the professor change his behavior?

Responding Make your response by using the above information.

In his lecture, the professor talks about

Because of his actions,

He states that

The professor's actions are related to

Speaking ▶ Now say your response out loud and record your time. While you are speaking, do not look at the written response.

Response time: 60 seconds   Your speaking time: _____ seconds

Comparing ▶ Listen to a sample response and compare it with yours.

03-24

Self-Rating Rate your response based on the following criteria.

Delivery	Score			
How clearly did you speak your response?	1	2	3	4

Language Use	Score			
How well did you control language structures to convey your ideas?	1	2	3	4
How appropriately did you use vocabulary to convey your ideas?	1	2	3	4

Topic Development	Score			
How fully did you answer the question?	1	2	3	4
How coherently did you present your ideas?	1	2	3	4

Exercise Read, listen, and answer the question following each step.

Reading Read the following passage about an academic subject.

Compulsions

Some people repeatedly and consistently engage in actions that can be troubling and that are negative in some manner. These are known as compulsions or compulsive behaviors. A wide variety of behaviors can become compulsions. Some people are shopaholics who spend too much money or who buy unneeded items. Some people never throw away items but hoard them instead. Others may have compulsions concerning food, gambling, and even exercise. People who suffer from these compulsions tend to have anxiety issues. While their anxiety can be relieved by engaging in their compulsive behavior, their feelings of relief do not last long.

📖 Words & Phrases

consistently adv on a regular basis
shopaholic n a person who shops too much
hoard v to collect and keep something

anxiety n a feeling of uneasiness or nervousness
relieve v to ease; to lower

Comprehension Answer the following questions to make sure you understand the passage.

1 What are compulsions?

2 What do shopaholics do?

3 What do people who hoard do?

4 What do other people have compulsions concerning?

5 What do people with compulsions often suffer from?

Listening Listen to a lecture about the same topic and take notes.

🖊 Note Taking

03-25

📖 **Words & Phrases**

hoarder [n] a person who saves things and does not throw them out

clutter [v] to fill or cover so much that movement is difficult

literally [adv] completely accurately

cruise [n] a trip on a ship or boat

therapy [n] a medical treatment for some kind of problem

Q The professor describes her parents and their activities. Explain how they relate to compulsions.

Organization Ask yourself the following questions and organize your ideas.

1 What does the professor say about her parents?

2 What did the professor's parents' house look like?

3 What was painful for the professor's parents?

4 What did the professor and her brother do?

5 How did the professor's parents recover?

Responding Make your response by using the above information.

In her lecture, the professor tells

She remarks that

She then adds that

To solve the problem,

Speaking Now say your response out loud and record your time. While you are speaking, do not look at the written response.

Response time: 60 seconds   Your speaking time: _____ seconds

Comparing Listen to a sample response and compare it with yours.

03-26

Self-Rating Rate your response based on the following criteria.

Delivery	Score			
How clearly did you speak your response?	1	2	3	4

Language Use	Score			
How well did you control language structures to convey your ideas?	1	2	3	4
How appropriately did you use vocabulary to convey your ideas?	1	2	3	4

Topic Development	Score			
How fully did you answer the question?	1	2	3	4
How coherently did you present your ideas?	1	2	3	4

Exercise Read, listen, and answer the question following each step.

Reading Read the following passage about an academic subject.

Retention Marketing

Many businesses focus on acquiring new customers. Yet more than ever nowadays, businesses are doing their best to retain the customers they already have. They are also attempting to increase the profitability of each purchase by these customers. This is known as retention marketing. This is a particularly popular marketing method with companies doing e-commerce, yet other businesses engage in it as well. Companies practice it by catering to customers in certain ways. Examples are by having sales, by providing fast, cheap shipping, by requesting regular feedback, and by helping make customers satisfied with their shopping experiences.

Words & Phrases

retain v to keep
profitability n the act of yielding positive returns
cater v to supply something that is desired

feedback n information about an action or event
satisfied adj pleased

Comprehension Answer the following questions to make sure you understand the passage.

1 What are many businesses focusing on doing nowadays?

2 What are businesses attempting to do with these customers?

3 What companies often practice retention marketing?

4 How do companies practice retention marketing?

5 What are some examples of practices that companies use?

Listening ▶ Listen to a lecture about the same topic and take notes.

> 🖊 Note Taking
>
>
>
> 03-27

📖 Words & Phrases

regional adj relating to a local area
expand v to increase in size
claim v to declare; to state

valuable adj having a high worth
discount n a reduction in price

Q The professor discusses Jackson Airlines. Explain how the airline relates to retention marketing.

Organization ▶ Ask yourself the following questions and organize your ideas.

1 What does the professor say about Jackson Airlines?

2 What does Jackson Airlines put first?

3 What does Jackson Airlines focus on doing?

4 What is a benefit that repeat customers of Jackson Airlines get?

5 What has the professor done when flying on Jackson Airlines?

Responding ▶ Make your response by using the above information.

In his lecture, the professor talks about

In addition,

For instance,

This is an example of

Speaking ▶ Now say your response out loud and record your time. While you are speaking, do not look at the written response.

Response time: 60 seconds   Your speaking time: _____ seconds

Comparing ▶ Listen to a sample response and compare it with yours.

03-28

Self-Rating   Rate your response based on the following criteria.

Delivery	Score			
How clearly did you speak your response?	1	2	3	4

Language Use	Score			
How well did you control language structures to convey your ideas?	1	2	3	4
How appropriately did you use vocabulary to convey your ideas?	1	2	3	4

Topic Development	Score			
How fully did you answer the question?	1	2	3	4
How coherently did you present your ideas?	1	2	3	4

Read, listen, and answer the question following each step.

Reading Read the following passage about an academic subject.

The Misinformation Effect

Not all memories remain the same. Sometimes it is possible for memories to change on account of outside influences. For instance, people may witness a certain event and develop memories of it. However, later, they may learn or be told something new—something either correct or incorrect—about the event which causes their memories of what happened to change. This misinformation effect shows how easy it is for people to be misled about what occurred in the past by having their memories changed through the actions of others.

📖 Words & Phrases

memory 🄝 the ability to recall something one has seen, learned, or heard

influence 🄝 the power or ability to have an effect on something

witness 🅥 to see

develop 🅥 to create

mislead 🅥 to take in a wrong direction, often on purpose

Comprehension Answer the following questions to make sure you understand the passage.

1 What can happen to memories?

2 How can memories change?

3 What can make people's memories change?

4 What is one result of the misinformation effect?

5 How are people's memories changed due to the misinformation effect?

✎ Note Taking

03-29

📖 Words & Phrases

psychologist Ⓝ a person who studies the mind and behavior

accident Ⓝ an unfortunate event

smash into ⓟʰʳ to hit very hard

respond Ⓥ to answer

recall Ⓥ to remember

Q The professor describes an experiment that was conducted by Elizabeth Loftus. Explain how this experiment relates to the misinformation effect.

Organization Ask yourself the following questions and organize your ideas.

1 Who was Elizabeth Loftus?

2 What were the group of people shown?

3 What question were the people asked?

4 How was the question changed for some people?

5 What was the question that was asked a few days later?

Responding Make your response by using the above information.

The professor lectures about

The study involved

One question asked

This is an instance of

Speaking ▶ Now say your response out loud and record your time. While you are speaking, do not look at the written response.

Response time: 60 seconds	Your speaking time: _____ seconds

Comparing ▶ Listen to a sample response and compare it with yours.

03-30

Self-Rating Rate your response based on the following criteria.

Delivery	Score			
How clearly did you speak your response?	1	2	3	4
Language Use	**Score**			
How well did you control language structures to convey your ideas?	1	2	3	4
How appropriately did you use vocabulary to convey your ideas?	1	2	3	4
Topic Development	**Score**			
How fully did you answer the question?	1	2	3	4
How coherently did you present your ideas?	1	2	3	4

Exercise Read, listen, and answer the question following each step.

Reading ▷ Read the following passage about an academic subject.

Pheromones

Not all communication is done orally or visually. There are chemicals secreted by various organisms which are capable of transmitting messages to others of the same species. Pheromones are used by insects, crustaceans, and vertebrates. They are typically secreted by glands but may be found in substances such as urine when it is removed from the body. They have a number of purposes. Animals such as insects frequently use pheromones to conduct complex activities enabling them to work together as a single mind. They may also be used as warnings and as signs of attraction.

📖 Words & Phrases

orally adv by sound
visually adv by sight
transmit v to send

crustacean n a marine animal with a hard shell, such as a lobster or a crab
urine n liquid waste removed from a body

Comprehension ▷ Answer the following questions to make sure you understand the passage.

1 What are two ways communication can be done?

2 What are pheromones?

3 What animals use pheromones?

4 How are pheromones secreted?

5 How do insects use pheromones?

Listen to a lecture about the same topic and take notes.

✐ Note Taking

03-31

📖 Words & Phrases

complex adj complicated
release v to set free; to let go
detect v to notice; to recognize

rush v to hurry
stimulate v to excite to activity

Q The professor describes how bees have complex societies. Explain how this relates to pheromones.

Organization Ask yourself the following questions and organize your ideas.

1 How do bees keep their colonies running smoothly?

2 Why do some animals attack beehives?

3 How do bees respond to attacks?

4 What do bees do when they need more food?

5 How do bees respond in this case?

Responding Make your response by using the above information.

In his lecture, the professor points out

According to the reading passage,

The first example the professor uses is

The second example concerns

Speaking Now say your response out loud and record your time. While you are speaking, do not look at the written response.

Response time: 60 seconds	Your speaking time: _____ seconds

Comparing Listen to a sample response and compare it with yours.

03-32

Self-Rating Rate your response based on the following criteria.

Delivery		Score		
How clearly did you speak your response?	1	2	3	4

Language Use		Score		
How well did you control language structures to convey your ideas?	1	2	3	4
How appropriately did you use vocabulary to convey your ideas?	1	2	3	4

Topic Development		Score		
How fully did you answer the question?	1	2	3	4
How coherently did you present your ideas?	1	2	3	4

PART IV

Integrated Speaking Task 3
Lecture

....

In this task, you will be presented with a short lecture about an
academic topic. Typically, the professor will provide two examples of
the topic being discussed. Then, you will provide a response based upon
what you heard. You will be asked to discuss the examples provided
in the professor's lecture. You will be given 20 seconds to prepare your
answer after the question is presented, and you will have 60 seconds to
respond to the question.

Integrated Speaking Task 3 | Lecture

Overview

For this task, you will first listen to a professor present a brief lecture on an academic subject, and then you will be asked a question about what you have heard. The topics will vary but will not require you to have any prior knowledge of any field in particular. The professor will typically introduce a concept and go on to discuss examples about it. You will be asked to explain the main concept by using the given examples in the lecture.

Sample TOEFL iBT Task

Listen to a lecture about an academic subject.

> **Script**
>
>
> 04-01
>
> **M Professor**: We've discussed a lot of different aspects about marketing, but there's one thing that's the most important of all. You need to know this. So let me tell you what it is . . . A successful marketer will ensure that a product grabs people's attention, which will then convince people to purchase that product. I think I can best explain this by providing a couple of examples.
>
> You've all probably gone shopping for cereal at the local supermarket. There are so many colorful boxes you'd just think that they'd all stand out, wouldn't you? Well, one cereal company once decided to market the same product in two different ways to determine which one was better. The first way it did that was by designing a colorful cereal box that was filled with the most amazing pictures and descriptions of its product. It was a complete masterpiece. Unfortunately, when it went on the store shelves, it didn't look any different from the dozens of other cereal boxes that were right next to it. So shoppers failed to notice it. Accordingly, it failed to make significant sales.
>
> However, the company also marketed the same cereal in a plain, white box that simply had the word "Cereal" written across the front of it in big black letters. While you might think that this was a nonsensical design, the box's plainness made it stand out from the other cereal boxes. People noticed it. And they started purchasing that cereal because they had noticed it. The company found that its sales of the cereal in the plain box began increasing rapidly. That box, while simple, was an example of successful marketing.

Q Using points and examples from the lecture, explain what marketers need to do to ensure that their product sells well.

PREPARATION TIME
00 : 20 : 00

RESPONSE TIME
00 : 60 : 00

04-02

Sample Response

The main idea is that in order for a product to sell well, marketers need to guarantee that their product will somehow attract people's attention. The professor gives two examples of the same company selling the same product but with different marketing strategies. The first is that the company made a colorful, attractive cereal box with lots of pictures and descriptions. However, the professor points out that this box wasn't any different from the other cereal boxes, so no one noticed it. Therefore, the cereal sold poorly. On the other hand, when the same cereal was put in a plain white box with the word "Cereal" in big, black letters, it stood out from the other boxes and therefore sold quite well. The reason is that the simple design made the box look different from the other boxes, so more people noticed it.

For Task 4, you must give your response based on a lecture given by a professor. The score you receive will be similar to the ones in Tasks 1, 2, and 3:

- ◆ **Weak** (0 - 1)
- ◆ **Limited** (1.5 - 2)
- ◆ **Fair** (2.5 - 3)
- ◆ **Good** (3.5 - 4)

Again, the scores are given based on the following components: delivery, language use, and topic development.

- ◇ **Delivery**: This describes how clearly and intelligibly you speak. Pronunciation, intonation, pacing, and flow are all included in this component.
- ◇ **Language Use**: This is based upon the vocabulary and the grammar that you use.
- ◇ **Topic Development**: This part refers to how well you create your response in terms of discussing the two examples that the professor discusses in the lecture.

Each score on the Integrated Speaking task represents the following:

Score	Description
4	The speaker fully addresses the task and may only make small errors. The response is highly intelligible and flows well.
3	The response mostly addresses the task but may not be developed completely. It is mostly intelligible and has good flow. However, the speaker may not express some ideas clearly or properly.
2	The response addresses the task but it not well developed. The response is somewhat intelligible, but there are problems with the delivery and coherence. At time, the meanings of the speaker's words may be unknown.
1	The response is short with a limited amount of contact. It is not particularly coherent, and some parts of the response may be unrelated to the task or mostly not intelligible.
0	The speaker does not make a response, the response is not intelligible, or the response is given in a foreign language.

To receive a 4, the response does not need to be perfect. However, the response should be easy to understand, it should be based on the lecture, and it should contain details about both of the examples that the professor provides.

A score of 1 or 2 shows that the speaker has a limited amount of proficiency in English. These responses may be hard to understand, may use basic grammar and have grammar mistakes, and may use basic vocabulary or use words incorrectly. They also typically do not discuss the topic of the lecture or barely cover it.

Tips for Getting a High Score

1 While you are listening to the lecture, pay close attention to what the professor is saying. Write down details of both examples that the professor provides.

2 Be sure that your answer is related to the question. The question will ask about the two points that the professor makes in the lecture. Only discuss that information. Do not discuss anything else.

3 You should only use the information that appears in the lecture. Do not make up other information or use knowledge about the topic that you may possess. Simply focus on the information that is presented in the lecture.

4 The professor usually provides two examples. Be sure to include information about both of them in your response.

5 Be sure to use a wide variety of grammar structures in your response. Try to use complex sentences—sentences with subordinating conjunctions such as *because*, *since*, *as*, and *although*—when you give your response. That will increase the quality of your response.

6 Be sure to use advanced vocabulary. That will show that you have a high level of English. But also try to paraphrase the information stated by the professor instead of repeating it word for word.

7 Do not repeat yourself when you give a response. Discuss the first example the professor gives and then move on to the next example. Repeating yourself is a time waster, and you will lose points for doing it.

Exercise Listen to a lecture and answer the question following each step.

Listening Listen to a lecture and take notes.

> ✏ Note Taking
>
>
>
> 04-03

📖 **Words & Phrases**

potential adj possible; prospective
categorize v to classify; to sort out; to put into categories
vital adj important; essential

flexible adj elastic; movable
ram v to attack head on; to slam into

Q Using points and examples from the lecture, explain the two different types of physical variations some animals use to defend themselves.

Organization Ask yourself the following questions and organize your ideas.

1 What is the subject of the professor's lecture?

2 What is the first kind of adaptation the professor mentions?

3 What example does the professor provide for this adaptation?

4 What is the second kind of adaptation that the professor discusses?

5 Which animal makes use of this kind of way to protect itself?

Responding Make your response by using the above information.

The topic of the lecture is

During the lecture, the professor mentions

The first one he discusses is

The second example the professor cites is

Speaking Now say your response out loud and record your time. While you are speaking, do not look at the written response.

| Response time: 60 seconds | Your speaking time: _____ seconds |

Comparing Listen to a sample response and compare it with yours.

04-04

Self-Rating Rate your response based on the following criteria.

Delivery		Score		
How clearly did you speak your response?	1	2	3	4
Language Use		Score		
How well did you control language structures to convey your ideas?	1	2	3	4
How appropriately did you use vocabulary to convey your ideas?	1	2	3	4
Topic Development		Score		
How fully did you answer the question?	1	2	3	4
How coherently did you present your ideas?	1	2	3	4

Exercise Listen to a lecture and answer the question following each step.

Listening Listen to a lecture and take notes.

Note Taking

04-05

Words & Phrases

pitch v to advertise; to try to sell
reiterate v to repeat; to say again
undoubtedly adv surely; certainly

wind up v to end up
welfare n wellbeing

Q Using points and examples from the lecture, describe how name recognition can affect how much of a product a company sells.

Organization Ask yourself the following questions and organize your ideas.

1 What topic does the professor cover in his lecture?

2 What aspect of name recognition does the professor first focus upon?

3 How is this related to making successful advertisements?

4 What is the second aspect of name recognition the professor focuses on?

5 According to the professor, what is the result of this aspect of name recognition?

Responding ▶ Make your response by using the above information.

The entire lecture covered

First, the professor mentions

According to the professor,

The professor's second explanation focuses on

Speaking ▶ Now say your response out loud and record your time. While you are speaking, do not look at the written response.

Response time: 60 seconds	Your speaking time: _____ seconds

Comparing ▶ Listen to a sample response and compare it with yours.

04-06

Self-Rating Rate your response based on the following criteria.

Delivery	Score			
How clearly did you speak your response?	1	2	3	4

Language Use	Score			
How well did you control language structures to convey your ideas?	1	2	3	4
How appropriately did you use vocabulary to convey your ideas?	1	2	3	4

Topic Development	Score			
How fully did you answer the question?	1	2	3	4
How coherently did you present your ideas?	1	2	3	4

Exercise Listen to a lecture and answer the question following each step.

Listening Listen to a lecture and take notes.

> 📝 Note Taking
>
>
> 04-07

📖 **Words & Phrases**

patron ⓝ a sponsor
inaccessible adj unavailable
retain ⓥ to keep; to maintain

drawback ⓝ a disadvantage
strive for phr to pursue; to endeavor

Q Using points and examples from the lecture, explain two methods artists used to enable more of the public to view their work.

Organization Ask yourself the following questions and organize your ideas.

1 What idea does the professor try to convey in the lecture?

2 How did artists guarantee they would own the works they created?

3 What benefit did artists gain from being the owners of their works?

4 What is the second way that artists made their works available for public viewing?

5 What examples does the professor give of works that could be seen in public?

Responding ▶ Make your response by using the above information.

The main idea of the lecture is

In her first example, she says

The professor then discusses how

In her view,

Speaking ▶ Now say your response out loud and record your time. While you are speaking, do not look at the written response.

| Response time: 60 seconds | Your speaking time: _____ seconds |

Comparing ▶ Listen to a sample response and compare it with yours.

04-08

Self-Rating ▶ Rate your response based on the following criteria.

Delivery	Score			
How clearly did you speak your response?	1	2	3	4

Language Use	Score			
How well did you control language structures to convey your ideas?	1	2	3	4
How appropriately did you use vocabulary to convey your ideas?	1	2	3	4

Topic Development	Score			
How fully did you answer the question?	1	2	3	4
How coherently did you present your ideas?	1	2	3	4

Exercise Listen to a lecture and answer the question following each step.

Listening Listen to a lecture and take notes.

✎ Note Taking

04-09

📖 **Words & Phrases**

in concert phr together
exploit v to take advantage of; to use
fawn n a baby deer

textbook case n a perfect example; a typical example
hive n a place where bees, hornets, or wasps live

Q Using points and examples from the lecture, explain two different activities that animals engage in to cooperate with one another.

Organization Ask yourself the following questions and organize your ideas.

1 What does the professor focus on in her lecture?

2 What is the example of defense cooperation that the professor mentions?

3 In what ways does this cooperation help the deer?

4 What is another method in which animals cooperate with one another?

5 What is the end result of the honeybees working together?

Responding Make your response by using the above information.

The professor looks into two different ways in which

She emphasizes that

In her first example,

On the same topic, the professor then cites the example of

Speaking Now say your response out loud and record your time. While you are speaking, do not look at the written response.

Response time: 60 seconds   Your speaking time: .... seconds

Comparing Listen to a sample response and compare it with yours.

04-10

Self-Rating Rate your response based on the following criteria.

Delivery		Score		
How clearly did you speak your response?	1	2	3	4
Language Use		**Score**		
How well did you control language structures to convey your ideas?	1	2	3	4
How appropriately did you use vocabulary to convey your ideas?	1	2	3	4
Topic Development		**Score**		
How fully did you answer the question?	1	2	3	4
How coherently did you present your ideas?	1	2	3	4

Exercise Listen to a lecture and answer the question following each step.

Listening Listen to a lecture and take notes.

> 📝 Note Taking
>
>
> 04-11

📖 **Words & Phrases**

pollination (n) the transfer of pollen to fertilize a plant
irresistible (adj) appealing; tempting
colorblind (adj) unable to see certain colors

scent (n) a smell; an aroma
get a load of (phr) to listen to; to pay attention to

Q Using points and examples from the lecture, describe two ways in which flowers attract insects for the purpose of pollination.

Organization Ask yourself the following questions and organize your ideas.

1 What does the professor discuss in his lecture?

2 What does the professor first discuss as a way flowers attract insects for pollination?

3 According to the professor, why is color so important to flowers?

4 What is the next attractor that flowers use as described by the professor?

5 What example does the professor give to describe how flowers use this attractor?

Responding Make your response by using the above information.

The professor discusses two of the ways that

First of all,

The professor then points out that

The example cited by the professor is

Speaking Now say your response out loud and record your time. While you are speaking, do not look at the written response.

| Response time: 60 seconds | Your speaking time: _____ seconds |

Comparing Listen to a sample response and compare it with yours.

04-12

Self-Rating Rate your response based on the following criteria.

Delivery	Score			
How clearly did you speak your response?	1	2	3	4

Language Use	Score			
How well did you control language structures to convey your ideas?	1	2	3	4
How appropriately did you use vocabulary to convey your ideas?	1	2	3	4

Topic Development	Score			
How fully did you answer the question?	1	2	3	4
How coherently did you present your ideas?	1	2	3	4

Exercise Listen to a lecture and answer the question following each step.

Listening Listen to a lecture and take notes.

🖉 Note Taking

04-13

📖 **Words & Phrases**

ominous adj threatening; dangerous
take off v to become common; to become popular
celebrate v to honor; to respect

light n an image; a representation
demonize v to represent as evil or something very bad

Q Using points and examples from the lecture, explain how photographers portrayed industrialization in different centuries.

Organization Ask yourself the following questions and organize your ideas.

1 What topic does the professor cover during his lecture?

2 Which century's opinion of industrialization does the professor discuss first?

3 What does the professor conclude about the way people felt about industrialization then?

4 How did people's opinions of industrialization change in the twentieth century?

5 What is the significance of the picture the professor shows?

During the course of the talk,

According to the professor,

On the other hand,

As an example,

Speaking ▶ Now say your response out loud and record your time. While you are speaking, do not look at the written response.

Response time: 60 seconds	Your speaking time: _____ seconds

Comparing ▶ Listen to a sample response and compare it with yours.

04-14

Self-Rating Rate your response based on the following criteria.

Delivery	Score			
How clearly did you speak your response?	1	2	3	4
Language Use	**Score**			
How well did you control language structures to convey your ideas?	1	2	3	4
How appropriately did you use vocabulary to convey your ideas?	1	2	3	4
Topic Development	**Score**			
How fully did you answer the question?	1	2	3	4
How coherently did you present your ideas?	1	2	3	4

Exercise Listen to a lecture and answer the question following each step.

Listening Listen to a lecture and take notes.

🖊 Note Taking

04-15

📖 **Words & Phrases**

recall Ⓥ to remember
promote Ⓥ to advertise; to endorse
cite Ⓥ to mention; to quote

economical ⓐⓓⓙ money-saving; cost-effective
scener Ⓝ a view; a landscape

　Using points and examples from the lecture, describe two ways in which companies use persuasion to try to sell their products.

Organization Ask yourself the following questions and organize your ideas.

1 What does the professor talk about in his lecture?

2 What is the first advertising method the professor discusses?

3 What are some examples car companies may use to advertise with this method?

4 What is another method of persuasion that the professor mentions?

5 How is this method different from the first one?

Responding Make your response by using the above information.

The professor focuses on

The example given by the professor involves

Meanwhile,

Again,

Speaking Now say your response out loud and record your time. While you are speaking, do not look at the written response.

Response time: 60 seconds   Your speaking time: _____ seconds

Comparing Listen to a sample response and compare it with yours.

04-16

Self-Rating Rate your response based on the following criteria.

Delivery	Score			
How clearly did you speak your response?	1	2	3	4

Language Use	Score			
How well did you control language structures to convey your ideas?	1	2	3	4
How appropriately did you use vocabulary to convey your ideas?	1	2	3	4

Topic Development	Score			
How fully did you answer the question?	1	2	3	4
How coherently did you present your ideas?	1	2	3	4

Exercise Listen to a lecture and answer the question following each step.

Listening Listen to a lecture and take notes.

┌───┐
│ 🖊 Note Taking   │
│   04-17 │
│   │
│   │
│   │
│   │
└───┘

📖 **Words & Phrases**

loathe v to despise; to hate
undesirable adj unwanted
morning people phr people who enjoy waking up in the morning

reward n a prize
dread v to fear; to be afraid of

Q Using points and examples from the lecture, explain two ways to convince oneself to do an activity that one does not enjoy.

Organization Ask yourself the following questions and organize your ideas.

1 What is the subject of the professor's lecture?

2 Which method does the professor mention first?

3 How does the professor define this method?

4 What is the next method that the professor explains?

5 In what way does a person go about doing this method?

Responding > Make your response by using the above information.

The professor tells his class about

The first one he mentions is

The second explanation deals with

Therefore,

Speaking > Now say your response out loud and record your time. While you are speaking, do not look at the written response.

Response time: 60 seconds	Your speaking time: _____ seconds

Comparing > Listen to a sample response and compare it with yours.

04-18

Self-Rating   Rate your response based on the following criteria.

Delivery	Score			
How clearly did you speak your response?	1	2	3	4
Language Use	**Score**			
How well did you control language structures to convey your ideas?	1	2	3	4
How appropriately did you use vocabulary to convey your ideas?	1	2	3	4
Topic Development	**Score**			
How fully did you answer the question?	1	2	3	4
How coherently did you present your ideas?	1	2	3	4

Exercise Listen to a lecture and answer the question following each step.

Listening Listen to a lecture and take notes.

Note Taking

04-19

Words & Phrases

convey v to send; to transmit
significance n importance
subject n a person who is ruled by a king or queen

elevate v to raise; to lift
utter adj complete; total

Q Using points and examples from the lecture, describe two types of film shots and the messages they convey to audiences.

Organization Ask yourself the following questions and organize your ideas.

1 What topic is covered by the professor in her lecture?

2 What kind of film shot does the professor discuss first?

3 What message do these film shots send to the audience?

4 What is another kind of film shot described by the professor?

5 What example does the professor use to help explain this film shot?

Responding Make your response by using the above information.

The professor tells her students about

The first example given is

The professor mentions that

The professor describes

Speaking Now say your response out loud and record your time. While you are speaking, do not look at the written response.

Response time: 60 seconds   Your speaking time: _____ seconds

Comparing Listen to a sample response and compare it with yours.

04-20

Self-Rating Rate your response based on the following criteria.

Delivery	Score			
How clearly did you speak your response?	1	2	3	4

Language Use	Score			
How well did you control language structures to convey your ideas?	1	2	3	4
How appropriately did you use vocabulary to convey your ideas?	1	2	3	4

Topic Development	Score			
How fully did you answer the question?	1	2	3	4
How coherently did you present your ideas?	1	2	3	4

Exercise Listen to a lecture and answer the question following each step.

Listening Listen to a lecture and take notes.

Note Taking

04-21

📖 **Words & Phrases**

as opposed to phr in opposition to; rather than

drastically adv dramatically; greatly

meteorologist n a person who studies and predicts the weather

flu season n a time of year—usually winter—when many people catch colds

treat v to take care of; to cure; to make better

Q Using points and examples from the lecture, describe how positive thinking affects the ways in which people behave.

Organization Ask yourself the following questions and organize your ideas.

1 What is the focus of the professor's lecture?

2 What does the professor begin his lecture by discussing?

3 How does the professor explain the students' actions?

4 Why does the professor bring up medicine bottles?

5 What does the professor say about the medicine bottles?

▶ Responding ▷ Make your response by using the above information.

The professor focuses his lecture on

He states that

However,

He next compares

Although,

▶ Speaking ▷ Now say your response out loud and record your time. While you are speaking, do not look at the written response.

| Response time: 60 seconds | Your speaking time: _____ seconds |

▶ Comparing ▷ Listen to a sample response and compare it with yours.

04-22

🗒 Self-Rating ▷ Rate your response based on the following criteria.

Delivery	Score			
How clearly did you speak your response?	1	2	3	4

Language Use	Score			
How well did you control language structures to convey your ideas?	1	2	3	4
How appropriately did you use vocabulary to convey your ideas?	1	2	3	4

Topic Development	Score			
How fully did you answer the question?	1	2	3	4
How coherently did you present your ideas?	1	2	3	4

Exercise Listen to a lecture and answer the question following each step.

Listening Listen to a lecture and take notes.

> **Note Taking**
>
>
> 04-23

Words & Phrases

engage in phr to take part in; to practice
brainstorm v to think of a wide variety of ideas
ideal adj perfect

eliminate v to rule out; to get rid of
unfeasible adj not practical; not capable of being done

Q Using points and examples from the lecture, explain two types of thinking required when planning an event.

Organization Ask yourself the following questions and organize your ideas.

1 What is the subject of the professor's lecture?

2 What is the first kind of thinking the professor mentions?

3 What does the professor indicate about this type of thinking?

4 What is the second kind of thinking that the professor discusses?

5 What does the professor indicate about this type of thinking?

Responding Make your response by using the above information.

The topic of the lecture is

She points out that

First,

She gives examples such as

Speaking Now say your response out loud and record your time. While you are speaking, do not look at the written response.

Response time: 60 seconds   Your speaking time: _____ seconds

Comparing Listen to a sample response and compare it with yours.

04-24

Self-Rating Rate your response based on the following criteria.

Delivery		Score		
How clearly did you speak your response?	1	2	3	4

Language Use		Score		
How well did you control language structures to convey your ideas?	1	2	3	4
How appropriately did you use vocabulary to convey your ideas?	1	2	3	4

Topic Development		Score		
How fully did you answer the question?	1	2	3	4
How coherently did you present your ideas?	1	2	3	4

Exercise Listen to a lecture and answer the question following each step.

Listening Listen to a lecture and take notes.

Note Taking

04-25

Words & Phrases

process n a method; a way of doing something
marine adj relating to the sea
larva n an immature insect that hatches from an egg

protrusion n something that sticks out
apparent adj clear; obvious

Q Using points and examples from the lecture, explain two ways in which organisms use bioluminescence.

Organization Ask yourself the following questions and organize your ideas.

1 What is the lecture about?

2 What is the first reason organisms use bioluminescence that the professor mentions?

3 What examples does the professor provide for this reason?

4 What is the second reason organisms use bioluminescence that the professor mentions?

5 What examples does the professor provide for this reason?

▌Responding Make your response by using the above information.

The lecture is about

According to the professor,

The first reason that he gives is

He then adds

▌Speaking Now say your response out loud and record your time. While you are speaking, do not look at the written response.

| Response time: 60 seconds | Your speaking time: _____ seconds |

▌Comparing Listen to a sample response and compare it with yours.

04-26

▌Self-Rating Rate your response based on the following criteria.

Delivery	Score			
How clearly did you speak your response?	1	2	3	4

Language Use	Score			
How well did you control language structures to convey your ideas?	1	2	3	4
How appropriately did you use vocabulary to convey your ideas?	1	2	3	4

Topic Development	Score			
How fully did you answer the question?	1	2	3	4
How coherently did you present your ideas?	1	2	3	4

Exercise Listen to a lecture and answer the question following each step.

Listening Listen to a lecture and take notes.

> 📝 Note Taking
>
>
> 04-27

📖 **Words & Phrases**

entice ⓥ to lure; to attract
immediately adv at once
rapid adj fast; swift

senior citizen ⓝ an elderly person, usually sixty years of
age or older
inexpensive adj not costly; cheap in price

Q Using points and examples from the lecture, explain two successful types of marketing promotions.

Organization Ask yourself the following questions and organize your ideas.

1 What does the professor lecture to the students about?

2 What is the first type of marketing promotion the professor mentions?

3 What kinds of stores often use this promotion?

4 What is the second type of marketing promotion the professor mentions?

5 What examples of this type of promotion does the professor give?

Responding Make your response by using the above information.

The professor lectures to the students about

The first example that he

The second example the professor gives

He provides one example of

Speaking Now say your response out loud and record your time. While you are speaking, do not look at the written response.

Response time: 60 seconds	Your speaking time: _____ seconds

Comparing Listen to a sample response and compare it with yours.

04-28

Self-Rating Rate your response based on the following criteria.

Delivery	Score			
How clearly did you speak your response?	1	2	3	4

Language Use	Score			
How well did you control language structures to convey your ideas?	1	2	3	4
How appropriately did you use vocabulary to convey your ideas?	1	2	3	4

Topic Development	Score			
How fully did you answer the question?	1	2	3	4
How coherently did you present your ideas?	1	2	3	4

Exercise Listen to a lecture and answer the question following each step.

Listening Listen to a lecture and take notes.

> 🖉 Note Taking
>
>
> 04-29

📖 **Words & Phrases**

soil n dirt; ground; earth
continually adv at all times
loosen v to make something less compact

aerate v to provide or supply something with air
consume v to eat

Q Using points and examples from the lecture, explain two benefits of worms.

Organization Ask yourself the following questions and organize your ideas.

1 What is the subject of the professor's lecture?

2 What is the first benefit of worms that the professor discusses?

3 How do worms provide this benefit?

4 What is the second benefit of worms that the professor discusses?

5 How do worms provide this benefit?

Responding Make your response by using the above information.

The professor talks to the class about

The first benefit she mentions

In addition,

She notes that

Speaking Now say your response out loud and record your time. While you are speaking, do not look at the written response.

Response time: 60 seconds   Your speaking time: _____ seconds

Comparing Listen to a sample response and compare it with yours.

04-30

Self-Rating Rate your response based on the following criteria.

Delivery		Score		
How clearly did you speak your response?	1	2	3	4

Language Use		Score		
How well did you control language structures to convey your ideas?	1	2	3	4
How appropriately did you use vocabulary to convey your ideas?	1	2	3	4

Topic Development		Score		
How fully did you answer the question?	1	2	3	4
How coherently did you present your ideas?	1	2	3	4

Unit 60 Biology V

Exercise Listen to a lecture and answer the question following each step.

Listening Listen to a lecture and take notes.

04-31

Note Taking

Words & Phrases

enormous adj huge; very large
click n a short, sharp noise
universal adj important; essential

pod n a group of whales
vibration n a continuous, fast shaking motion that may produce a low sound

Q Using points and examples from the lecture, explain how sperm whales and elephants communicate.

Organization Ask yourself the following questions and organize your ideas.

1 What topic does the professor discuss?

2 What do sperm whales use to communicate?

3 What have scientists noticed about sperm whales?

4 What do elephants use to communicate?

5 What do scientists think about this method of communication?

Responding Make your response by using the above information.

The professor talks to the students about

The first method he discusses is

So scientists believe that

Next, the professor tells

Speaking Now say your response out loud and record your time. While you are speaking, do not look at the written response.

| Response time: 60 seconds | Your speaking time: _____ seconds |

Comparing Listen to a sample response and compare it with yours.

04-32

Self-Rating Rate your response based on the following criteria.

Delivery	Score			
How clearly did you speak your response?	1	2	3	4

Language Use	Score			
How well did you control language structures to convey your ideas?	1	2	3	4
How appropriately did you use vocabulary to convey your ideas?	1	2	3	4

Topic Development	Score			
How fully did you answer the question?	1	2	3	4
How coherently did you present your ideas?	1	2	3	4

Actual Test

Actual Test

01

CONTINUE | VOLUME

Speaking Section Directions

05-01

 Make sure your headset is on.

This section measures your ability to speak about a variety of topics. You will answer four questions by speaking into the microphone. Answer as completely as possible.

In the first question, you will speak about a familiar topic. Your response will be scored on your ability to speak clearly and coherently.

In the next two questions, you will first read a short reading passage. This passage will go away, and you will then listen to a talk on the same topic. You will be asked about the information you have read and heard. You will need to combine information from the reading passage and the talk to provide a complete answer. Your response will be scored on your ability to speak clearly and coherently and how accurately you convey information about what you read and heard.

In the last question, you will listen to part of a lecture. You will be asked about what you have heard. Your response will be scored on your ability to speak clearly and coherently and how accurately you convey information about what you heard.

You may take notes while you read and while you listen to the conversations and lectures. You may use your notes to help prepare your response.

Listen carefully to the directions for each question. The directions will not be written on the screen.

For each question you will be given a short time to prepare your response (15 to 30 seconds, depending on the question). A clock will show how much preparation time is remaining. When the preparation time is up, you will be told to begin your response. A clock will show how much response time is remaining. A message will appear on the screen when the response time has ended.

Task **1**

05- 02

Some people enjoy watching television. Others prefer to read the newspaper or to use the Internet. Which activity do you prefer to do and why? Use specific reasons and examples to support your preference.

PREPARATION TIME
00 : 15 : 00

RESPONSE TIME
00 : 45 : 00

Sample Response ▶

05- 03

Task **2**

05-04

All Students to Live in Dormitories

At the start of the new school year next fall, all students will be required to take residence in the university dormitories. By having all students live on campus, the university will not have to increase student housing fees as it has been forced to do in each of the past five years. The fact that all students will be spending more time on campus will permit them to take part in more extracurricular activities. The university administration feels it is important for students to engage in activities outside of class in order to attain a complete college experience.

The man expresses his opinion of the university's regulation on living in the dormitories. State his opinion and explain the reasons he gives for holding that opinion.

PREPARATION TIME
00 : 30 : 00

RESPONSE TIME
00 : 60 : 00

Sample Response

05-05

Task **3**

05-06

Sampling Error

    In any kind of survey or scientific study where data is analyzed, researchers try as much as possible to obtain a true random sampling of the data they are studying. However, there is always some element of error in their studies. This is called the sampling error. The sampling error is usually expressed as a percentage, which shows the possibility for error in the study. Researchers attempt to get the sampling error to as low of a number as possible. As a general rule, the lower the sampling error is, the more accurate the research being performed.

The professor describes the results of two recent surveys. Explain how the results are related to sampling error.

PREPARATION TIME
00 : 30 : 00

RESPONSE TIME
00 : 60 : 00

Sample Response ❯

05-07

VOLUME HELP NEXT

Task **4**

05-08

Using points and examples from the lecture, explain two ways children make mistakes when they are learning.

PREPARATION TIME
00 : 20 : 00

RESPONSE TIME
00 : 60 : 00

Sample Response ≫

05-09

Actual Test

02

05-10

Speaking Section Directions

 Make sure your headset is on.

This section measures your ability to speak about a variety of topics. You will answer four questions by speaking into the microphone. Answer as completely as possible.

In the first question, you will speak about a familiar topic. Your response will be scored on your ability to speak clearly and coherently.

In the next two questions, you will first read a short reading passage. This passage will go away, and you will then listen to a talk on the same topic. You will be asked about the information you have read and heard. You will need to combine information from the reading passage and the talk to provide a complete answer. Your response will be scored on your ability to speak clearly and coherently and how accurately you convey information about what you read and heard.

In the last question, you will listen to part of a lecture. You will be asked about what you have heard. Your response will be scored on your ability to speak clearly and coherently and how accurately you convey information about what you heard.

You may take notes while you read and while you listen to the conversations and lectures. You may use your notes to help prepare your response.

Listen carefully to the directions for each question. The directions will not be written on the screen.

For each question you will be given a short time to prepare your response (15 to 30 seconds, depending on the question). A clock will show how much preparation time is remaining. When the preparation time is up, you will be told to begin your response. A clock will show how much response time is remaining. A message will appear on the screen when the response time has ended.

Task **1**

05-11

Do you agree or disagree with the following statement?
It is important to have a friend with different interests from yourself.
Give specific reasons and examples to support your opinion.

PREPARATION TIME
00 : 15 : 00

RESPONSE TIME
00 : 45 : 00

Sample Response ❯

05-12

Task 2

05-13

No More Bicycles on Campus

Recently, there have been a number of bicycle-related accidents, both with automobiles and pedestrians, on campus. Some have been so severe as to have required the hospitalization of those involved. The school administration has therefore decided to ban all bicycles from campus. The reckless behavior of most bicyclists on campus has been the sole reason for these accidents, so until our student-bicyclists learn to be respectful of others, they may not ride on campus anymore. The school will, however, increase the number of buses on campus. With more buses, students should have no problem getting to their classes on time.

The man expresses his opinion on the regulation against bicycles. State his opinion and explain the reasons he gives for holding that opinion.

PREPARATION TIME
00 : 30 : 00

RESPONSE TIME
00 : 60 : 00

Sample Response ▶

05-14

Task **3**

05-15

Animal Tameability

There are thousands of species of animals on the Earth, yet only a small number have been domesticated. One important factor in domesticating animals is the species' tameability. This refers to the ease with which an animal may be domesticated. An animal's disposition is crucial for determining its tameability. Those with pleasant dispositions may be tamed much more easily than animals aggressive or hostile toward humans. Another is the ability to change the animal's social hierarchy. In other words, animals must be able to recognize humans as their new pack leaders, thereby easing their ability to be domesticated.

The professor describes the difference in trying to domesticate dogs and wolves. Explain how this relates to animal tameability.

PREPARATION TIME
00 : 30 : 00

RESPONSE TIME
00 : 60 : 00

Sample Response ❯

05-16

Task **4**

05-17

Using points and examples from the lecture, explain two ways artists in the Renaissance used perspective in their paintings.

PREPARATION TIME
00 : 20 : 00

RESPONSE TIME
00 : 60 : 00

Sample Response ❯

05-18

Appendix

Useful Expressions
for the Speaking Tasks

This part provides some essential expressions and collocations that can be used in each unit. They will be given with sample sentences through which their applications as well as their meanings can be clarified. Once in your memory, these lexical chunks will help you give sophisticated responses.

Useful Expressions for the Speaking Tasks

1 Stating Your Preference

I prefer A to B
I **prefer** studying online **to** studying in a classroom.
I **prefer** outgoing friends **to** introverted ones.

I like A better [more] than B
I **like** summer vacation **more than** winter vacation since I can do more outdoor activities in summer.
I **like** traveling abroad **better than** staying home during time off from school.

I'd rather A than B
I**'d rather** read fiction **than** nonfiction because novels and short stories stimulate my imagination.
I**'d rather** save money in the bank **than** spend it on something useless.

I think [believe] (that) A is better than B
I **think** riding on the bus **is better than** taking the subway.
I **believe that** recycling **is better than** throwing everything away.

In my opinion, A is better than B
In my opinion, organic food **is better than** mass-produced food.
In my opinion, reading a physical book **is better than** reading an e-book.

Given the choice of A and [or] B, I would choose
Given the choice of working online **or** in an office, **I would choose** to work online.
Given the choice of studying during summer vacation **or** doing a part-time job, **I would choose** the job.

2 Giving Reasons

I prefer ~ because S + V
I **prefer** healthy food **because** nutrition is important to me.
I **prefer** individual activities to group ones **because** I work better on my own.

There are several reasons why I prefer
There are several reasons why I prefer wearing a school uniform to casual clothes.
There are several reasons why I prefer living in a small town to living in a big city.

The first reason is that S + V
The first reason is that we can become close to one another.
The first reason is that small towns are not as crowded as big cities.

The second reason is that S + V
The second reason is that I feel connected with other students who wear the same uniform.
The second reason is that we can have many things in common.

The last [final] reason is that S + V

The last reason is that I can mingle more easily with other students from different economic backgrounds.

The last reason is that houses in small towns are bigger and cheaper than those in big cities.

3 Giving Supporting Details

Comparing & Contrasting

S + V, but S + V

Some people think college education is essential for one's success in life, **but** I don't think so.

Some people like doing experiments in labs, **but** I prefer doing computer simulations.

S + V while S + V

I prefer going to college in a small town **while** many other students want to go to college in a big city.

Studying at the library is ideal **while** studying in a dorm room would be noisy.

On the other hand, S + V

If you study with others, you can save more time. **On the other hand,** you can get distracted easily.

Having an internship can be a great experience. **On the other hand,** you have less time to study.

Although [Though] S + V, S + V

Though attending school provides a lot of benefits, homeschooling also has advantages.

Although shopping at department stores may be convenient, shopping at smaller places has more advantages.

Clarifying

That means (that) S + V

Many students like to study music and art. **That means that** they tend to be creative.

A lot of people rarely save money. **That means that** they may have financial problems in the future.

What I'm saying is (that) S + V

What I'm saying is that more people should use their local libraries.

What I'm saying is that governments should stop taxing people so much.

TASK 2 **Reading & Conversation**

1 Stating the Speaker's Position

Agreeing

The man [woman] agrees with / The man [woman] agrees that S + V

The woman agrees with the university's policy to renovate the art building instead of constructing a new one.

The man agrees with the school's decision that classes in the Physics Department will be canceled.

The man [woman] approves of

The woman approves of the decision to increase tuition.

The man approves of the announcement that a new parking lot will be built.

The man [woman] supports

The woman supports the school's decision to provide milk and water instead of soft drinks.

The man supports the school's decision to build another parking lot.

The man [woman] thinks [believes] ~ is a good idea

The man believes keeping the library open twenty-four hours a day during final exams **is a good idea**.

The woman thinks that offering classes during winter vacation **is a good idea**.

The man [woman] likes the idea of / The man [woman] likes the idea that S + V

The woman likes the idea of prohibiting cars from the on-campus street during part of the day.

The man likes the idea of extending the hours the dining halls are open during final exams.

Disagreeing

The man [woman] disagrees with / The man [woman] disagrees that S + V

The woman disagrees that freshman students should be allowed to live off campus instead of living in the dormitory for a semester.

The man disagrees with the decision that students must pay to use the facilities at the university gym.

The man [woman] is against

The man is against the decision to charge a subscription fee for the school newspaper.

The woman is against the decision to make three students live together in some dormitory rooms.

The man [woman] opposes

The man opposes having a dorm only for seniors.

The woman opposes the school's decision to stop publishing a daily newspaper.

2 Talking about the Reasons

He [She] gives two reasons why he [she]

He gives two reasons why he cannot pay money to use the university health club.

She gives two reasons why she does not want to take an extra required course.

The [His, Her] first reason is that S + V

His first reason is that the school is charging the students for lots of different things.

The first reason is that students already pay too much money in tuition.

The [His, Her] other reason is that S + V

His other reason is that it is unfair that members of the school's sports teams do not pay for the university health club.

The second reason is that the school offers a limited number of scholarships to students.

3 Quoting

According to the announcement [letter, article], S + V

According to the letter, students are not allowed to drive cars on campus.

According to the announcement, the movie club will start charging admission to its weekly movie screenings.

The announcement [letter, article] says (that) S + V

The announcement says that the university has a funding problem.

The article says that the school will not have a baseball team next year.

According to the student [man, woman], S + V

According to the man, he can learn more things if he shares a room with someone from a different major.
According to the woman, she takes the shuttle to the subway station every day.

He [She] mentions (that) S + V

He mentions it is unfair for the university to raise the parking price by a third in just one semester.
She mentions that some students have trouble getting to their classes on time in the morning.

He [She] points out (that) S + V

She points out that poor students are not able to participate in the student exchange program.
He points out that the school already offers a tutoring service.

He [She] argues (that) S + V

He argues that the online tutoring system will cost him a lot because he needs to buy a new computer to get the service.
She argues that the computers in the labs are old and need to be replaced.

TASK 3 **Reading & Lecture**

1 Talking about the Topic

The reading defines A as B

The reading defines invasive species **as** plants or animals that are not native to a habitat.
The reading defines camouflage **as** the ability of an animal to hide itself from others.

According to the reading, S + V

According to the reading, our decision about a certain thing changes depending on the way it is presented.
According to the reading, erosion is something that happens for a variety of reasons.

The professor explains

The professor explains why people can remember to do various activities.
The professor explains the concept of audience effects in more detail.

The professor talks about

The professor talks about the balance of the food chain in the ecosystem.
The professor talks about how advertising can influence purchasing decisions.

According to the professor, S + V

According to the professor, certain chemicals give off a distinct color when exposed to an open flame.
According to the professor, many animals make migrations that are hundreds of kilometers long.

The lecture is about

The lecture is about why companies must prepare for disasters.
The lecture is about the gestation period of various land mammals.

According to the lecture, S + V

According to the lecture, different kinds of clouds can be found in the atmosphere.
According to the lecture, the world is currently in the middle of an ice age.

2 Explaining the Details

Talking about Subtopics

There are two main A of B
There are two main types **of** mountain ranges.
There are two main principles **of** interior design.

One is A, and the other is B
One is long-term memory, **and the other** is short-term memory.
One is the principle of unity, **and the other** is the principle of contrast.

There are two (different) kinds of
There are two kinds of theories of animal communication.
There are two different kinds of charges: positive and negative.

The first (one) is A, and the second (one) is B
The first is information transfer theory, **and the second is** behavioral manipulation theory.
The first one is fish that live in fresh water, **and the second one is** saltwater fish.

Talking about Examples

The professor talks about A as an example of B
The professor talks about dead grass **as an example of** drought.
The professor talks about Antarctica **as an example of** a cold desert.

The professor gives an example of A by discussing B
The professor gives an example of the nature-nurture controversy **by discussing** children's behavior in a classroom setting.
The professor gives an example of invasive species **by discussing** the snakehead fish.

The professor bases his [her] example on
The professor bases his example on relics dug up by archaeologists.
The professor bases his examples on research by the famous architect, Frank Lloyd Wright.

The professor discusses ~ to demonstrate [illustrate]
The professor discusses the company she owned **to illustrate** why small businesses often fail.
The professor discusses animal echolocation **to demonstrate** how it has been applied to human life.

The first example shows how S + V
The first example shows how migratory birds can fly exactly to their winter homes.
The first example shows how marketing can be done online.

Another example the professor gives is
Another example the professor gives is a robin's ability to feel the vibration of worms underground.
Another example the professor gives is marketing that is done in print media.

1 Stating the Topic of the Lecture

The lecture is (mainly) about
The lecture is **mainly about** the kinds of propaganda used in advertising.
The lecture is **mainly about** animals that live in deserts.

The topic of the lecture is
The topic of the lecture is how flowers attract insects to pollinate them.
The topic of the lecture is common fallacies.

The professor talks about
The professor talks about some animals that change their skin color to protect themselves.
The professor talks about animals that can survive in extreme conditions.

The professor discusses [explains]
The professor discusses how to prevent food decay by keeping bacteria in check.
The professor explains how people used to preserve food in the past.

According to the lecture [professor], S + V
According to the professor, there were two main schools of art during that century.
According to the lecture, shaping is teaching someone new behavior through selective reinforcement.

According to the lecture [professor], A refers to B
According to the professor, marketing **refers to** business activities to attract people's attention to a certain product and to make them buy it.
According to the lecture, instinct **refers to** behavior that an animal naturally engages in.

2 Explaining the Details

Talking about Subtopics

The professor says there are two ways (for something) to
The professor says there are two ways to vaccinate people.
The professor says there are two ways to solve the problem.

The first (one) is A, and the second (one) is B
The first one is by fragrance, **and the second one is** by color.
The first one is strip mining, **and the second one is** digging in the ground.

According to the professor, there are two types [kinds] of
According to the professor, there are two kinds of camels.
According to the professor, there are two kinds of utility in economics.

According to the lecture, there are two factors in
According to the lecture, there are two factors in food decay.
According to the lecture, there are two factors in preventing erosion.

One is A, and the other is B
One is proper temperature, **and the other is** a proper level of moisture.
One is creating barriers, **and the other is** eliminating conditions that lead to erosion.

Talking about Examples

The professor gives two examples of

The professor gives two examples of plant adaptations to the environment.

The professor gives two examples of defensive methods that fish use.

The professor explains ~ by giving two examples

The professor explains the extinction of dinosaurs **by giving two examples**.

The professor explains the causes of recessions **by giving two examples**.

The professor talks [speaks] about A as an example of B

The professor talks about pulsars **as an example of** an astronomical phenomenon.

The professor talks about the Great Lakes **as an example of** lakes carved by glaciers.

The professor gives A as an example of B

The professor gives printer flyers **as an example of** advertising.

The professor gives free samples **as an example of** marketing.

The professor gives one more example that shows

The professor gives one more example that shows how lunar eclipses happen.

The professor gives one more example that shows animal defense methods.

The other example (of something) is

The other example of overgeneralization **is** the case in which a child regards every four-legged animal as a dog.

The other example of greenwashing **is** a business claiming it cares about the environment but then refusing to recycle anything.

MEMO

How to
Master Skills for the
TOEFL® iBT
SPEAKING

▍ Answers, Scripts, and Translations

Advanced

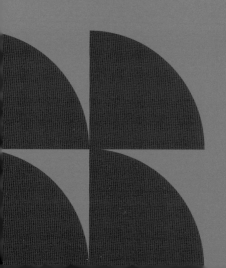

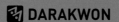

How to
Master Skills for the

Second Edition

TOEFL® iBT

SPEAKING   Advanced

Answers, Scripts,
and Translations

 DARAKWON

Unit 01 Cell Phones

Exercise p.14

Organization

Choice A	Choice B
Agree I am the kind of person who believes cell phones should definitely be prohibited in public places.	**Disagree** In my opinion, people should not be prohibited from using their cell phones in public.
First reason For starters, people speak too loudly on their phones when in public.	**First reason** To begin with, people should have the right to speak on their phones anywhere in public.
Details These places are already noisy enough from the hustle and bustle of daily life, so we do not need to add hundreds of more people chatting away loudly on their phones.	**Details** I live in a country where people have freedom of speech, so no one should make other people be quiet.
Second reason Additionally, many people forget their manners and use all sorts of bad language in public when using their phones.	**Second reason** Another important thing is that many people use their cell phones for their jobs.
Details People—especially young children—should not be subjected to that kind of language.	**Details** We live in a mobile society, and cell phones enable people to get to where they need to be and to work at the same time.

Comparing

Sample Response I Choice A

Script 🎧 01-02

I'm the kind of person who believes cell phones should definitely be prohibited in public places. For starters, people speak too loudly on their phones when in public. These places are already noisy enough from the hustle and bustle of daily life, so we don't need to add hundreds of more people chatting away loudly on their phones. In other words, these people are adding to local noise pollution. Additionally, many people forget their manners and use all sorts of bad language in public when using their phones. People—especially young children—shouldn't be subjected to that kind of language. If cell phone users can't control their mouths, then the government should step in and prohibit people from talking in places where others can overhear them.

해석

나는 공공 장소에서 휴대 전화 사용을 반드시 금지해야 한다고 믿는 쪽이다. 우선 사람들은 공공 장소에서 너무 큰 소리로 통화를 한다. 이러한 장소는 혼잡하고 소란스러운 일상 생활에서 비롯되는 소음으로 이미 충분히 시끄럽기 때문에 전화 통화를 하는 수백 명의 시끄러운 목소리까지 더할 필요가 없다. 다시 말해 이러한 사람들은 지역적인 소음 공해를 악화시키고 있다. 뿐만 아니라 많은 사람들이 예의를 잊고 공공 장소에서 전화 통화를 하면서 온갖 나쁜 말들을 내뱉는다. 사람들은, 특히 어린 아이들은, 그러한 언어를 들어서는 안 된다. 휴대 전화 사용자들이 입조심을 하지 못한다면 정부가 개입해서 다른 사람이 통화 내용을 들을 수 있는 장소에서는 통화를 금지시켜야 한다.

Sample Response I Choice B

Script 🎧 01-03

In my opinion, people should not be prohibited from using their cell phones in public. To begin with, so long as they are not disturbing others, people should have the right to speak on their phones anywhere in public. I live in a country where people have freedom of speech, so no one should make other people be quiet. Another important thing is that many people use their cell phones for their jobs. We live in a mobile society, and cell phones enable people to get to where they need to be and to work at the same time. While some people may be very annoying while talking on their cell phones, we should not punish everyone by prohibiting the use of cell phones in public.

해석

내 생각에는 공공 장소에서의 휴대 전화 사용을 금지해서는 안 된다. 우선, 다른 사람에게 방해를 주지 않는 한, 사람들은 어떤 공공 장소에서도 전화 통화를 할 수 있는 권리를 갖는다. 나는 언론의 자유가 있는 나라에서 살고 있으며 누구도 다른 사람을 침묵하도록 만들 수 없다. 또 다른 중요한 점은 많은 사람들이 업무 때문에 휴대 전화를 사용한다는 것이다. 우리는 모바일 사회에서 살고 있고, 휴대 전화 덕분에 가야할 곳에 가면서 그와 동시에 일을 할 수가 있다. 휴대 전화로 통화를 하면서 심하게 민폐를 끼치는 사람들도 있지만 공공 장소에서 휴대 전화 사용을 금지함으로써 모든 사람들에게 벌을 주는 일은 없어야 한다.

Exercise ··· p.16

Organization

Choice A	Choice B
Live together with one another Personally, I prefer a situation in which all first-year students live together in dormitories.	**Live together with students from other years** I would rather attend a school that had first-year students living with upperclassmen than one where freshmen lived with other freshmen.
First reason First off, it is always ideal to have students in the same year room with each other.	**First reason** One of the main reasons for this is that upperclassmen could be incredibly helpful to first-year students.
Details The reason is that students in the same year will have similar experiences, so they should be with those who can share these experiences.	**Details** An upperclassman roommate could help a freshman get acquainted with the campus more quickly.
Second reason Another important thing is that mixing freshmen with upperclassmen will not benefit the older students at all.	**Second reason** Second of all, many freshmen go to college with bad study habits.
Details They would constantly be stuck explaining things or having to show the freshmen around.	**Details** Upperclassmen know what it takes to do well in college, so they would be able to impart their knowledge to their younger roommates, thereby helping them do better at school.

Comparing

Sample Response | Choice A
Script 🎧 01-04

Personally, I prefer a situation in which all first-year students live together in dormitories. I feel this would have a number of benefits for them. First off, it's always ideal to have students in the same year room with each other. In other words, freshmen should live with freshmen, sophomores with sophomores, and so on. The reason is that students in the same year will have similar experiences, so they should be with those who can share

these experiences. Another important thing is that mixing freshmen with upperclassmen won't benefit the older students at all. They'd constantly be stuck explaining things or having to show the freshmen around. However, by having freshmen live with each other, they'd be able to assist one another in getting used to the school.

해석

개인적으로 나는 모든 신입생이 기숙사에서 함께 생활하는 상황을 선호한다. 그렇게 되면 그들에게 많은 혜택이 돌아갈 것으로 생각한다. 우선 동급생끼리 같은 방을 쓰게 하는 것은 언제나 이상적인 일이다. 다시 말해서 1학년은 1학년과, 2학년은 2학년과 지내야 하며, 계속 이런 식이 되어야 한다. 그 이유는 학년이 같으면 비슷한 경험을 하는데, 학생들은 이러한 경험을 공유할 수 있는 사람과 지내야 하기 때문이다. 또 다른 중요한 점은 신입생을 상급생과 섞어 놓을 경우 기존 학생에게는 아무런 도움이 되지 않는다는 것이다. 그들은 계속해서 이것저것을 설명하거나 신입생들에게 안내를 해 주어야 한다. 하지만 신입생들끼리 함께 생활을 한다면 학교 생활에 적응하는데 있어서 서로 도움을 주고받을 수 있을 것이다.

Sample Response | Choice B
Script 🎧 01-05

I would rather attend a school that had first-year students living with upperclassmen than one where freshmen lived with other freshmen. One of the main reasons for this is that upperclassmen could be incredibly helpful to first-year students. It often takes freshmen several weeks simply to learn where the various buildings on campus are. However, upperclassmen are much more familiar with the campus. An upperclassman roommate could help a freshman get acquainted with the campus more quickly. Second of all, many freshmen go to college with bad study habits. They don't study much, so their grades suffer. Upperclassmen are more disciplined and know what it takes to do well in college. They'd be able to impart their knowledge to their younger roommates, thereby helping them do better at school.

해석

나라면 신입생들끼리만 같이 사는 곳보다 신입생과 상급생이 함께 생활하는 학교에 다닐 것이다. 이렇게 생각하는 주요한 이유 중 하나는 상급생이 신입생에게 엄청난 도움이 될 수 있기 때문이다. 신입생의 경우 캠퍼스 내 여러 건물들의 위치를 파악하는 일에만 종종 여러 주가 걸린다. 하지만 상급생들은 캠퍼스에 훨씬 더 익숙하다. 상급생 룸메이트는 신입생이 캠퍼스에 보다 빨리 적응할 수 있도록 도움을 줄 수 있다. 두 번째로 많은 신입생들이 좋지 않은 학습 습관을 가지고 대학에 진학한다. 공부를 많이 하지 않기 때문에 성적도 좋지 않다. 상급생들은 보다 규율을 잘 따르고 대학에서 어떻게 해야 성적이 올라가는지 알고 있다. 그들은 하급생인 룸메이트들에게 자신이 아는 것을 나누어 줌으로써 그들이 학교 생활을 더 잘 하도록 도와 줄 수 있다.

Exercise p.18

Organization

Choice A	Choice B
Agree I support the idea of having students take classes during the day and work part time either at night or on the weekend.	**Disagree** I believe college students should not be expected to study during the day and then find part-time jobs at night or on the weekend.
First reason For one, studying and working at the same time would teach students about time management.	**First reason** The first reason is that doing both activities at once would be too tiring for them.
Details This would help them learn to use their time more wisely and to study more effectively while using less time.	**Details** When students are too exhausted from working, their grades are bound to suffer. They might not even attend all their classes, which would cause them to learn less and to get low grades.
Second reason Another lesson students would learn is the value of hard work.	**Second reason** Second of all, working part time would detract from students enjoying their college experience as much as possible.
Details By working and studying simultaneously, students would get to know what the real world after college is like.	**Details** Having to work part time would prevent students from doing extracurricular activities and making lifelong friendships and would thus deprive them of some valuable aspects of college life.

Comparing

Sample Response | Choice A
Script 🎧 01-06

I support the idea of having students take classes during the day and work part time either at night or on the weekend. For one, studying and working at the same time would teach students about time management. By having to work many hours each week, students would have less time to spend on other activities. This would help them learn to use their time more wisely and to study more effectively while using less time. Another lesson students would learn is the value of hard work. Many students don't exert themselves in college, but by working and studying simultaneously, they'd get to know what the real world after college is like. Additionally, when they work hard, they'll feel better about both themselves and everything that they've accomplished.

해석

나는 학생들이 낮에 수업을 듣고 밤이나 주말에는 아르바이트를 하는 아이디어에 찬성한다. 우선 학업과 일을 동시에 하면 학생들이 시간 관리하는 법을 익힐 수 있다. 매주 여러 시간 동안 일을 해야 하면 학생들이 다른 활동에 쓸 수 있는 시간이 적어진다. 이로써 시간을 보다 현명하게 사용하는 법과 더 적은 시간으로 보다 효율적으로 공부할 수 있는 법을 배울 수 있을 것이다. 학생들이 배울 수 있는 또 다른 교훈은 힘든 노동의 가치이다. 많은 학생들이 대학 생활을 열심히 하지 않지만 학업과 일을 병행하면 대학 졸업 후의 실제 상황이 어떤지를 알 수 있을 것이다. 뿐만 아니라 열심히 일을 하면 자기 자신과 자신이 성취한 모든 것들에 대해 보다 자부심을 느끼게 될 것이다.

Sample Response | Choice B
Script 🎧 01-07

I believe college students shouldn't be expected to study during the day and then find part-time jobs at night or on the weekend. The first reason is that doing both activities at once would be too tiring for them. When students are too exhausted from working, their grades are bound to suffer. They might not even attend all their classes, which would cause them to learn less and to get low grades. Second of all, working part time would detract from students enjoying their college experience as much as possible. Attending college is not just about going to classes; it involves extracurricular activities and making lifelong friendships. Having to work part time would prevent students from doing these things and would thus deprive them of some valuable aspects of college life.

해석

나는 대학생들이 낮에 공부하면서 밤이나 주말에 일을 해서는 안 된다고 생각한다. 첫 번째 이유는 한꺼번에 두 가지 일을 하면 너무 피곤할 것이기 때문이다. 일 때문에 너무 지치는 경우 반드시 성적이 떨어질 것이다. 심지어 수업에 출석하지 못할 수도 있는데, 그렇게 되면 배우는 양도 적어지고 성적도 떨어질 것이다. 두 번째로 아르바이트를 하면 학생들이 대학 생활을 최대한으로 즐길 수가 없을 것이다. 대학에 다닌다는 것은 수업을 듣는다는 것만 의미하지 않는다. 여기에는 과외 활동 및 평생의 친구를 사귀는 것과 같은 일도 포함된다. 아르바이트를 하면 학생들이 이런 것들을 할 수가 없으며 그 결과 대학 생활의 몇몇 중요한 측면들을 경험하지 못하게 될 것이다.

Unit 04 Life after High School

Exercise ·· p.20

Organization

Choice A	Choice B
Go to college or university immediately In my opinion, a person should attend college or university immediately after graduating from high school.	**Take a year off** I believe it is better for people to take a year off between high school and college.
First reason To begin with, it is ideal to continue straight through with one's schooling so that the person will not forget how to study.	**First reason** For one, a person can use this year off to rest after twelve consecutive years of attending school.
Details Students can actually unlearn the study habits they developed if they do not attend school, so by heading straight to college, they can ensure this does not happen to them.	**Details** By taking a year off, a person can be completely rested and ready to attend four years of college, which will be harder than high school.
Second reason Something else to consider is that by going immediately to college, people can guarantee they will get a college education.	**Second reason** Another thing is that a person could take a year off to get some life experience in the real world.
Details Many people delay going to college for a year but then never get around to attending school again, thereby depriving themselves of a college education.	**Details** For example, a person could find a job and earn some money. This would enable the person to help pay for college, which is expensive.

Comparing

Sample Response | Choice A
Script 🎧 01-08

In my opinion, a person should attend college or university immediately after graduating from high school. To begin with, it's ideal to continue straight through with one's schooling so that the person will not forget how to study. Students can actually unlearn the study habits they developed if they don't attend school, so by heading straight to college, they can ensure this doesn't happen to them. Something else to consider is that by

going immediately to college, people can guarantee they will get a college education. Many people delay going to college for a year but then never get around to attending school again, thereby depriving themselves of a college education. A college diploma is crucial to a person's success nowadays, so it's better to start one's working life off with a college degree rather than to have to return to college in one's thirties or forties.

해석

내 생각에는 고등학교를 졸업한 즉시 대학이나 대학교에 진학해야 한다. 우선 공부하는 법을 잊지 않기 위해서는 학업을 중단하지 않고 계속 이어가는 것이 이상적이다. 실제로 학생들은 학교를 다니지 않으면 익혔던 공부 습관을 잊어버릴 수 있기 때문에 곧바로 대학에 진학함으로써 그런 일이 일어나지 못하게 할 수 있다. 고려해야 할 또 한 가지는 대학에 바로 진학을 해야 확실히 대학 교육을 받게 된다는 점이다. 많은 사람들은 1년 정도 대학 진학을 미루다가 이후 입학을 하지 못해서 대학 교육을 받을 수 있는 기회를 잃어버린다. 오늘날 성공하기 위해서는 대학 졸업장이 꼭 필요하기 때문에 30대나 40대에 다시 대학에 진학하는 것보다 대학 학위를 가진 채 직장 생활을 시작하는 것이 더 낫다.

Sample Response | Choice B
Script 🎧 01-09

I believe it's better for people to take a year off between high school and college. For one, a person can use this year off to rest after twelve consecutive years of attending school. High school and middle school aren't easy, and a person can get burned out from studying hard for so many years. By taking a year off, a person can be completely rested and ready to attend four years of college, which will be harder than high school. Another thing is that a person could take a year off to get some life experience in the real world. For example, a person could find a job and earn some money. This would enable the person to help pay for college, which is expensive. By working, a person would also be able to develop a better appreciation of the value of hard work.

해석

나는 고등학교와 대학교 사이에 1년 동안 쉬는 것이 더 좋다고 생각한다. 우선 12년 연속으로 학교 생활을 하고 난 후 이러한 시간을 이용해서 휴식을 취할 수가 있다. 중학교 및 고등학교는 쉬운 곳이 아니며 여러 해 동안 열심히 공부하면 번아웃을 겪을 수도 있다. 1년간 휴식을 취하면 기력을 완전히 회복할 수 있고 고등학교보다 힘든 4년간의 대학 생활에 대한 대비를 할 수 있다. 또 다른 이유는 1년간의 시간을 이용해 현실 세계에 대한 인생 경험을 쌓을 수 있기 때문이다. 예를 들어 일자리를 구해서 돈을 벌 수도 있다. 그러면 비싼 대학 등록금을 납부하는데 도움이 될 것이다. 또한 일을 함으로써 고된 노동의 가치를 더 잘 이해하게 될 수도 있다.

Exercise p.22

Organization

Choice A	Choice B
Agree I would agree that money and power are the two best measures of a person's success.	**Disagree** I could not disagree more that money and power are the most important indicators of success.
First reason First of all, we live in an age that is defined by how much money a person has or makes.	**First reason** To begin with, I would argue that a person's accomplishments are much better measures of success.
Details With money, people have the freedom to live anywhere, to buy anything, and to do whatever they want to do.	**Details** A man like Jonas Salk, who invented the polio vaccine but never got rich from it, was definitely successful, even without money.
Second reason Power is also another way to determine how successful someone is.	**Second reason** Another example of a better measure of success is the respect others have for someone.
Details Powerful people, like presidents, prime ministers, and CEOs, are able to come up with plans and ideas and make sure people follow them.	**Details** For example, volunteers at hospitals help save people's lives every day. They are greatly respected for this, which makes them successful people.

Comparing

Sample Response | Choice A
Script 🎧 01-10

I'd agree that money and power are the two best measures of a person's success. First of all, we live in an age that's defined by how much money a person has or makes. With money, people have the freedom to live anywhere, to buy anything, and to do whatever they want to do. People admire and try to emulate the wealthy, so it's no surprise that money is an important measure of success. Power is also another way to determine how successful someone is. A person with power can control other people and have them follow his orders. Powerful people, like presidents, prime ministers, and CEOs, are able to come up with plans and ideas and make sure people follow them. That makes them very successful people.

해석
나는 돈과 권력이 성공을 평가하는 가장 좋은 두 가지 척도라는 점에 동의한다. 우선 우리는 재산과 수입으로 정의되는 시대에 살고 있다. 돈이 있으면 어디에서나 지낼 수 있고, 어떤 것이든 살 수 있으며, 그리고 원하는 무엇이든 할 수 있는 자유가 생긴다. 사람들은 부자를 존경하고 본받으려고 하기 때문에 돈이 성공의 중요한 척도라는 점은 당연하다. 권력 역시 성공 여부를 판단할 수 있는 또 다른 방법이다. 권력을 가진 사람은 타인을 통제할 수 있으며 그들이 자신의 명령을 따르도록 만들 수 있다. 대통령, 수상, 그리고 기업 회장과 같이 권력을 가진 자들은 계획과 아이디어를 생각해 내서 사람들이 이를 따르도록 만들 수 있다. 그러한 점 때문에 그들은 매우 성공한 사람이 된다.

Sample Response | Choice B
Script 🎧 01-11

I couldn't disagree more that money and power are the most important indicators of success. To begin with, I'd argue that a person's accomplishments are much better measures of success. People's accomplishments are what make the world go forward. A man like Jonas Salk, who invented the polio vaccine but never got rich from it, was definitely successful, even without money. Another example of a better measure of success is the respect others have for someone. There are many people on the Earth who are respected by others yet are neither rich nor powerful. For example, volunteers at hospitals help save people's lives every day. They are greatly respected for this, which makes them successful people. They don't need money or power to win in life.

해석
나는 돈과 권력이 성공을 평가하는 가장 좋은 두 가지 척도라는 점에 결코 동의할 수 없다. 우선 나는 개인의 업적이 성공 여부를 판단하는 훨씬 나은 척도라고 주장하고 싶다. 인간의 업적이 세상을 발전시키는 것이다. 소아마비 백신을 발명했지만 그것으로 부자가 되지 못했던 조너스 솔크와 같은 사람들이, 비록 가진 돈은 없었지만, 분명 성공한 사람이었다. 성공을 판단하는 보다 나은 척도의 또 다른 예는 누군가에게 다른 사람들이 보이는 존경심이다. 세상에는 부유하지도 않고 권력을 가지지도 않았지만 다른 사람들로부터 존경을 받는 많은 사람들이 존재한다. 예를 들면 병원에서 일하는 자원봉사자들은 매일 사람들의 목숨을 살리고 있다. 이에 대해 그들은 많은 존경을 받고 있는데, 이로써 그들은 성공한 사람이 된다. 그들은 인생에서 승리하기 위해 돈이나 권력을 필요로 하지 않는다.

Unit 06 Kinds of Books

Exercise p.24

Organization

Choice A	Choice B
Reading nonfiction books I prefer to read nonfiction books much more than fiction books.	**Reading fiction books** I love reading books, and most of all, I prefer to read works of fiction instead of nonfiction.

First reason	First reason
For starters, nonfiction books are, quite frankly, more relevant than works of fiction.	The first reason is that many fiction books are some of the greatest works of literature that man has ever produced.
Details	Details
By reading nonfiction books, I can learn so much more about the world.	I love reading works by Hemingway, C.S. Lewis, Tolkien, and many other writers.
Second reason	Second reason
Another reason why I prefer them is that the truth is often stranger than fiction.	In addition, reading fiction allows me to let my imagination run wild.
Details	Details
While fiction books can be entertaining, the plots and stories of nonfiction books are often more imaginative than anything a fiction writer could ever create.	I also enjoy reading science-fiction books, which are often about space, future civilizations, and other fascinating topics.

Comparing

Sample Response | Choice A

Script 🎧 01-12

I prefer to read nonfiction books much more than fiction books. For starters, nonfiction books are, quite frankly, more relevant than works of fiction. They tell true stories about various people, places, things, and events. By reading nonfiction books, I can learn so much more about the world. Another reason why I prefer them is that the truth is often stranger than fiction. While fiction books can be entertaining, the plots and stories of nonfiction books are often more imaginative than anything a fiction writer could ever create. They have the added benefit of being true, so you know what you're reading is both unique and true. Therefore, not only are nonfiction books educational, but they can also be pleasurable works to read.

해석

나는 픽션보다 논픽션 작품을 읽는 것을 더 좋아한다. 우선 솔직히 말해서 논픽션 작품이 픽션 작품보다 더 현실적이다. 논픽션 작품은 다양한 사람, 장소, 물건, 그리고 사건에 관한 실제 이야기를 들려 준다. 논픽션 작품을 읽으면 세상에 대해 훨씬 더 많은 것을 배울 수 있다. 내가 논픽션을 선호하는 또 다른 이유는 진실이 픽션보다 더 이상한 경우가 종종 있기 때문이다. 픽션 작품이 재미있을 수는 있지만, 논픽션 작품의 플롯이나 줄거리는 픽션 작가가 쓸 수 있는 어떠한 내용보다도 더 상상력을 자극하는 경우가 많다. 논픽션은 진실이라는 장점까지 가지고 있기 때문에 읽고 있는 내용이 독특하면서도 사실이라는 점을 알 수 있다. 따라서 논픽션은 교육적일 뿐만 아니라 즐겁게 읽을 수 있는 작품일 수도 있다.

Sample Response | Choice B

Script 🎧 01-13

I love reading books, and, most of all, I prefer to read works of fiction instead of nonfiction. The first reason is that many fiction books are some of the greatest works of literature that man has ever produced. I love reading works by Hemingway, C.S. Lewis, Tolkien, and many other writers. They all wrote great works of fiction that are pleasures to read. In addition, reading fiction allows me to let my imagination run wild. I also enjoy reading science-fiction books, which are often about space, future civilizations, and other fascinating topics. While these stories aren't about true subjects, they let me think about the future a lot while I read them, and this lets me enter new, unknown worlds just from reading books.

해석

나는 책 읽기를 좋아하며 무엇보다 논픽션이 아닌 픽션 작품을 읽는 것을 좋아한다. 첫 번째 이유는 인간이 이제까지 썼던 가장 위대한 문학 작품 중에 많은 픽션 작품들이 포함되기 때문이다. 나는 헤밍웨이, C. S. 루이스, 톨킨, 그리고 기타 많은 작가의 작품들을 정말 좋아한다. 그들 모두 재미있게 읽을 수 있는 위대한 픽션 작품들을 썼다. 뿐만 아니라 픽션을 읽으면 상상력이 발휘된다. 나는 공상 과학 소설도 좋아하는데, 이러한 소설들은 종종 우주, 미래 문명, 그리고 기타 흥미로운 주제들을 다룬다. 이러한 이야기는 현실의 주제를 다루지는 않지만, 나는 이를 읽는 동안 미래에 대해 많은 생각을 하게 되고 따라서 책을 읽는 것만으로 미지의 새로운 세계에 들어갈 수가 있다.

Unit 07 Films & Concerts

Exercise ·· p.26

Organization

Choice A	Choice B
Watching films	**Attending concerts**
As for me, I prefer watching films to attending concerts.	I would say I prefer attending concerts rather than watching films.
First reason	**First reason**
First of all, watching films is a very relaxing activity.	One of the main reasons is that there are so many different genres of music I like.
Details	**Details**
They usually last around two hours, so during that time, I can forget about what is going on in my life and get lost in the movie, especially if it is an action movie, which I love.	In the past few months, I have attended concerts performed by musicians in three different genres, thereby enabling me to hear some of my favorite songs performed live.

Second reason	Second reason
Secondly, I think of films as artwork, so I try to appreciate them as works of art.	Another reason why I like attending concerts is that music is better when I hear it performed live.

Details	Details
When they come together successfully, like in *Citizen Kane*, I realize I am watching something more than a movie.	My family went to a classical music concert recently. Attending the concert in person was better than listening to the same music on a CD.

Comparing

Sample Response | Choice A
Script 🎧 01-14

As for me, I prefer watching films to attending concerts. First of all, watching films is a very relaxing activity. They usually last around two hours, so during that time, I can forget about what's going on in my life and get lost in the movie, especially if it's an action movie, which I love. For example, no matter how many times I watch movies like *Spiderman* and *Mission Impossible*, I get lost in the stories and forget about the outside world. Secondly, I think of films as artwork, so I try to appreciate them as works of art. For example, the acting, the camerawork, the lighting, and many other aspects of a film are all important. When they come together successfully, like in *Citizen Kane*, I realize I'm watching something more than a movie.

해석

나로서는 콘서트에 가는 것보다 영화를 보러 가는 것이 더 좋다. 우선, 영화 관람은 매우 편안히 즐길 수 있는 활동이다. 영화는 보통 두 시간 정도 지속되는데, 그 시간 동안 나는 내 삶에서 일어나는 일들을 잊고, 특히 내가 좋아하는 액션 영화인 경우, 영화에 몰입할 수 있다. 예를 들어 나는 *스파이더맨*과 *미션 임파서블*과 같은 영화를 몇 번이고 볼 때마다 이야기에 빠져서 바깥 세상 일은 잊게 된다. 둘째, 나는 영화를 예술 작품이라고 생각하기 때문에 영화를 예술 작품으로서 감상하려고 노력한다. 예를 들어 연기, 카메라 워크, 조명, 그리고 기타 영화의 여러 요소들이 모두 중요하다. *시민 케인*의 경우처럼 이러한 요소들이 성공적으로 결합되면 나는 영화 이상의 것을 보고 있다는 점을 깨닫게 된다.

Sample Response | Choice B
Script 🎧 01-15

I'd say I prefer attending concerts rather than watching films. One of the main reasons is that there are so many different genres of music I like. I enjoy classical music, pop, rock, and other kinds of music. Fortunately, musicians performing these genres come to my city. In the past few months, I've attended concerts performed by musicians in three different genres, thereby enabling

me to hear some of my favorite songs performed live. Another reason why I like attending concerts is that music is better when I hear it performed live. The musicians put more feeling and emotion into playing than they do when they're in the recording studio. My family went to a classical music concert recently. Attending the concert in person was better than listening to the same music on a CD.

해석

나는 영화를 보는 것보다 콘서트에 가는 것이 더 좋다. 한 가지 주요한 이유는 내가 정말로 여러 장르의 음악을 좋아하기 때문이다. 클래식, 팝, 락, 그리고 기타 종류의 음악을 좋아한다. 다행히도 이러한 장르의 음악가들이 우리 도시에 온다. 지난 몇 달간 나는 서로 다른 세 가지 장르의 음악가들의 공연을 보러 가서 내가 가장 좋아하는 곡들을 라이브 연주로 들을 수 있었다. 내가 콘서트에 가는 것을 좋아하는 또 다른 이유는 라이브로 듣는 음악이 더 좋기 때문이다. 음악가들은 녹음실에서 연주를 할 때보다 더 많은 느낌과 감정을 연주에 쏟아 붓는다. 최근 우리 가족은 클래식 음악 콘서트에 갔다. 직접 콘서트에 가니 똑같은 음악을 CD로 들을 때보다 더 좋았다.

Unit 08 Summer Vacation Activities

Exercise p.28

Organization

Choice A	Choice B
Take classes In my opinion, it is better for students to remain on campus and to take classes during summer.	**Work off campus** I truly believe college students would be wise to get jobs and to work off campus during their summer vacations.
First reason For starters, summer school students typically only take one or two classes during the entire session.	**First reason** One reason I prefer this choice is that students should get some work experience to prepare for life after graduation.
Details By focusing on one or two classes, students can greatly improve their knowledge in these subjects.	**Details** Many companies are also willing to hire students or offer internships in summer, which makes getting jobs after graduating much easier.
Second reason In addition, since the cost of attending college is rising, students should take summer school classes.	**Second reason** Another important thing is that students ought to earn some money during their college years.

Details	Details
Summer school classes are often cheaper than regular ones, and if students take enough summer school classes, they can graduate one or two semesters early and save thousands of dollars.	Many summer jobs offer reasonably good salaries, so students should take the opportunity to improve their finances.

Comparing

Sample Response | Choice A

Script 🎧 01-16

In my opinion, it's better for students to remain on campus and to take classes during summer. For starters, summer school students typically only take one or two classes during the entire session. This enables them to focus exclusively on these classes. This is much unlike the regular semester, when students might take five or more classes at one time. By focusing on one or two classes, students can greatly improve their knowledge in these subjects. In addition, since the cost of attending college is rising, students should take summer school classes. One reason is that summer school classes are often cheaper than regular ones. Another reason is that if students take enough summer school classes, they can graduate one or two semesters early, potentially saving themselves thousands of dollars.

해석

내 생각에는 학생들이 여름에 캠퍼스에 머물면서 수업을 듣는 편이 더 낫다. 우선 여름 학기에는 학기 내내 학생들이 보통 한두 과목만 수강한다. 그러면 그러한 수업에만 집중을 할 수가 있다. 이는 한꺼번에 다섯 과목 이상을 듣는 정규 학기와 크게 다른 점이다. 한두 수업에 집중할 경우 학생들은 이러한 과목에서 매우 많은 것을 배울 수 있다. 또한 대학 등록금이 인상되고 있기 때문에 학생들은 여름 학기 수업을 들어야 한다. 한 가지 이유는 여름 학기 수업이 정규 수업보다 수강료가 저렴하기 때문이다. 또 다른 이유는 학생들이 여름 학기 수업을 충분히 들으면 한두 학기 정도 먼저 졸업을 할 수 있는데, 그러면 수천 달러를 아낄 수도 있다.

Sample Response | Choice B

Script 🎧 01-17

I truly believe college students would be wise to get jobs and to work off campus during their summer vacations. One reason I prefer this choice is that students should get some work experience to prepare for life after graduation. Since many students don't have time to work during the semester, summer vacation is the perfect time to do this. Many companies are also willing to hire students or offer internships in summer, which makes getting jobs after graduating much easier. Another

important thing is that students ought to earn some money during their college years. They could use the money either to help pay for college or to save for after graduation. Many summer jobs offer reasonably good salaries, so students should take the opportunity to improve their finances.

해석

나는 여름 방학에 대학생들이 일자리를 구해서 캠퍼스 밖에서 일을 하는 것이 현명한 일이라고 굳게 믿는다. 내가 그렇게 생각하는 한 가지 이유는 학생들이 졸업 후를 대비해 실무 경험을 쌓아야 하기 때문이다. 많은 학생들이 학기 중에는 시간이 없기 때문에 여름 방학은 그럴 수 있는 완벽한 시간이 된다. 많은 기업들 역시 여름에 학생을 고용하거나 인턴 자리를 기꺼이 제공하는데, 이러한 기회는 졸업 후 취업을 훨씬 더 용이하게 만든다. 또 다른 중요한 점은 학생들이 대학생일 때 돈을 벌어야 한다는 것이다. 그 돈을 학비에 보탤 수도 있고 졸업 후를 대비해 저축할 수도 있다. 많은 여름 일자리들이 상당히 괜찮은 수준의 임금을 지급하기 때문에 학생들은 재정 상황을 향상시킬 수 있는 그러한 기회를 잡아야 할 것이다.

Unit 09 Comfort in Different Generations

Exercise p.30

Organization

Choice A	Choice B
Agree I must agree that people in modern society have lives vastly more comfortable than the lives which my grandparents' generation lived.	Disagree I actually disagree with the statement and feel that my grandparents' generation led more comfortable lives.
First reason First off, there are so many more machines that make life more comfortable.	First reason One reason I feel like this is that they had much simpler lives.
Details People today have access to inventions, including TVs, computers, jet planes, and so many more.	Details We have so many different activities to choose from that this can really be burdensome.
Second reason Second of all, people living during my grandparents' time had inferior health care and medicine.	Second reason Second, my grandparents' generation had much slower-paced lives.

Details	Details
We know how to take care of ourselves better. In addition, when we do have health problems, doctors can cure us quickly.	For example, my grandparents farmed and spent the majority of their time on their land. They were never in a rush to do anything, which must have surely been comfortable for them.

Comparing

Sample Response | Choice A

Script 🎧 01-18

I must agree that people in modern society have lives vastly more comfortable than the lives which my grandparents' generation lived. First off, there are so many more machines that make life more comfortable. People today have access to inventions, including TVs, computers, jet planes, and so many more. All of these have made our lives simpler and have, naturally, made them more comfortable, too. Second of all, people living during my grandparents' time had inferior health care and medicine. Nowadays, our lives are more comfortable because we know how to take care of ourselves better. In addition, when we do have health problems, doctors can cure us quickly. Living a healthy life is a key aspect of living a comfortable life.

해석

나는 현대 사회의 사람들이 조부모 세대에 비해 훨씬 더 편안한 생활을 한다는 의견에 동의한다. 첫째, 삶을 보다 편안하게 만드는 정말 많은 기기들이 존재한다. 오늘날 사람들은 TV, 컴퓨터, 제트기, 그리고 기타 등등의 발명품들을 이용하고 있다. 이 모두는 우리 삶을 더 용이하게, 그리고 당연하게도, 더 편안하게 만들어 준다. 둘째, 조부모 시대에 살던 사람들의 경우 의료 관리 및 의약품 상태가 더 열악했다. 오늘날 우리는 스스로를 돌보는 법을 알고 있기 때문에 삶이 더 편안하다. 또한 건강상의 문제가 있으면 의사들이 빠르게 치료해 줄 수 있다. 건강한 삶은 편안한 삶에 있어서 핵심적인 부분이다.

Sample Response | Choice B

Script 🎧 01-19

I actually disagree with the statement and feel that my grandparents' generation led more comfortable lives. One reason I feel like this is that they had much simpler lives. Today, people have too many things to worry about. We have so many different activities to choose from that this can really be burdensome. Instead, my grandparents' generation had fewer options, which made their lives easier. Second, my grandparents' generation had much slower-paced lives. Today, people rush from one place to another for meeting after meeting. It was almost the

complete opposite in the past. For example, my grandparents farmed and spent the majority of their time on their land. They were never in a rush to do anything, which must have surely been comfortable for them.

해석

나는 사실 그러한 의견에 반대하며 조부모님 세대가 보다 편안한 삶을 살았다고 생각한다. 그렇게 생각하는 한 가지 이유는 그들이 훨씬 더 간소한 삶을 살았기 때문이다. 오늘날 사람들에게는 걱정해야 할 일들이 너무 많다. 선택할 수 있는 활동들이 너무 많은데, 이는 실제로 성가신 것일 수 있다. 대신 조부모님 세대에게는 선택의 여지가 적었기 때문에 삶이 더 용이했다. 두 번째로 조부모님 세대는 속도가 훨씬 느린 삶을 살았다. 오늘날 사람들은 이런 저런 만남을 위해 이곳저곳으로 급하게 뛰어다닌다. 과거에는 이와 정반대였다. 예를 들어 우리 조부모님께서는 농장을 운영하시면서 대부분의 시간을 그곳에서 보내셨다. 무언가를 하기 위해 한 번도 서두르신 적이 없으셨는데, 이러한 삶은 그분들에게 분명 편안한 것이었을 것이다.

Unit 10 Life Lessons

Exercise p.32

Organization

Choice A	Choice B
Agree I agree that people cannot learn important lessons about life in the classroom.	**Disagree** I could not disagree more with the statement that students cannot learn about life in the classroom.
First reason First of all, classrooms are places where students' minds are filled with knowledge about different subjects.	**First reason** On the contrary, it is possible for students to learn many things about life.
Details For example, my teachers always stick with the text and teach lessons that only relate to the subject we are learning. They never stress how our lessons relate to life.	**Details** For example, history lessons are filled with stories about people and how they reacted to certain events. Students always learn that people who do not learn history are doomed to repeat it.
Second reason Secondly, classrooms are sheltered environments that in no way resemble the real world.	**Second reason** Another reason is that teachers often fill their lessons with important facts or stories related to life.

Details	Details
Life is not fair, and not everyone gets the same opportunities as others. However, in classrooms, teachers try to be fair, so every student gets the same chances.	In my math class, we do not simply solve addition or subtraction problems. Instead, we learn to calculate interest, to balance a checkbook, and to do other practical skills we'll need in the future.

Comparing

Sample Response | Choice A

Script 🎧 01-20

I agree that people cannot learn important lessons about life in the classroom. First of all, classrooms are places where students' minds are filled with knowledge about different subjects. This means they're taught math, English, science, history and other subjects but aren't taught anything about life. For example, my teachers always stick with the text and teach lessons that only relate to the subject we're learning. They never stress how our lessons relate to life. Secondly, classrooms are sheltered environments that in no way resemble the real world. Life isn't fair, and not everyone gets the same opportunities as others; however, in classrooms, teachers try to be fair, so every student gets the same chances. This isn't like the real world, so it's hard to imagine how students can learn about life in classrooms.

해석

나는 사람들이 교실 안에서 삶에 대한 중요한 내용을 배울 수 없다는 점에 동의한다. 첫째, 교실은 학생들의 머리에 다양한 과목에 대한 지식이 채워지는 공간이다. 다시 말해 수학, 영어, 과학, 역사, 그리고 기타 과목들이 가르쳐지지만 삶에 대해서는 아무것도 가르쳐지지 않는다. 예를 들어 우리 선생님들은 항상 문구에 집착하시고 우리가 배우는 과목과 관련된 내용만 가르치신다. 우리가 배우는 내용이 인생과 어떤 관련이 있는지는 결코 강조하지 않으신다. 둘째, 교실은 지나친 보호를 받는 환경이라 현실 세상과 결코 닮아 있지 않다. 인생은 공평하지 않으며 모든 사람들이 남들과 동일한 기회를 얻는 것도 아니다. 이는 현실 세계와 다른 점으로, 교실에서 학생들이 삶에 대해 어떻게 배울 수 있는지를 상상하는 일은 힘들다.

Sample Response | Choice B

Script 🎧 01-21

I couldn't disagree more with the statement that students can't learn about life in the classroom. On the contrary, it's possible for students to learn many things about life. To begin with, many subjects students learn are related to life. For example, history lessons are filled with stories about people and how they reacted to certain events. Students always learn that people who don't learn history are doomed to repeat it. History is essentially a story

about life, meaning much can be learned about it in classrooms. Another reason is that teachers often fill their lessons with important facts or stories related to life. In my math class, we don't simply solve addition or subtraction problems. Instead, we learn to calculate interest, to balance a checkbook, and to do other practical skills we'll need in the future.

해석

나는 교실에서 학생들이 인생에 대해 배울 수 없다는 주장에 결코 동의할 수 없다. 그와 반대로 학생들은 인생에 대해 많은 것을 배울 수 있다. 우선 학생들이 배우는 많은 과목들이 인생과 관련이 있다. 예를 들어 역사는 사람들에 대한 이야기와 그들이 특정 사건에 대응한 방식에 관한 이야기로 채워져 있다. 역사를 배우지 않는 사람은 그것을 반복할 수밖에 없다는 점을 학생들은 항상 배운다. 역사는 본질적으로 인생에 대한 이야기이며, 이는 교실에서도 인생에 대해 많은 것을 배울 수 있다는 점을 의미한다. 또 다른 이유는 교사들이 인생과 관련된 중요한 사실이나 이야기들을 수업 내용에 끼워 넣기 때문이다. 수학 수업에서 우리는 단순히 더하기 빼기 문제만 푸는 것은 아니다. 대신 이자를 계산하고, 결산을 하며, 그리고 미래에 필요한 기타 실용적인 기술들을 익힌다.

Unit 11 Class Times

Exercise ·· p.34

Organization

Choice A	Choice B
Taking classes in the morning I would much rather take classes in the morning.	**Taking classes in the afternoon** Of the two choices, taking classes in the afternoon is more appealing to me than taking classes in the morning.
First reason For one thing, I am a morning person, so I always wake up early.	**First reason** One of the reasons is that I often stay awake past midnight, so I tend to get up late in the morning.
Details I am ready to study by seven o'clock. I am very alert at that time since I'm a morning person, so it's better for me to take classes when my brain is working at its best.	**Details** After I wake up, I take my time preparing for school. As a result, it's more convenient for me to have classes in the afternoon so that I don't have to hurry.
Second reason Another reason I prefer morning classes is that I like to do various activities in the afternoon.	**Second reason** Another reason is that I have always performed better in afternoon classes than I have in morning classes.

Details	Details
If I finish my classes by noon, I can play sports, go to the gym, or just relax with a book in the afternoon.	For instance, when I take tests in the afternoon, my grades are typically high. However, the same is not true when I have exams in the morning.

Comparing

Sample Response l Choice A
Script 🎧 01-22

While many people prefer to take classes in the afternoon, I feel the opposite way. I would much rather take classes in the morning. For one thing, I am a morning person, so I always wake up early. I get up around six in the morning, take a shower, get dressed, and have breakfast. I am ready to study by seven o'clock. I am very alert at that time since I'm a morning person, so it's better for me to take classes when my brain is working at its best. Another reason I prefer morning classes is that I like to do various activities in the afternoon. If I finish my classes by noon, I can play sports, go to the gym, or just relax with a book in the afternoon.

해석

많은 사람들이 오후에 수업을 듣는 것을 선호하지만 나는 그 반대이다. 나는 오히려 오전에 수업을 듣고 싶다. 우선 나는 아침형 인간이기 때문에 항상 일찍 일어난다. 오전 6시에 기상을 해서 샤워를 하고 옷을 입은 후 아침 식사를 한다. 7시쯤이면 공부할 준비를 마친다. 나는 아침형 인간이라 그 시간에 정신이 매우 맑기 때문에 나로서는 뇌가 최고의 성능을 발휘하는 시간에 수업을 듣는 것이 더 좋다. 내가 오전 수업을 듣는 것을 좋아하는 또 다른 이유는 오후에 다양한 활동들을 하고 싶기 때문이다. 12시에 수업을 마치면 오후에 스포츠 경기를 하거나 체육관에 갈 수도 있으며, 혹은 책을 읽으면서 휴식을 취할 수도 있다.

Sample Response l Choice B
Script 🎧 01-23

Of the two choices, taking classes in the afternoon is more appealing to me than taking classes in the morning. One of the reasons is that I often stay awake past midnight, so I tend to get up late in the morning. After I wake up, I take my time preparing for school. As a result, it's more convenient for me to have classes in the afternoon so that I don't have to hurry. Another reason is that I have always performed better in afternoon classes than I have in morning classes. For instance, when I take tests in the afternoon, my grades are typically high. However, the same is not true when I have exams in the morning. So to get the best grades possible, I should take afternoon classes.

해석

나로서는 두 가지 선택 사항 중에서 오후 수업을 듣는 것이 오전 수업을 듣는 것보다 더 좋아 보인다. 한 가지 이유는 내가 종종 자정이 지난 시간까지 깨어 있고 오전 늦게 일어나는 편이기 때문이다. 깨어난 후에는 수업 준비를 하느라 시간을 보낸다. 따라서 나로서는 서두를 필요가 없기 때문에 오후 수업을 듣는 것이 더 편하다. 또 다른 이유는 오전 수업에서보다 오후 수업에서의 성적이 항상 더 좋기 때문이다. 예를 들어 나는 오후에 시험을 보면 성적이 보통 높게 나오는 편이다. 하지만 오전에 시험을 보면 그렇지가 못하다. 따라서 가장 좋은 성적을 받기 위해서는 오후 수업을 들어야 한다.

Unit 12 Volunteer Work

Exercise p.36

Organization

	Choice A	Choice B
	Agree I strongly agree that all students should do volunteer work on weekends.	**Disagree** I disagree that all students should do volunteer work on weekends.
	First reason First off, it is always ideal to have students in the same year room with each other.	**First reason** The primary reason is that people should do volunteer work because they want to rather than because they are required to.
	Details As for me, I volunteer at a food kitchen sometimes, so I help serve meals to people who can't afford their own for various reasons.	**Details** My brother's school makes all of the students do volunteer work, and many of them are unhappy about it because they are being forced to do it.
	Second reason Second, lots of students don't do anything constructive on weekends.	**Second reason** Another reason is that many students are busy doing other activities on weekends.
	Details For instance, they just stay home and either watch television or play computer games. Others might just spend most of their time on social media sites.	**Details** As an example, I attend some private academies to improve my abilities every weekend. If I have to volunteer somewhere, I might not be able to improve myself by attending those classes.

Sample Response | Choice A
Script 🎧 01-24

I strongly agree that all students should do volunteer work on weekends. First, doing volunteer work is a wonderful way to give back to the members of the community who need assistance in some ways. As for me, I volunteer at a food kitchen sometimes, so I help serve meals to people who can't afford their own for various reasons. Doing that makes me feel good about myself and also lets me help others. Second, lots of students don't do anything constructive on weekends. For instance, they just stay home and either watch television or play computer games. Others might just spend most of their time on social media sites. Instead of wasting their time like that, they should be productive and help others by volunteering.

해석

나는 모든 학생들이 주말마다 자원봉사를 해야 한다는 점에 전적으로 동의한다. 자원봉사는 여러가지 면에서 도움을 필요로 하는 지역 주민들에게 봉사할 수 있는 멋진 방법이다. 내 경우, 나는 때때로 주방에서 자원봉사를 하며 다양한 이유로 식비를 낼 수 없는 사람들에게 음식을 내어 주고 있다. 그렇게 하면 스스로에 대한 만족감을 느낄 수 있고 다른 사람에게도 도움이 된다. 둘째, 많은 학생들이 주말에 어떠한 건설적인 활동도 하지 않는다. 예를 들어 그저 집에서 머물면서 텔레비전을 보거나 컴퓨터 게임을 한다. 소셜 미디어 사이트에서 대부분의 시간을 보내는 사람도 있을 것이다. 그처럼 시간을 낭비하는 대신 자원봉사를 함으로써 생산적인 일을 하고 다른 사람에게 도움을 주어야 할 것이다.

Sample Response | Choice B
Script 🎧 01-25

I'm a big believer in doing volunteer work; however, I disagree that all students should do volunteer work on weekends. The primary reason is that people should do volunteer work because they want to rather than because they are required to. My brother's school makes all of the students do volunteer work, and many of them are unhappy about it because they are being forced to do it. This makes them feel both angry at and upset with their school. Another reason is that many students are busy doing other activities on weekends. As an example, I attend some private academies to improve my abilities every weekend. If I have to volunteer somewhere, I might not be able to improve myself by attending those classes.

해석

나는 자원봉사 활동을 크게 찬성하는 입장이다. 하지만 모든 학생들이 주말마다 자원봉사를 해야한다는 점에는 동의하지 않는다. 첫 번째 이유는 사람들이 해야 해서가 아니라 하고 싶어서 자원봉사를 해야 하기 때문이다. 내 동생의 학교는 모든 학생들에게 자원봉사를 시키고 있는데, 그들 중 다수가 자신들이 억지로 자원봉사를 해야 하기 때문에 기분이 상해 있다. 이는 학생들로 하여금 학교에 대한 분노와 불만을 갖도록 만든다. 또 다른 이유는 많은 학생들이 주말마다 기타

Unit 13 Recycling

Exercise ·· p.38

Organization

Choice A	Choice B
Agree I believe that everyone should be required to recycle, so I agree with the statement.	Disagree I do not agree with the statement that everyone should have to recycle.
First reason One thing to remember is that the Earth has limited amounts of various natural resources.	First reason For one thing, it's not necessary to recycle items such as paper.
Details As a result, it is vital that we recycle these resources so that we can use them again and again.	Details Paper is biodegradable, so it can break down rather quickly, and it's also a renewable resource. After all, we can plant more trees.
Second reason Something else to consider is that we create tons and tons of garbage every year, so landfills are starting to overflow.	Second reason Secondly, even though people recycle lots of items these days, most of the time, they still wind up in garbage dumps.
Details If everyone has to recycle paper, plastic, glass, and metal objects, we can slow down the rate that landfills become larger.	Details Take plastic for instance. It is often taken from recycling centers and sent to garbage dumps because it cannot be reused for anything.

Comparing ▶

Sample Response | Choice A
Script 🎧 01-26

I believe that everyone should be required to recycle, so I agree with the statement. One thing to remember is that the Earth has limited amounts of various natural resources. As a result, it is vital that we recycle these resources so that we can use them again and again.

If everyone has to recycle, then we can help future generations by not using up all of our natural resources today. Something else to consider is that we create tons and tons of garbage every year, so landfills are starting to overflow. If everyone has to recycle paper, plastic, glass, and metal objects, we can slow down the rate that landfills become larger. By creating much less garbage, we can help make the Earth a cleaner place.

해석

나는 모든 사람들이 재활용을 해야 한다고 믿기 때문에 그러한 주장에 동의한다. 기억해야 할 한 가지는 지구에 한정된 양의 다양한 천연 자원들이 존재한다는 점이다. 따라서 이들을 계속 사용하기 위해서는 자원을 재활용하는 일이 반드시 필요하다. 모두가 재활용을 한다면 현재의 천연 자원들을 모두 소모하지 않음으로써 후손들에게 도움을 줄 수 있다. 고려해야 할 또 한 가지는 우리가 해마다 엄청난 양의 쓰레기를 배출하기 때문에 매립지가 포화되기 시작할 것이라는 점이다. 모두가 종이, 플라스틱, 유리, 그리고 금속 물건들을 재활용한다면 그러한 속도를 늦춰서 매립지를 확대시킬 수 있다. 쓰레기 배출량을 크게 줄임으로써 지구를 보다 깨끗한 곳으로 만들 수 있다.

Sample Response | Choice B
Script 🎧 01-27

I do not agree with the statement that everyone should have to recycle. For one thing, it's not necessary to recycle items such as paper. Paper is biodegradable, so it can break down rather quickly, and it's also a renewable resource. After all, we can plant more trees. So there's no need to force people to recycle paper and other similar items. Secondly, even though people recycle lots of items these days, most of the time, they still wind up in garbage dumps. Take plastic for instance. It is often taken from recycling centers and sent to garbage dumps because it cannot be reused for anything. In other words, recycling many products is a huge waste of time and money, so people should not be forced to do it.

해석

나는 모두가 재활용을 해야 한다는 주장에 동의하지 않는다. 우선, 종이와 같은 제품들은 재활용을 할 필요가 없다. 종이는 생분해성이라서 빠르게 분해되며 또한 재생이 사용이 가능한 자원이다. 어쨌거나 더 많은 나무를 심으면 된다. 따라서 사람들에게 강제로 종이 및 기타 유사한 제품들을 재활용하도록 만들 필요가 없다. 둘째, 오늘날 사람들이 많은 제품을 재활용하고 있지만 대부분의 경우 이들은 결국 쓰레기 처리장으로 보내진다. 플라스틱을 예로 들어 보자. 종종 재활용 센터에서 온 플라스틱은 재사용이 불가능하기 때문에 쓰레기 처리장으로 보내진다. 다시 말해 많은 제품들을 재활용하는 일은 막대한 시간 낭비이며 돈 낭비이기 때문에 사람들에게 재활용을 강요해서는 안 된다.

Exercise p.40

Organization

Choice A	Choice B
Camping and sleeping outdoors I absolutely love to spend time outdoors, so given the two choices, I would prefer to go camping and to sleep outdoors.	**Staying at hotels** Of the two choices I was given, I would take the latter one, so I prefer to sleep at hotels on my trips.
First reason Firstly, I live in a place that has a lot of great camping spots, so I frequently spend time camping with my family.	**First reason** One reason is that when I take a trip, I want to be comfortable.
Details There is nothing better than having a campfire, watching the stars, and then going to sleep in a tent outdoors.	**Details** I can sleep in a nice, soft bed, take a long, hot shower, and then wake up and enjoy a delicious breakfast buffet.
Second reason Another benefit is that I can get away from modern technology.	**Second reason** A second reason is that I prefer to take trips to cities, where it is impossible to go camping.
Details When I go camping, my smartphone doesn't have Internet connectivity, so I can't get online.	**Details** Instead, when my family travels, we always stay at hotels that are located downtown, so there's no way we can go camping even if we want to.

Comparing

Sample Response | Choice A
Script 🎧 01-28

I absolutely love to spend time outdoors, so given the two choices, I would prefer to go camping and to sleep outdoors. Firstly, I live in a place that has a lot of great camping spots, so I frequently spend time camping with my family. There is nothing better than having a campfire, watching the stars, and then going to sleep in a tent outdoors. I have a lot of great memories from my time spent camping. Another benefit is that I can get away from modern technology. When I go camping, my smartphone doesn't have Internet connectivity, so I can't get online. It's nice to spend time away from the Internet and to do other activities, which is something I can do when I go camping.

나는 정말로 야외에서 시간을 보내는 것을 좋아하기 때문에 두 가지 선택 사항 중에서는 캠핑을 가서 야외에서 잠을 자는 것을 좋아한다. 첫째, 나는 멋진 캠핑 장소가 많은 지역에서 살기 때문에 종종 가족들과 캠핑을 하며 시간을 보낸다. 모닥불을 피우고, 별을 바라보며, 그 후에는 야외 텐트에서 잠을 자는 것보다 더 좋은 것은 없다. 나는 캠핑을 하면서 보낸 시간에 대한 멋진 기억들이 많이 있다. 또 다른 이점은 내가 현대의 첨단 기술로부터 벗어날 수 있기 때문이다. 캠핑을 가면 내 스마트폰이 인터넷에 연결되지 않기 때문에 나는 온라인에 접속할 수가 없다. 인터넷으로부터 떨어져 시간을 보내고 다른 활동을 하는 것은 멋진 일이며, 이것이 바로 내가 캠핑을 가면 하는 일이다.

Sample Response I Choice B

Script 🎧 01-29

> Of the two choices I was given, I would take the latter one, so I prefer to sleep at hotels on my trips. One reason is that when I take a trip, I want to be comfortable. Camping is not comfortable at all, but hotels are. I can sleep in a nice, soft bed, take a long, hot shower, and then wake up and enjoy a delicious breakfast buffet. When I take a trip like that, I come back home feeling refreshed. A second reason is that I prefer to take trips to cities, where it is impossible to go camping. Instead, when my family travels, we always stay at hotels that are located downtown, so there's no way we can go camping even if we want to.

해석

나는 주어진 두 가지 선택 사항 중 후자를 선택함으로써 여행 기간 동안 호텔에 묵고 싶다. 한 가지 이유는 여행할 때 편안히 지내고 싶어서이다. 캠핑은 전혀 편안하지 않지만 호텔은 편안하다. 나는 안락하고 부드러운 침대에서 잠을 잘 수 있고, 따뜻한 물로 오래 샤워를 할 수 있으며, 잠에서 깨어 맛있는 조식 뷔페를 즐길 수 있다. 그러한 여행을 함으로써 나는 개운한 상태로 집에 돌아오게 된다. 두 번째 이유는 내가 캠핑이 불가능한 도시에서 여행하는 것을 좋아하기 때문이다. 가족 여행을 하는 경우 우리는 항상 시내 중심가에 위치한 호텔에서 머물기 때문에 설령 원하는 경우라도 캠핑을 할 수 있는 방법이 없다.

Unit 15 Types of Books

Exercise p.42

Organization

Choice A	Choice B
Reading printed books	**Reading e-books**
I would much rather read printed books than e-books for a couple of reasons.	I know that many people prefer printed books, but I love technology, so I would much rather read e-books.

First reason	First reason
One of them is that I love to hold a book in my hands and to turn the pages when I read.	For one thing, I can carry hundreds or even thousands of books around on an e-reader.
Details	**Details**
There is nothing better than sitting outside underneath a tree and reading a printed book. That is something which I can do for hours at a time.	This means that if I am out somewhere and want to read a book, I can do that instantly instead of having to go home or to the library.
Second reason	**Second reason**
A second reason is that once a book is printed, it cannot be changed.	A second advantage of e-books is that they are much cheaper than printed books.
Details	**Details**
However, e-books can be updated or changed automatically, which is something that I really dislike.	As a result, I have built up an enormous collection of e-books, which is something I can't do with printed books since they are frequently expensive.

Comparing

Sample Response I Choice A

Script 🎧 01-30

> I would much rather read printed books than e-books for a couple of reasons. One of them is that I love to hold a book in my hands and to turn the pages when I read. There is nothing better than sitting outside underneath a tree and reading a printed book. That is something which I can do for hours at a time. A second reason is that once a book is printed, it cannot be changed. However, e-books can be updated or changed automatically, which is something that I really dislike. When I purchase a printed book or check one out from the library, I can be certain that not a single word will have been changed from when it was first printed.

해석

나는 두 가지 이유에서 전자책보다 종이책을 읽는 것을 훨씬 더 좋아한다. 한 가지 이유는 내가 손에 책을 들고 다니는 것과 책을 읽을 때 페이지를 넘기는 것을 좋아하기 때문이다. 야외에서 나무 밑에 앉아 종이책을 읽는 것보다 더 좋은 것은 없다. 나는 그런 일을 때때로 몇 시간 동안 할 수 있다. 두 번째 이유는 책이 인쇄되면 수정이 불가능하기 때문이다. 하지만 전자책은 자동으로 업데이트되거나 수정될 수 있는데, 나는 이러한 점을 정말로 좋아하지 않는다. 종이책을 구입하거나 도서관에서 대출하는 경우, 나는 처음 인쇄된 이후로 단 한 글자도 바뀌지 않을 것이라는 점을 확신할 수 있다.

Script 🎧 01-31

I know that many people prefer printed books, but I love technology, so I would much rather read e-books. For one thing, I can carry hundreds or even thousands of books around on an e-reader. This means that if I am out somewhere and want to read a book, I can do that instantly instead of having to go home or to the library. For me, that is extremely convenient. A second advantage of e-books is that they are much cheaper than printed books. A lot of e-books just cost one or two dollars, and many are actually free. As a result, I have built up an enormous collection of e-books, which is something I can't do with printed books since they are frequently expensive.

해석

많은 사람들이 종이책을 좋아한다는 점을 알지만 나는 과학 기술을 좋아하기 때문에 전자책을 읽는 것이 훨씬 더 좋다. 우선 나는 수백 혹은 수천 권의 책을 전자책 단말기에 넣어서 가지고 다닐 수 있다. 이러한 점은 내가 외부에 있는데 책을 읽고 싶은 경우, 집이나 도서관에 갈 필요없이 즉시 그렇게 할 수 있다는 점을 의미한다. 나로서는 정말로 편한 일이다. 전자책의 두 번째 장점은 이들이 종이책보다 훨씬 더 저렴하다는 것이다. 많은 전자책의 가격이 1달러나 2달러에 불과하며 실제로 무료인 책들도 많다. 따라서 나는 막대한 양의 전자책을 수집할 수 있는데, 이는 종종 값이 비싼 종이책으로는 할 수 없는 일이다.

PART II Integrated Speaking Task 1 **Reading & Conversation**

Unit 16 School Facilities

Exercise p.50

Reading

해석

지나치게 붐비는 학생 센터 식당

편집자님께,

저는 학생 센터 식당에 대한 생각을 나타내고자 이 편지를 씁니다. 입학생이 증가한 이후로 식당이 지나치게 붐비고 있습니다. 이러한 점은 학생들이 앉아서 식사를 할 수 있는 충분한 자리가 없기 때문에 아침, 점심, 그리고 저녁 식사 시간에 매우 심각한 문제가 되고 있습니다. 뿐만 아니라 도서관에도 자리가 충분하지 않아서 많은 학생들이 식당에서 공부를 합니다. 안타깝게도 식당에는 학생들이 앉을 수 있는 자리가 부족합니다. 저는 학교 당국이 학생 센터를 리모델링해서 식당을 확장할 것을 강력히 촉구합니다.

David Thompson
2학년생

Comprehension

1 The letter complains about the lack of space in the cafeteria in the student center.
2 First of all, the writer states that the cafeteria is too crowded during mealtimes.
3 The letter writer mentions that there are not enough places for the students to sit and to have their meals.
4 The author also notes that the cafeteria is crowded because many students study in the cafeteria.
5 There are not enough spaces in the library, so the students have to go to the cafeteria to find a place to sit and study.

Listening

Script 🎧 02-03

M Student: You know . . . The author of this letter is right. The school should renovate the student center cafeteria.

W Student: Hold on a second. They don't need to do that. After all, there are small eateries all over campus. We have choices of where we want to eat.

M: Sure, but the cafeteria is so convenient.

W: Yes, but you don't have to eat there. I mean . . . I go outdoors to eat when the weather's nice. And don't you eat at that little café inside Robinson Hall? I've seen you there before.

M: Okay, yes, I eat there sometimes.

W: See. We have choices.

M: But what about the studying aspect? That's important.

W: Oh, come on. The student center is always full of students doing lots of different activities. People are always chatting, and it's really loud. How can anyone study in that kind of an environment?

M: But we can't study at the library.

W: That's true. The desks are always occupied, and there's no room to study. You know, the school should renovate the library instead of the cafeteria. That would help us out a lot more.

M Student: 알겠지만… 이 편지를 쓴 사람 말이 맞아. 학교측이 학생 센터 식당을 리모델링해야 해.

W Student: 잠깐만. 그럴 필요는 없어. 어찌되었든 캠퍼스 도처에 간이 식당들이 있잖아. 어디에서 식사할지 선택할 수가 있다고.

M: 그건 그렇지만 구내 식당이 정말 편하지.

W: 그래, 하지만 꼭 거기에서 먹을 필요는 없어. 내 말은… 나는 날씨가 좋으면 밖에서 먹어. 그리고 너도 Robinson 홀 안에 있는 그 조그만 카페에서 식사를 하지 않니? 전에 거기에서 널 본 적이 있어.

M: 그래, 맞아, 가끔 거기에서 식사를 해.

W: 거봐. 선택할 수가 있잖아.

M: 하지만 공부는 어떡하고? 그게 중요하지.

W: 오, 이런. 학생 센터는 여러 다양한 활동을 하는 학생들로 항상 북적거려. 사람들이 항상 대화를 하고 있어서 정말로 시끄럽지. 그런 환경에서 누가 공부를 할 수 있겠어?

M: 하지만 도서관에서 공부를 할 수가 없잖아.

W: 맞는 말이야. 자리들은 항상 주인이 있고 공부할 공간이 없지. 알겠지만 학교측은 식당이 아니라 도서관을 리모델링해야 해. 그러면 더 많은 도움이 될 거야.

Organization

1 The woman disagrees with the writer of the letter.

2 She claims that the students do not all have to eat at the cafeteria.

3 She mentions that there are many eateries around campus and even tells the male student that she has seen him eating at a café elsewhere on campus.

4 She claims that the student center is always too noisy.

5 She mentions that because of all the people chatting there, the student center is a bad study environment.

Comparing

Sample Response

Script 🎧 02-04

The letter to the editor states that the school should renovate the student center cafeteria because it's too crowded and doesn't have enough room for students both to eat and to study in. The woman disagrees with the writer of the letter. First, she claims that the students don't all have to eat at the cafeteria. For example, she mentions that there are many eateries around campus and even tells the male student that she has seen him eating at a café elsewhere on campus. In addition, she claims that the student center is always too noisy anyway, so it's fairly useless for the students to study there. She mentions that because of all the people chatting there, the student center is a bad study environment. She claims that the school should renovate the library, not the cafeteria, to enable students to study better.

편집자에게 보내는 편지는 학생 센터 식당이 너무 붐비고 학생들이 식사하고 공부할 수 있는 공간이 부족하기 때문에 학교측이 그곳을 리모델링해야 한다고 주장한다. 여자는 편지를 쓴 사람의 주장에 동의하지 않는다. 우선 그녀는 학생들이 모두 그 식당에서 식사를 할 필요는 없다고 주장한다. 예를 들어 그녀는 캠퍼스 주변에 간이 식당들이 많으며 남학생이 캠퍼스 안의 또 다른 한 카페에서 식사하는 모습을 본 적이 있다고 말한다. 또한 그녀는 학생 센터가 어쨌거나 항상 시끄러운 곳이라서 학생들이 그곳에서 공부하는 것은 거의 소용없는 일이라고 주장한다. 그녀는 그곳에서 떠드는 사람들 때문에 학생 센터가 공부하기에 좋지 않은 환경이라고 언급한다. 그녀는 학생들이 공부를 더 열심히 하도록 만들기 위해서는 식당이 아니라 도서관을 리모델링해야 한다고 주장한다.

Unit 17 Dormitory Policies I

Exercise p.53

Reading

신입생은 전원 기숙사 생활이 가능합니다

다음 학기부터 신입생 전원이 교내 기숙사에서 지낼 수 있습니다. 신입생 전원에게 기숙사 생활을 보장해 주지 못했던 이전 규정이 학생 및 학부모들로부터 수많은 불만에 의해 변경되었습니다. 이러한 새 규정으로 1학년생들은 캠퍼스 내에서 친구들과 보다 쉽게 스터디 그룹을 결성할 수 있을 것입니다. 이로 인해 학생들의 전체적인 평균 평점이 향상될 수 있을 것입니다. 또한 대학측은 신입생들이 주차할 수 있도록 추가 차량들을 위한 주차 공간을 충분히 확보하기로 결정했는데, 이로써 주차 문제가 발생하지 않을 것입니다.

1 The announcement mentions that all freshmen will now be able to live in on-campus housing.

2 Students will now be able more easily to form study groups with others on campus.

3 Because freshmen can form on-campus study groups, this should help them study better, which will, in turn, help their grades increase.

4 All freshmen will be able to park their cars on campus next semester.

5 The university determined that it had enough parking space for all of the extra cars.

Listening

Script 🎧 02-05

M Student: Hey, they're letting freshmen live in the dorms. Great!

W Student: The school means well, but I must say that their reasoning is completely illogical.

M: I disagree. That idea about forming study groups sounds good. I could've used one when I was a freshman. But I didn't get to live on campus.

W: I lived in the dorms when I was a freshman.

M: How was it?

W: Noisy. Really noisy. I didn't have a study group because the atmosphere in the dorms just wasn't conducive to studying. People were making noise at all hours of the day and never studying. That's why I moved off campus my sophomore year, when, incidentally, I actually joined a study group. It was much quieter off campus.

M: Okay, but what about this parking situation? That's nice, isn't it?

W: The school's not planning to build any new parking lots. That's a huge mistake.

M: Do you think so?

W: If every freshman living on campus has a car, the parking lots are going to be jam packed. Nobody from off campus will get to park here. You can count on that.

해석

M Student: 와, 신입생들이 기숙사에서 살게 되었네. 잘됐군!

W Student: 학교측의 의도는 좋지만 그들의 논리는 완전 터무니없어.

M: 난 그렇게 생각하지 않아. 스터디 그룹의 결성에 관한 아이디어도 좋게 들려. 내가 신입생일 때 스터디 그룹을 활용하면 좋았을 텐데. 하지만 난 교내에서 지내지 못했지.

W: 난 신입생일 때 기숙사 생활을 했어.

M: 어땠는데?

W: 시끄러웠지. 정말로 시끄러웠어. 기숙사 분위기가 공부와는 거리가 멀어서 스터디 그룹도 없었어. 사람들이 하루 종일 시끄럽게 굴기만 하고 공부는 전혀 하지 않았거든. 그래서 나는 2학년 때 기숙사를 나왔는데, 이때 우연히도 스터디 그룹에 들어가게 되었지. 캠퍼스 밖이 훨씬 조용했어.

M: 좋아, 그렇지만 이 주차 방안은 어때? 괜찮지 않아?

W: 학교측은 새로운 주차장 건설을 계획하고 있지 않아. 이는 커다란 실수라고.

M: 그렇게 생각해?

W: 캠퍼스 내에 사는 모든 신입생들이 차를 가지고 있으면 주차장이 엄청 붐빌 거야. 캠퍼스 밖에 사는 사람은 누구도 이곳에 주차를 못하게 되겠지. 두고 보라고.

Organization

1 The woman opposes this change in the university's policy.

2 One reason she gives is that the dorms her freshmen year were too noisy, so they were not good study environments.

3 She states that it was not until her sophomore year, when she moved off campus, that she actually joined a study group.

4 The second reason the woman mentions she is against the change is that the parking situation on campus is going to get worse.

5 The woman believes that the school is not planning to build any new parking lots, so if all the freshmen living on campus drive, there will not be enough space to park.

Comparing

Sample Response

Script 🎧 02-06

The announcement mentions that all freshmen will now be able to live in on-campus housing whereas previously they hadn't been guaranteed dormitory rooms. However, the woman opposes this change in the university's policy. One reason she gives is that the dorms her freshmen year were too noisy, so they weren't good study environments. She states that it wasn't until her sophomore year, when she moved off campus, that she actually joined a study group. The second reason the woman is against the change is that the parking situation on campus is going to get worse. The woman believes that the school isn't planning to build any new parking lots, so if all the freshmen living on campus drive, there won't be enough space to park. She clearly believes not letting all freshmen live on campus is better than guaranteeing them all dormitory rooms.

해석

공지에 따르면 이전에는 신입생들 전원에게 기숙사가 배정되지 못했지만 이제 신입생 전원이 기숙사 생활을 할 수 있게 되었다. 하지만 여자는 이러한 대학 정책의 변경을 반대한다. 그녀가 제시하는 한 가지 이유는 그녀가 신입생일 때 기숙사가 너무 시끄러워서 기숙사가 공부를 하기에 좋은 환경이 아니었기 때문이다. 그녀는 자신이 2학년이 되어 캠퍼스를 나온 후 실제로 스터디 그룹에 가입하게 되었다고 언급한다. 여자가 그러한 변경에 반대하는 두 번째 이유는 캠퍼스 내 주차 상황이 악화될 것이기 때문이다. 여자는 학교측이 주차장을 새로 건설할 계획을 갖고 있지 않기 때문에 캠퍼스 내에 거주하는 모든 신입생들이 차를 몬다면 주차 공간이 부족해질 것이라고 생각한다. 그녀는 분명 신입생 전원에게 기숙사 방을 배정하는 것보다 그들 중 일부에게만 캠퍼스 생활을 허용하는 것이 더 낫다고 생각한다.

Unit 18 Dormitory Policies II

Exercise ··· p.56

Reading

해석

하계 기숙사 정책

심각한 공간상의 제약으로 인해 재학생들은 여름 학기 동안 이전처럼 기숙사에 소지품을 남겨둘 수 없게 되었습니다. 여름 학기의 특별 프로그램이 확대됨에 따라 평소보다 많은 기숙사 방이 사용될 예정입니다. 따라서 학생들은 여름 동안 세 상자에 해당하는 짐만 남겨둘 수 있습니다. 많지 않은 것처럼 보일 수도 있지만, 모든 학생들을 최대한 공정하고 공평하게 대우하기 위해 이러한 정책이 실시될 예정입니다. 이번 정책과 관련된 보다 자세한 사항은 기숙사 사무실로 문의해 주시기 바랍니다.

Comprehension

1 The announcement declares that students will no longer be allowed to leave all of their possessions in the dormitories over summer break but may only leave a small amount of them instead.
2 The school is having a large number of special programs during the summer.
3 This means that there will be fewer dormitory rooms available in which students may store their possessions.
4 The school is trying to be as fair as possible to all of the students.
5 By limiting each student to three boxes, the school can ensure that every student is able to leave at least a small amount of their possessions at school during the summer.

Listening

Script 🎧 02-07

W Student: I'm so aggravated about this new policy. I was planning to leave everything I owned here like last year.

M Student: Yeah, it's unfortunate. But I'm just going to bring everything home. Why don't you do the same?

W: I live all across the country, not in the same city like you do. There's no way to get all my things home unless I hire a mover, and I don't have that kind of money.

M: Oh, right. I forgot about where you live.

W: It's just that there are so many empty dorm rooms during summer.

M: But the announcement said there won't be many available. That's why they've changed the policy.

W: I've done the math, but it doesn't add up. Remember that we recently built that new dorm, which has over 300 rooms. There can't be that many new summer programs on campus. I think they don't want to be bothered with going through all the trouble this year.

M: Can you blame them?

W: Yes, I can. The school should be serving our needs. We're the customers after all.

해석

W Student: 이번 새 정책 때문에 정말 화가 나는군. 나는 작년과 마찬가지로 내 모든 짐을 두고 갈 생각이었어.

M Student: 그래, 안 된 일이야. 하지만 난 짐을 모두 집에 가져갈 거야. 너도 똑같이 하는 것이 어때?

W: 나는 너처럼 이 도시에 사는 것이 아니라 우리나라 반대편에 살아. 이삿짐 센터를 부르지 않는 한 집으로 짐을 옮겨다 놓을 방법이 없는데, 그런 돈은 없어.

M: 오, 그래. 네가 어디에 사는지 잊고 있었어.

W: 여름에는 기숙사에 빈 방들이 정말 많을 것 같은데.

M: 하지만 공지에 남는 방이 많지 않을 거라고 나와 있잖아. 그것이 바로 규정을 바꾼 이유이지.

W: 계산을 해 보니 말이 안 되더라고. 방이 300개가 넘는 새 기숙사가 최근에 지어졌다는 점을 기억해 봐. 캠퍼스에 그렇게 많은 여름 방학 프로그램이 신설되었을 리가 없어. 내 생각에는 그들이 올해 그러한 수고를 하고 싶어하지 않는 것 같아.

M: 그들을 탓하는 거니?

W: 그래, 맞아. 학교측은 학생들 요구를 들어 줘야 해. 어찌되었든 학생이 고객이니까.

Organization

1 The woman speaks out against this policy.
2 To begin with, unlike the man, she states that she lives all the way across the country, so it is too far for her to take all of her possessions with her.
3 She could only do that by hiring a mover, which is too expensive for her.
4 Her next point of contention is that she believes there is enough room on campus for students to leave all of their possessions.

5 She says that the school has just opened a new dorm with 300 rooms, so that should provide more than enough space.

Comparing

Sample Response

Script 🎧 02-08

The announcement declares that students will no longer be allowed to leave all of their possessions in the dormitories over summer break but may only leave a small amount of them instead. The woman speaks out against this policy. To begin with, unlike the man, she states that she lives all the way across the country, so it's too far for her to take all of her possessions with her. She could only do that by hiring a mover, which is too expensive for her. Her next point of contention is that she believes there's enough room on campus for students to leave all of their possessions. She says that the school has just opened a new dorm with 300 rooms, so that should provide more than enough space. She feels that the school ought to take better care of its students instead of making things difficult for them.

해석

공지에 따르면 학생들이 여름 방학 동안 기숙사에 짐을 전부 남겨두는 것은 더 이상 허용되지 않으며 그 대신 소량의 짐만 남겨둘 수 있다. 여자는 이러한 정책을 반대한다. 우선 여자는 남자와 달리 나라 반대편에 살기 때문에 짐을 모두 옮기기에는 그 거리가 너무 멀다고 말한다. 그녀는 이삿짐 센터를 이용하면 그럴 수 있지만 이는 그녀에게 너무나 비용이 많이 드는 일이다. 그녀의 그 다음 논점은 학생들이 짐 전체를 남겨둘 수 있는 공간이 캠퍼스에 충분하다고 그녀가 생각한다는 점이다. 그녀는 학교에서 최근 300개가 넘는 방을 갖춘 새로운 기숙사가 문을 열었기 때문에 남을 정도로 충분한 공간이 제공될 것이라고 말한다. 그녀는 학교가 학생들의 상황을 힘들게 만드는 대신 학생들을 더 많이 배려해야 한다고 생각한다.

Unit 19 Class Size Increases

Exercise p.59

Reading

해석

세미나 수업의 수강 인원 확대

이제 더 이상 세미나 수업의 수강생이 15명으로 제한되지 않습니다. 대신 세미나 수업의 수강생 수가 25명으로 확대될 것입니다. 인기는 많지만 강사의 부족으로 이 토론식 세미나 수업에 등록할 수 있는 학생의 수는 많지 않았습니다. 이번 변경으로 학생들은 자신이 선택한 세미나 수업에 등록할 수 있을 것입니다. 1학년과 2학년 학생들이 예상보다 훨씬 더 많아졌기 때문에 이번 조치로 모든

학생들이 최소한 하나의 세미나 수업을 들어야 한다는 졸업 요건을 분명 충족시킬 수 있을 것입니다.

Comprehension

1 The topic of the notice is the change in the university's policy, which will now allow twenty-five students, as opposed to fifteen, to register for each seminar.

2 Many students have not been able to register for the seminars which they wanted to take.

3 While the seminars are popular with students, there are not enough professors to teach them.

4 The first-and second-year student classes are much bigger than the school had expected.

5 Students must complete a seminar before they can graduate, so the school needs to ensure that there are enough spaces for students to enroll in them.

Listening

Script 🎧 02-09

W Student: It looks like getting into a seminar has just gotten a lot easier. That's good to hear.

M Student: Yes, it's sounds nice, but there's a slight problem.

W: I don't see anything wrong.

M: Well, these seminars are discussion based. You can't have a discussion with twenty-five students in a class, especially if everyone is supposed to speak during them. The entire class will suffer because of this.

W: Okay, that might be a problem, but I'm not too disturbed.

M: How come?

W: Well, I wanted to get into a seminar last semester, but it was full before I could register. There just aren't enough seminars being offered.

M: Exactly. The school needs to open more of them. But we have an insufficient number of teachers.

W: I heard we're going to hire a large number of part-time professors.

M: Yeah, I saw that too, but it's a misguided idea. Part-time professors often aren't qualified to teach university classes. Or else they're busy teaching part-time at several different schools. So they won't be able to guarantee the students a quality education. The school needs to reconsider this policy immediately.

해석

W Student: 세미나 수업을 듣기가 훨씬 수월해질 것 같은데. 반가운 소식이군.

M Student: 그래, 좋은 것 같지만 약간의 문제가 있어.

W: 내가 보기에는 잘못된 것이 없는데.

M: 음, 이러한 세미나 수업들은 토론식 수업이잖아. 한 반에 25명의 학생들이 있으면, 특히 모두가 수업에서 말을 해야 하는 경우, 토론을 할 수가 없지. 이 때문에 수업 전체가 힘들어질 거야.

W: 좋아, 그 점은 문제가 될 수도 있겠지만 나는 크게 신경이 쓰이지 않아.

M: 어째서?

W: 음, 나는 지난 학기에 세미나 수업을 들으려고 했는데, 등록을 하기 전에 정원이 다 찼거든. 개설되는 세미나 수업이 충분치 않아.

M: 바로 그래. 학교측이 더 많은 세미나 수업을 개설해야 하지. 하지만 강사의 수가 충분하지 않다고.

W: 나는 시간제 강사를 다수 고용할 예정이라는 말을 들었는데.

M: 그래, 나도 그랬는데, 그건 잘못된 아이디어야. 시간제 강사들은 대학 수업을 맡기에 종종 자격이 부족한 경우가 있어. 혹은 여러 다른 학교에서 수업을 하느라 바쁠 수도 있고. 그래서 학생들에게 양질의 교육이 보장되지 못할 수도 있지. 학교측은 이번 정책을 즉시 재고해야 해.

Organization

1 The male student opposes letting so many students into the seminars.

2 He claims that seminars are classes which are based on students having discussions with one another.

3 The student points out the difficulty of having twenty-five students in a discussion class, especially since everyone is required to speak in them.

4 Furthermore, the man declares that the school's plan to hire part-time professors is mistaken.

5 He first mentions that these professors are often unqualified to teach college classes. He then points out that a lot of these teachers are employed elsewhere, which makes them too busy.

Comparing

Sample Response

Script 🎧 02-10

The topic of the notice is the change in the university's policy, which will now allow twenty-five students, as opposed to fifteen, to register for each seminar. The male student opposes letting this many students into the seminars. He claims that seminars are classes which are based on students having discussions with one another. The student points out the difficulty of having twenty-five students in a discussion class, especially since everyone is required to speak in them. He's concerned that students' educations will suffer. Furthermore, the man declares that the school's plan to hire part-time professors is mistaken. He first mentions that these professors are often unqualified to teach college

classes. He then points out that a lot of these teachers are employed elsewhere, which makes them too busy. Overall, he feels that they won't be able to provide the students with a quality education.

해석

공지의 주제는 각 세미나 수업의 수강 인원이 15명이 아니라 25명으로 바뀔 것이라는 대학 정책의 변경 사항이다. 남학생은 이처럼 많은 학생들에게 세미나 수업을 허용하는 것을 반대한다. 그는 세미나 수업이 학생들 상호간의 토론에 기반하는 수업이라고 주장한다. 특히 이러한 수업에서는 모든 학생들이 말을 해야 하기 때문에 25명의 학생들이 토론 수업에 참여하는 것은 어려운 일이라고 지적한다. 그는 학생들의 교육이 문제를 겪게 될 것이라고 걱정한다. 더 나아가 남자는 시간제 강사를 고용하려는 학교측의 계획이 잘못된 것이라고 주장한다. 우선 이러한 교수들이 대학 수업을 담당하기에는 종종 자질이 부족한 경우가 있다고 언급한다. 그런 다음 이러한 강사들이 다른 학교에도 고용되어 있기 때문에 매우 바쁘다는 점을 지적한다. 전체적으로 그는 이들이 학생들에게 양질의 교육을 제공할 수 없을 것이라고 생각한다.

Unit 20 School Policies

Exercise p.62

Reading

해석

신입생에게 수업을 할 수 있는 4학년생 모집

Central 대학에서 가을 학기에 새로운 프로그램이 시작될 예정입니다. 이제 자격을 갖춘 4학년생들은 학과 교수님과 함께 공동으로 특정 수업을 가르칠 수 있습니다. 강사의 자질을 갖추기 위해서는 전체 과목 평점 및 전공 과목 평점 모두 3.50 이상이어야 합니다. 이번 프로그램은 교사가 되기 위한 필수 과정은 아니지만 교직을 생각하는 학생들은 이번 프로그램에 큰 관심을 가질 것입니다. 학생 교사는 수업 계획서를 준비해야 하며 또한 학생들을 위한 사무실 근무 시간을 낼 수 있어야 합니다. 보다 자세한 사항에 대해서는 학생 서비스 센터로 문의하시기 바랍니다.

Comprehension

1 The topic of the notice is a new student-teaching program that the university has decided to create.

2 Students who are excelling academically both in their majors and overall may participate in the program.

3 Students must have GPAs of at least 3.50 in their major and overall in order to qualify as teachers.

4 Students considering teaching careers may be particularly interested in the program.

5 Students will have to turn in lesson plans and conduct office hours, which will give them valuable teaching experience.

W Student: What a silly idea. I can't believe the school is entertaining the notion of letting students teach classes.

M Student: It sounds intriguing to me.

W: You think so?

M: Why not? First, like the announcement says, it would be a great way to get some teaching experience. Think about it . . . It'd look great on an application to graduate school. It might help some students get accepted.

W: Okay, that's good for the student-teacher, but what about the students taking the classes? I can tell you this . . . I wouldn't want a student teaching my class. The student wouldn't have nearly as much knowledge as a real professor.

M: Well, there is the prospect of that, but the student will just be co-teaching, so I'm not terribly concerned. Anyway, you know, I like the part about the student keeping office hours.

W: Because?

M: My professors are always busy and often don't have time to chat. It'd be easier and, frankly, more comfortable, going to a student to ask my questions. It's not like my questions are so difficult that an upperclassman wouldn't be able to answer them.

해석

W Student: 정말 어리석은 아이디어야. 학교측이 학생들에게 수업을 시키려고 생각하다니 어이가 없어.

M Student: 나는 흥미롭게 들리는데.

W: 그렇게 생각해?

M: 안 될 게 있나? 우선 공지에 나와 있는 것처럼 교사 경험을 쌓을 수 있는 좋은 기회가 될 수 있어. 생각해 봐… 대학원 지원서에서도 멋지게 보일 거야. 대학원 입학에 도움이 될 수도 있을 것 같은데.

W: 그래, 학생 교사에게는 좋은 일이겠지만 수업을 듣는 학생들은 어떻게 하고? 다음과 같이 말할 수 있는데… 나는 학생이 내 수업을 가르치는 건 원하지 않아. 그 학생이 실제 교수님과 비슷한 정도로 많이 알고 있지는 않을 거야.

M: 음, 그럴 가능성도 있겠지만 학생은 단지 수업을 공동으로 맡을 것이기 때문에 난 크게 걱정되지는 않아. 어쨌든, 알겠지만, 학생에게 사무실 근무 시간이 있다는 점도 마음에 들어.

W: 왜?

M: 우리 교수님은 항상 바빠서 대화를 나눌 시간이 없으시지. 그래서 학생에게 질문하는 것이 더 쉽고, 솔직히 말하면, 더 편할 것 같아. 상급생이 대답을 못할 정도로 내 질문이 너무 어렵지는 않을 테니까.

Organization

1 In the man's mind, the program is a good idea and is worth supporting.

2 First, he thinks that doing student-teaching will benefit the students in the program.

3 He feels that putting it on their résumés will look good when they apply to graduate schools and might even help some of them get accepted.

4 Another reason is that he is encouraged by the fact that student-teachers will have to keep office hours.

5 He mentions that most of his professors have no time to chat, but he thinks students will.

Comparing

Sample Response
🎧 02-12

The topic of the notice is a new student-teaching program the university has decided to create. In the man's mind, the program is a good idea and is worth supporting. He cites a couple of reasons to defend his opinion. First, he thinks that doing student-teaching will benefit the students in the program. He feels that putting it on their résumés will look good when they apply to graduate schools and might even help some of them get accepted. Another reason is that he's encouraged by the fact that the student-teachers would have to keep office hours. He believes students having office hours is better than professors having them. He mentions that most of his professors have no time to chat, but he thinks students will. In addition, most of his questions could be answered by upperclassmen, so he wouldn't have to bother his professors so much.

해석

공지의 주제는 대학측이 실시하기로 결정한 새로운 학생 교사 프로그램이다. 남자의 생각으로 이 프로그램은 괜찮은 아이디어이며 지지할만한 가치가 있는 것이다. 그는 자신의 의견을 옹호하기 위해 두 가지 이유를 제시한다. 첫째, 그는 학생 교사 일을 함으로써 프로그램에 참가하는 학생들에게 혜택이 있을 것으로 생각한다. 그는 그러한 경험을 이력서에 적으면 대학원 진학 시 좋게 보여서 일부 학생들의 진학에 도움이 될 수 있다고 생각한다. 또 다른 이유는 학생 교사들에게 사무실 근무 시간이 있을 것이라는 사실에 그가 고무되었기 때문이다. 그는 교수들보다 학생 교사들에게 사무실 근무 시간이 있는 것이 더 낫다고 생각한다. 대부분의 교수들에게는 이야기를 나눌 수 있는 시간이 없지만 학생에게는 있을 것이라고 언급한다. 또한 자신의 질문은 대부분 상급생이 대답해 줄 수 있는 것이기 때문에 그가 교수를 귀찮게 만들 일이 없어질 것이다.

Exercise p.65

Reading

해석

야간 수업 개설

폭발적인 요구에 따라 학교측은 1월에 시작하는 이번 봄 학기부터 제한적으로 야간 수업을 개설할 예정입니다. 야간 수업은 저녁 6시와 10시 사이에 진행됩니다. 하지만 이들 강의는 현재 정규직으로 고용되어 있는 학생들만 수강이 가능합니다. 등록을 하기 위해서는 재직 증명서를 제출해야 합니다. 야간 수업은 모든 학과에서 개설될 것이며 일을 하면서 공부하는 학생들이 직장 생활에 차질을 빚지 않고 학업을 지속할 수 만들어 줄 것입니다.

Comprehension

1 The university has decided to open a night school program and to offer classes on a somewhat limited basis.

2 Many students have requested that the university teach night classes.

3 The notice mentions that there is overwhelming demand for these courses.

4 The night school program will be of great benefit to students who are currently working.

5 The program should help the students study well since they will not have to interrupt their work schedules in order to attend classes.

Listening

Script 🎧 02-13

M Student: I must confess that I'm rather displeased with this news.

W Student: What? The night classes?

M: Yeah, it's unfair that only those with jobs can sign up for the courses. That just doesn't seem right. These classes should be open to all interested students.

W: Maybe . . . But perhaps the coursework will be tailored to those who have jobs. You know, the professors might give less homework or something. Regular students would have an unfair advantage.

M: That's possible, but I'd love to take night classes myself. Unfortunately, I'm being denied that opportunity.

W: Oh, well. You could always get a job. Then you'd qualify.

M: Good one. Here's another problem.

W: What's that?

M: Well, the school hasn't mentioned anything about hiring new professors, right?

W: Okay.

M: So that means the school's going to be offering fewer classes during the day. That could wreak havoc with a lot of students' schedules. I mean, there are going to be fewer classes being offered to those students without jobs.

W: Hmm, perhaps the school ought to reconsider this new policy.

해석

M Student: 사실대로 말하면 난 이번 소식이 다소 불만스러워.

W Student: 어떤 소식? 야간 수업?

M: 맞아, 일을 하는 사람만 강의를 들을 수 있다는 점은 공평하지 않아. 올바른 결정처럼 보이지 않는걸. 이러한 수업은 관심이 있는 모든 학생들에게 열려 있어야 해.

W: 그럴지도 모르지… 하지만 아마도 일을 하고 있는 사람들에게 교과 과정이 맞춰질 거잖아. 알다시피 교수님들이 과제를 줄여 주는 등의 조치를 내리실 수도 있어. 일반 학생들은 불공평하게 이득을 취하게 될 거야.

M: 그럴 수도 있지만 나도 정말 야간 수업을 듣고 싶어. 안타깝게도 나는 그러한 기회를 거부당하고 있는 거야.

W: 오, 글쎄. 언제라도 일자리를 구할 수 있잖아. 그러면 자격이 생길 텐데.

M: 좋은 지적이군. 그런데 또 다른 문제가 있어.

W: 무슨 문제인데?

M: 음, 학교측이 신규 교수 임용에 대해서는 아무런 말도 하지 않았잖아, 그렇지?

W: 그래.

M: 그건 학교측이 개설되는 주간 수업을 줄일 것이라는 의미지. 그러면 많은 학생들의 시간표에 큰 차질이 생길 수 있어. 즉 일을 하지 않는 학생에게 제공되는 수업이 적어질 것이라는 말이야.

W: 흠, 어쩌면 학교측이 이번 새로운 정책을 재고해야 할 수도 있겠네.

Organization

1 The man's opinion is that the night school program is not a good idea.

2 More than anything else, the reason is that the program is being restricted to students with jobs.

3 He feels that he is being discriminated against because he wants to register for the night classes, yet the school will not allow him to do so.

4 Another reason he gives is that there are going to be fewer classes available for day students to take.

5 Since the school's professors will be teaching night school, they will naturally be holding fewer classes during the day, which will cause problems with many students' schedules.

Sample Response

Script 🎧 02-14

According to the notice, the university has decided to open a night school program and to offer classes on a somewhat limited basis. The man's opinion is that the night school program isn't a good idea. More than anything else, the reason is that the program is being restricted to students with jobs. He feels that he's being discriminated against because he wants to register for the night classes, yet the school won't allow him to do so. He claims that's unfair. Another reason he gives is that there are going to be fewer classes available for day students to take. He points out that the school hasn't commented about hiring any new professors for the coming semester. Therefore, since the school's professors will be teaching night school, they will naturally be holding fewer classes during the day. The man thinks this will cause problems with many students' schedules.

해석

공지에 따르면 대학측은 야간 수업 프로그램을 신설해서 일정 조건하에 수업을 제공하기로 결정했다. 남자의 의견으로 야간 수업 프로그램은 좋은 아이디어가 아니다. 그 이유는 무엇보다 그 프로그램이 일을 하는 학생들만을 대상으로 삼기 때문이다. 그는 야간 수업에 등록을 하고 싶지만 학교가 이를 허락하지 않기 때문에 자신이 차별을 받고 있다고 생각한다. 그는 그것이 불공평하다고 주장한다. 그가 제시하는 또 다른 이유는 주간 수업의 학생들이 들을 수 있는 수업이 줄어들 것이기 때문이다. 그는 학교측이 다음 학기의 신규 교수 임용에 대해 언급하지 않았다는 점을 지적한다. 따라서 교내 교수들이 야간 수업을 진행할 것이기 때문에 당연히 주간에 진행하는 수업은 줄어들게 될 것이다. 남자는 이로써 많은 학생들의 시간표에 문제가 생길 것이라고 생각한다.

Unit 22 Student Affairs

Exercise p.68

Reading

해석

학부생도 대학원 수업을 수강할 수 있습니다

이제 3학년과 4학년생들도 해당 학과의 대학원 과정에서 제공되는 수업에 등록할 수 있습니다. 모든 대학원 강의는 500번대와 600번대 강의입니다. 학생들이 이들 수업에 등록하기 위해서는 지도 교수님으로부터 서면 허가를 받아야 하며, 학기당 들을 수 있는 수업은 하나로 제한됩니다. 이로 인해 최상위권 학생들이 학부생 자격으로 양질의 대학원 수준의 교육을 받을 수 있게 될 것입니다. 뿐만 아니라 학생들이 졸업과 동시에 대학원 입학에 관심이 있는지, 그리고 입학 자격을 갖추고 있는지를 판단하는데도 도움이 될 것입니다.

1 The notice mentions that some students are now allowed to enroll in graduate-level classes even though they are still undergraduates.

2 Students will be able to attend higher level classes.

3 They will be restricted to one graduate class per semester during their junior and senior years.

4 This will provide the students with a better education while they are still undergraduates.

5 By taking graduate-level classes, they will be able to determine if they are interested in and capable of doing the work necessary in graduate school.

Listening

Script 🎧 02-15

W Student: I can't wait to register for classes. I'm going to take that graduate-level anthropology class I told you about.

M Student: I hope you do well. But I fear you might not.

W: Why?

M: Graduate-level classes are a lot more comprehensive than undergrad ones. My sister's in grad school and has shown me her coursework. There's a reason why grad students typically take only two or three classes a semester. They tend to get a little, uh, overloaded.

W: Hmm, okay, then I'll be sure to do my best. But overall, don't you think this new rule is a good idea?

M: Not really. I actually feel sorry for most grad students.

W: The grad students? Why?

M: Think about it. Grad student classes are often small, say, around five to ten students. They work closely with their professors. Now, some of their classes might get flooded with undergrads, most of whom, I'm sorry to say, will be unqualified for the kind of upper-level work required. The value of their education might just decrease.

W: Hmm, I never looked at it that way until now.

해석

W Student: 빨리 수강 신청을 하고 싶은걸. 전에 내가 얘기했던 대학원 과정의 인류학 수업을 들을 생각이야.

M Student: 네가 잘 하기를 빌게. 하지만 그러지 못할 수도 있어.

W: 왜?

M: 대학원 수업은 학부 수업보다 훨씬 더 포괄적이거든. 우리 누나가 대학원을 다니는데, 나한테 교과 과정을 보여 준 적이 있어. 대학원생들이 한 학기에 한두 과목만 듣는 이유가 바로 거기에 있더라고. 보통은 약간, 어, 할 것들이 너무나 많지.

W: 음, 좋아, 그러면 최선을 다 해야겠네. 하지만 전반적으로 이번 새로운 규정이 좋은 아이디어라고 생각하지 않니?

M: 꼭 그렇지는 않아. 나는 사실 대부분의 대학원생들이 좀 안 됐어.

W: 대학원생들이? 왜?

M: 생각해 봐. 대학원 수업은, 이를테면 5명에서 10명 정도로, 인원이 적은 경우가 많아. 교수님들과도 가깝게 지내지. 그런데 이제 몇몇 수업이 학부생들로 넘쳐날 수도 있는데, 이들 중 대부분은, 이런 말해서 미안하지만, 보다 수준 높은 강의에 필요한 자격을 갖추고 있지 않아. 대학원 교육의 가치가 떨어질 수도 있어.

W: 흠, 지금까지 그런 생각은 한 번도 못 해 봤군.

Organization

1 The man is skeptical about the benefits of this new policy for a couple of different reasons.

2 First, the man thinks that most undergraduates cannot handle the workload in a typical graduate school class.

3 He mentions that he has seen his sister's graduate school coursework, and that has made him understand why graduate students take only a couple of classes each semester.

4 Second of all, the man believes the value of the graduate students' educations is going to decrease.

5 According to him, if lots of undergraduates start enrolling in these classes, the graduate students simply won't get the individual attention they had previously been receiving from their professors.

Comparing

Sample Response

Script 🎧 02-16

The notice mentions that some students are now allowed to enroll in graduate-level classes even though they are still undergraduates. The man is skeptical about the benefits of this new policy for a couple of different reasons. First, the man thinks that most undergraduates cannot handle the workload in a typical graduate school class. He mentions that he has seen his sister's graduate school coursework, and that has made him understand why graduate students take only a couple of classes each semester. He thinks the workload will be overwhelming for undergraduates. Second of all, the man believes the value of the graduate students' educations is going to decrease. He notes that graduate students work closely with their professors and take small classes. According to him, if lots of undergraduates start enrolling in these classes, the graduate students simply won't get the individual attention they'd previously been receiving from their professors.

해석

공지에는 이제 학부생일지라도 일부 학생들은 대학원 수업에 등록이 가능하다고 나와 있다. 남자는 각기 다른 두 가지 이유로 이러한 새로운 규정의 혜택에 대해 회의적이다. 첫째, 남자는 대부분의 학부생들이 전형적인 대학원 수업에서의 학습량을 감당할 수 없을 것이라고 생각한다. 그는 자신이 누나의 대학원 교과 과정을 보았는데, 이를 본 후 왜 대학원생들이 한 학기에 한두 과목만 듣는지 이해하게 되었다고 말한다. 그는 그러한 학습량이 학부생들에게는 압도적일 것이라고 생각한다. 둘째, 남자는 대학원생들의 교육의 가치가 떨어질 것이라고 믿는다. 남자는 대학원생들이 교수와 가깝게 지내며 소규모 수업을 듣는다는 점에 주목한다. 그에 따르면 많은 학부생들이 그러한 수업에 등록하기 시작하면 대학원생은 이전에 교수로부터 받았던 개별적인 관심을 받지 못하게 될 것이다.

Unit 23 Library Renovations

Exercise ·· p.71

Reading

해석

도서관 리모델링 공사가 진행됩니다

Sadowski 재단의 상당한 기부금 덕분에 이번 여름 Lufkin 도서관에서 리모델링 공사가 진행될 것이며, 이로써 도서관의 외관이 완전히 바뀌게 될 것입니다. 이번 리모델링 공사로 도서관은 보다 세련되고 현대적인 외형을 갖추게 될 것입니다. 예정된 많은 변화 가운데 특히 두 가지가 주목할만 합니다. 첫 번째는 기존의 콘크리트 바닥 대신 도서관에 마룻바닥이 설치될 예정입니다. 그리고 도서관 전체에, 내벽과 외벽 모두에, 페인트가 칠해질 것입니다. 도서관 이용객들이 도서관의 여러 부분들을 이용할 수 없는 경우가 몇 차례 있을 것입니다. 여러분의 이해와 협조를 부탁드립니다.

Comprehension

1 The purpose of the announcement is to declare that the school's library will be getting renovated during the summer.

2 The school received a donation from the Sadowski Foundation, so now it can afford to make the renovations.

3 Once the changes are made, the library will look more modern, especially because of the paint job the library will receive.

4 The library is going to have its concrete floors replaced with wooden ones, and the inside and the outside of the library are going to be painted.

5 During the renovations, patrons will sometimes be inconvenienced because they will not be able to access certain parts of the library.

M Student: Isn't it great that Lufkin Library is getting renovated? I worked there for a year, and let me tell you, it sure is dingy.

W Student: Well, yes, the repairs do sound nice, but . . .

M: But what?

W: For one thing, why are they installing wooden floors?

M: Come on. Wooden floors will give the library a classy look. You know, make it look, uh, like a real library.

W: I'm sure they'll look nice. But wooden floors are noisy. They squeak when you walk on them. How will students be able to concentrate while they're studying if the floor is making noise?

M: Oh, that's just a minor trifle.

W: But there's something else. You know, that foundation is donating a lot of money. And to be honest, our library's collection is, uh, not particularly stellar. Instead of painting the library, that money would be much more useful if it were spent on buying new books and periodicals. Don't you agree?

M: I don't know. I've never had any trouble finding the books I need.

W: Perhaps, but for people doing advanced research, our library is woefully inadequate.

해석

M Student: Lufkin 도서관을 리모델링 한다니 잘 됐지 않니? 나는 1년 동안 도서관에서 일했는데, 말하자면 그곳은 정말 우중충하거든.

W Student: 음, 그래, 공사는 좋은 것 같은데, 하지만…

M: 하지만 뭐?

W: 우선, 왜 마룻바닥을 설치하는 거지?

M: 들어 봐. 마룻바닥 때문에 도서관이 고급스럽게 보일 거야. 알겠지만, 어, 진짜 도서관처럼 보일 거라고.

W: 분명 좋아 보이겠지. 하지만 마룻바닥은 시끄러워. 그 위를 걸어 다니면 삐걱거리는 소리가 나잖아. 공부를 하고 있는데 바닥에서 소리가 나면 학생들이 어떻게 집중할 수 있겠어?

M: 오, 그건 사소한 문제일 뿐이야.

W: 또 다른 문제도 있어. 너도 알다시피 재단에서 많은 돈을 기부할 거잖아. 그리고 솔직히 말해서 우리 도서관에는 소장 도서들이, 어, 그렇게 많은 편이 아니야. 도서관에 페인트를 칠하는 대신 그 돈을 신간 도서나 정기 간행물을 사는데 쓴다면 훨씬 더 유익하겠지. 그렇게 생각하지 않아?

M: 모르겠어. 나는 필요한 책이 없어서 곤란했던 적이 한 번도 없었거든.

W: 그럴 수도 있지만 고급 과정의 연구를 진행하는 사람들에게 우리 도서관은 한심할 정도로 부적절해.

1 In the woman's mind, the school's plans for using the donation are inadequate and should be reconsidered.

2 During the conversation, the woman states her opposition to replacing the library's concrete floor with a wooden one.

3 She believes the floor will squeak and make too much noise, thereby serving as a distraction to students trying to study there.

4 She is also against the idea of painting the library.

5 She notes that the library's collections are inadequate for students doing advanced research, so the school should look to improve the quality of its materials rather than the appearance of the library.

Sample Response

Script 🎧 02-18

The purpose of the announcement is to declare that the school's library will be getting renovated during the summer. In the woman's mind, the school's plans for using the donation are inadequate and should be reconsidered. During the conversation, the woman states her opposition to replacing the library's concrete floor with a wooden one. She agrees that a wooden floor will look nice, but she believes it will squeak and make too much noise, thereby serving as a distraction to students trying to study there. She's also against the idea of painting the library. She believes spending more money on books and periodicals is better than painting the library's walls. She notes that the library's collections are inadequate for students doing advanced research, so the school should look to improve the quality of its materials rather than the appearance of the library.

해석

공지의 목적은 여름 동안 학교 도서관에 리모델링 공사가 진행될 것임을 알리는 것이다. 여자의 생각에 따르면 기부금 사용에 대한 학교측의 계획은 부적절한 것으로서 재고되어야 한다. 대화에서 여자는 자신이 도서관의 콘크리트 바닥을 마룻바닥으로 교체하는 것을 반대한다고 말한다. 그녀는 마룻바닥이 보기에 좋을 것이라는 점은 동의하지만, 삐걱거리는 시끄러운 소리가 나서 그곳에서 열심히 공부하는 학생들에게 방해가 될 것이라고 생각한다. 그녀는 또한 도서관에 페인트칠을 하는 것도 반대한다. 그녀는 도서관 벽에 페인트칠을 하는 것보다 도서 및 정기 간행물 구입에 돈을 더 써야 한다고 생각한다. 고급 과정의 연구를 하는 학생들에게는 도서관의 소장 도서가 부족하기 때문에 학교측이 도서관의 외관보다 소장 자료의 질을 높이는데 신경을 써야 한다고 그녀는 지적한다.

Unit 24 Online Library Materials

Exercise ··· p.74

Reading

해석

도서관의 온라인 참고 자료 구매

중앙 도서관의 공간을 극대화하기 위해 수석 사서인 John Hanlin은 이제부터 도서관의 참고 자료 구입 예산의 대부분을 온라인 자료를 구매하는데 쓰겠다고 발표했다. "이러한 자료들은 부피가 큰 참고 서적에 비해 공간을 훨씬 덜 차지합니다,"라고 Hanlin은 말했다. "이로써 공간은 덜 사용하면서도 보다 많은 자료를 구입하게 될 것입니다." Hanlin은 또한 많은 출판사들이 실제 도서를 구입하는 고객과는 달리 온라인 자료를 구매하는 고객들에게 할인을 제공하기 때문에 예산을 절약할 수 있다는 점도 강조했다. 이러한 변화는 3년 뒤 새로운 도서관 건물이 완공된 후에 이루어질 가능성이 크다.

Comprehension

1 The newspaper article covers the library's change in policy to where it will begin purchasing online reference materials instead of books.

2 Online materials take up much less room than reference books.

3 Not only are reference books large, but also by purchasing online materials, the library will be able to conserve its space.

4 It is cheaper to purchase online materials than it is to purchase printed books.

5 Because publishers give discounts to those buying online materials, the library will be able to save money.

Listening

Script 🎧 02-19

W Student: I just got back from the library. I was looking for a book, but the librarian told me the library doesn't have it in print. I've got to find it online.

M Student: Oh, the library has already got that new program up and running. Awesome.

W: No, it's not awesome. It's annoying.

M: I don't think so. I mean, the library is saving a ton of money and space. So it'll be able to purchase more reference materials. I've had to go to other schools countless times simply because our library didn't have something I needed. Hopefully, that'll change now.

W: Yeah, but searching for stuff online in the library is such a bother.

M: Well, you don't even have to go to the library anymore. You've got a computer in your dorm, right?

W: Yes.

M: So you can access the reference materials over the Internet. You can do a search from your room. And if you like reading books, then just print the information, and you'll have a paper version for yourself.

W: When you put it that way, it's starting to seem like a good idea.

해석

W Student: 방금 전에 도서관에 돌아왔어. 나는 책을 한 권 찾고 있었는데, 사서 선생님께서 인쇄된 것은 없다고 하시더라고. 온라인에서 찾아야 했지.

M Student: 오, 벌써 도서관에서 새 프로그램이 시작되어 운영되고 있군. 멋진걸.

W: 아냐, 멋지지 않아. 성가셔.

M: 난 그렇게 생각하지 않아. 내 말은, 도서관측이 엄청난 돈과 공간을 절약하고 있어. 그래서 보다 많은 참고 자료를 구입할 수 있을 거야. 나는 우리 도서관에 필요한 자료가 없어서 다른 학교에 간 적이 수없이 많아. 아마도 이제는 바뀌게 될 테지.

W: 그건 그렇지만 온라인에서 자료를 찾는 일은 정말 귀찮은 일이야.

M: 음, 이제 더 이상 도서관에 갈 필요조차 없는걸. 네 기숙사 방에 컴퓨터 있지?

W: 있어.

M: 그러면 인터넷으로 참고 자료를 볼 수 있어. 방에서 조사를 할 수가 있지. 그리고 네가 책 읽는 것을 좋아하는 경우에는 자료를 인쇄하기만 하면 너만의 인쇄본을 가지게 될 거야.

W: 그런 식으로 말을 하니 괜찮은 아이디어처럼 보이기 시작하네.

Organization

1 The man fully supports this change in the library's policy for a couple of separate reasons.

2 For one, he thinks that this decision will save the library both space and money.

3 This means that the school will get to purchase more materials and thus improve the library's collection.

4 Another reason is that students will not have to visit the library anymore to do their research.

5 Students can simply go online and gain access to the reference materials over the Internet.

Comparing

Sample Response
Script 🎧 02-20

The newspaper article covers the library's change in policy to where it will begin purchasing online reference materials instead of books. The man fully supports this change in the library's policy for a couple of separate reasons. For one, he thinks that this decision will save the library both space and money. This means that the school will get to purchase more materials and thus improve the library's collection. He feels this is important because he has had to visit other schools' libraries in the past to get the information that he needs. Another reason is that students won't have to visit the library anymore to do their research. Instead, they can simply go online and gain access to the reference materials over the Internet. He mentions that students who dislike reading off of computers can then print paper copies that they can read just like books.

해석

신문 기사는 도서 대신 온라인 참고 자료를 구입하는 것으로 도서관의 정책이 변경된다는 소식을 전한다. 남자는 서로 다른 두 가지 이유로 이러한 도서관의 정책 변화를 강력히 지지한다. 우선 그는 이번 결정으로 도서관이 공간과 돈 모두를 아끼게 될 것이라고 생각한다. 다시 말해서 학교측은 보다 많은 자료를 구입함으로써 도서관의 소장 자료를 늘릴 수 있다. 그는 과거에 필요한 자료를 얻기 위해 다른 학교 도서관에 가 본 적이 있기 때문에 그러한 점이 중요하다고 생각한다. 또 다른 이유는 학생들이 조사를 하기 위해 더 이상 도서관에 가지 않아도 되기 때문이다. 대신 온라인에 접속해서 인터넷으로 참고 자료를 볼 수가 있다. 그는 컴퓨터 화면으로 자료를 읽기를 싫어하는 학생들은 이를 출력해서 책처럼 읽으면 된다고 말한다.

Unit 25 Parking Policies

Exercise p.77

Reading

해석

주차 규정 변경

지난 학기에 학생, 교직원, 그리고 교수진들이 주차 공간을 찾느라 어려움을 겪었기 때문에 가을 학기에는 다음과 같은 변경 사항이 적용될 예정입니다. 신입생들은 더 이상 교내에 주차를 할 수 없습니다. 1학년생들에게는 주차권이 발급되지 않을 것입니다. 이러한 조치는 또한 캠퍼스에 만연한 교통 문제를 줄이려는 노력의 일환으로 실시될 것입니다. 자동차의 수를 줄이면 이러한 문제도 해결될 것입니다. 이번 조치로 주차 문제와 교통 문제가 모두 해결되기를 바랍니다. 보다 자세한 사항은 학생처장에게 문의해 주십시오.

Comprehension

1 The purpose of the announcement is to tell the students that freshmen will no longer be able to park their cars on campus any more.

2 Many students, staff, and faculty complained about the parking situation during the last semester.

3 They were unable to find parking spaces for their own cars.

4 There are many traffic problems throughout the campus.

5 The school believes that by reducing the number of cars on campus, it can make the traffic problems better.

Listening

Script 🎧 02-21

M Student: My brother's not going to be thrilled with this news.

W Student: Your brother?

M: He's starting school here in the fall. He was planning to bring his car, but I guess that won't happen any longer.

W: That's a good thing. The parking here is atrocious. And freshmen don't need cars anyway.

M: The traffic is bad, but did you know that only eighty-five freshmen applied for parking permits? That's just a drop in the bucket. Banning freshmen from having cars won't do much to alleviate the parking problems.

W: Well, every extra space counts. I've driven around for over half an hour looking for a parking spot before.

M: Yes, I understand. I have the same problems. But the school shouldn't be preventing freshmen from parking at school. It should, uh, build some more parking lots. What about all that empty land on the edge of campus? That would make a great new parking lot.

W: Well, you're right about that. It's not like building one would be too difficult or expensive.

M: Exactly. That way they could let everyone park and still have enough room.

해석

M Student: 내 동생이 이 소식을 들으면 크게 실망하겠군.

W Student: 동생?

M: 가을에 이곳 학교에 입학할 예정이야. 동생이 차를 가져올 생각이었는데 이제 그럴 수가 없을 것 같아.

W: 잘 된 일이지. 이곳 주차 상황은 말도 안 나오잖아. 그리고 어쨌든 신입생에게는 차가 필요하지 않고.

M: 교통이 안 좋기는 하지만 85명의 신입생들만 주차권을 신청했다는 점을 알고 있었어? 새 발의 피야. 신입생들로 하여금 차를 못 가져오게 한다고 해서 주차 문제가 크게 줄어들지는 않을 거야.

W: 음, 여분의 공간은 모두 다 중요해. 나는 전에 주차 공간을 찾느라 30분이 넘게 돈 적도 있어.

M: 그래, 이해해. 나도 같은 문제를 겪고 있거든. 하지만 학교측이 신입생들의 교내 주차를 금지해서는 안 돼. 학교측은, 어, 주차 공간을 더 많이 마련해야 하지. 캠퍼스 가장자리에 있는 공터는 뭔데? 그곳에 커다란 주차장을 지을 수도 있을 텐데 말이야.

W: 음, 그 점에 대해서는 네 말이 맞아. 주차장 하나를 건설하는 것이 특별히 어

렵거나 비용이 많이 드는 일은 아닐 것 같은데.

M: 바로 그거야. 그렇게 하면 모든 학생들이 주차를 해도 공간이 남을 수 있어.

Organization ▶

1 The man expresses his opposition to the university's new policy.

2 One reason he gives is that a very small number of freshmen applied for parking permits.

3 He says that only eighty-five freshmen wanted to park their cars on campus.

4 Additionally, he suggests that the school ought to build more parking lots on campus instead of banning freshmen from parking at school.

5 He points out that the school owns some empty land at the edge of campus, where the school should build a new parking lot.

Comparing ▶

Sample Response

`Script` 🎧 02-22

The purpose of the announcement is to tell the students that freshmen will no longer be able to park their cars on campus any more. The man expresses his opposition to the university's new policy. One reason he gives is that a very small number of freshmen applied for parking permits. He says that only eighty-five freshmen wanted to park their cars on campus. According to him, this number is so small that it couldn't possibly affect that parking situation on campus. Additionally, he suggests that the school ought to build more parking lots on campus instead of banning freshmen from parking at school. He points out that the school owns some empty land at the edge of campus. In his opinion, the school should build a new parking lot there, which would then enable everyone to park on campus.

`해석`

공지의 목적은 신입생들이 더 이상 교내에 주차를 할 수 없게 되었다는 점을 학생들에게 알리려는 것이다. 남자는 대학측의 새로운 규정에 반대 의견을 피력한다. 그가 제시하는 한 가지 이유는 주차권을 신청한 신입생의 수가 매우 적다는 점에 있다. 그는 85명의 신입생만이 교내에서 주차를 하고 싶어한다고 말한다. 그에 따르면 이 숫자가 너무 적어서 그로 인해 교내 주차 상황에 영향을 미치지는 못할 것이다. 또한 그는 학교측이 신입생들의 주차를 금지하는 대신 교내에 보다 많은 주차 시설을 마련해야 한다고 주장한다. 그는 캠퍼스 가장자리에 있는 공터가 학교 소유라는 점을 지적한다. 그는 학교측이 그곳에 주차장을 새로 지어야 하며, 그러면 모든 사람들이 교내에 주차를 할 수 있을 것이라고 생각한다.

`Exercise` ·· p.80

Reading ▶

`해석`

4학년생만 Madison 홀을 이용할 수 있습니다

350명의 학생을 수용할 수 있는 기숙사인 Madison 홀이 가을 학기부터 변화를 겪게 됩니다. 4학년생들만 해당 기숙사에서 생활할 수 있습니다. 이러한 변화는 상급생들이 1학년생 및 2학년생과 따로 떨어져 있어야 한다는 상급생들의 지속적인 요구 때문에 이루어진 것입니다. 자신들만의 기숙사를 가짐으로써 4학년생들은 마지막 학년 동안 학업을 마무리하는 일뿐만 아니라 또한 취업이나 대학원 진학에 집중할 수 있을 것입니다. 관심이 있는 4학년생들은 Anderson 가 45번지에 위치한 학생 주거 사무실을 방문하여 Madison 홀의 방을 신청할 수 있습니다.

Comprehension ▶

1 Madison Hall will be undergoing a change starting in the fall semester.

2 Only seniors can live in the dormitory.

3 The change is being made because upperclassman constantly requested to be separated from freshmen and sophomores.

4 Seniors will be able to focus on completing their studies during their final year as well as applying for jobs and to graduate schools.

5 They should visit the student housing office.

Listening ▶

`Script` 🎧 02-23

M Student: I can't believe it. Madison Hall is the best dorm on campus. I was hoping to live there next year, but I'll only be a sophomore.

W Student: Well, you can get a room there in two years then.

M: But I don't want to wait that long. It's just not fair.

W: Sure, but I completely understand the reason the school is making the dorm be only for seniors.

M: You do?

W: Of course. I can't stand how noisy the freshmen in dorms are. I have trouble concentrating on my studies even late at night because students are making so much noise. I would love to live there.

M: But you'll only be a junior next year.

W: I know. And that's very frustrating. There's one more thing that appeals to me.

M: What is it?

W: Freshmen and sophomores can be really annoying to upperclassmen. They're always asking the same questions about campus and life at school. Seniors who live in Madison Hall can get away from them, and that will be a big relief for them.

해석

M Student: 믿을 수가 없군. Madison 홀은 교내에서 가장 좋은 기숙사야. 내년에 그곳에서 생활할 수 있기를 바랐지만 나는 2학년인걸.

W Student: 음, 그러면 2년 후에 방을 얻으면 되잖아.

M: 하지만 그렇게 오래 기다리기는 싫어. 공정하지가 않아.

W: 그건 그렇지만, 나는 학교측이 그 기숙사를 오로지 4학년생들을 위한 곳으로 만들려는 이유는 전적으로 이해가 가.

M: 이해가 간다고?

W: 물론이지. 나는 기숙사에 사는 신입생들이 얼마나 시끄러운지 참을 수가 없어. 학생들이 하도 시끄럽게 굴어서 밤늦은 시간에도 공부에 집중하기가 힘들어. 나도 그곳에서 생활하면 좋겠어.

M: 하지만 너는 내년에 3학년이 되잖아.

W: 나도 알아. 그 점은 정말 불만이지. 그리고 마음에 드는 한 가지가 더 있어.

M: 그게 뭔데?

W: 1학년생과 2학년생들이 상급생에게 정말로 귀찮게 굴 수 있어. 그들은 캠퍼스 및 학교 생활에 대해 항상 똑같은 질문을 하니까. Madison 홀에서 사는 4학년생들은 그들로부터 떨어질 수 있는데, 그러면 큰 안도감을 느끼게 될 거야.

Organization

1 The woman understands the reason and supports the school's decision to let only seniors live in Madison Hall.

2 She says that they are too noisy, so she has trouble concentrating on her studies.

3 She feels frustrated because she cannot live in Madison Hall next year since she will only be a junior.

4 Getting away from freshmen and sophomores appeals to the woman.

5 She thinks some seniors will feel relieved to get away from freshman and sophomores.

Comparing

Sample Response

Script 🎧 02-24

The announcement reads that Madison Hall, a dormitory with room for hundreds of students, will be reserved only for seniors starting in the fall. The reason stated in the announcement is that upperclassman have requested

to be away from freshmen and sophomores. They want to be able to concentrate on their studies, to apply for jobs, and to apply to graduate schools. The woman supports this decision by the school and gives two reasons to defend her opinion. First, she remarks that the dormitories are very loud, even at night, so she has trouble focusing on her studies. She says that freshmen are the reason that the dorms are so noisy. In addition, she points out that first- and second-year students often ask upperclassmen the same questions, which can be very annoying. She thinks that seniors will be extremely happy to get away from underclassmen.

해석

공지에는 수백 명의 학생들을 수용할 수 있는 기숙사인 Madison 홀이 가을부터 4학년생만 예약을 받는다고 나와 있다. 공지에 적혀 있는 이유는 상급생들이 1학년생 및 2학년생들과 분리되기를 요청했기 때문이다. 그들은 학업에 집중하고, 취직을 하고, 그리고 대학원에 진학하고 싶어한다. 여자는 이러한 학교측의 결정을 지지하며 자신의 의견을 옹호하기 위해 두 가지 이유를 제시한다. 먼저 기숙사에서는 심지어 밤에도 매우 시끄럽기 때문에 공부에 집중하기가 힘들다고 언급한다. 그녀는 기숙사가 시끄러운 이유가 1학년생들 때문이라고 말한다. 또한 그녀는 1학년 및 2학년 학생들이 종종 상급생들에게 똑같은 질문을 하는데, 이는 매우 귀찮은 일일 수 있다. 그녀는 4학년생들이 하급생들로부터 떨어져 있게 되면 매우 기뻐할 것이라고 생각한다.

Unit 27 Intramural Sports

Exercise p.83

Reading

해석

교내 스포츠 행사 취소

현 시간부로 모든 교내 스포츠 행사가 취소됩니다. 여기에는 교내 미식축구, 축구, 배구, 그리고 야구가 포함됩니다. 학교측은 재정 위기를 겪고 있으며 이러한 행사들을 지원할 수 있는 자금이 부족합니다. 또한 교내 스포츠 행사의 참가율이 지난 5년동안 감소해 왔습니다. 이로써 학교측은 학생들이 거의 참여하지 않는 활동에 너무 많은 자금을 지출하고 있습니다. 교내 운동장 및 코트에서 이루어지는 학생들의 스포츠 경기는 여전히 환영합니다. 하지만 스스로 팀을 결성해서 자체적으로 경기 시간을 정해야 할 것입니다.

Comprehension

1 It mentions that all intramural sports are canceled.

2 It includes intramural football, soccer, volleyball, and baseball.

3 The school has a funding crisis and cannot afford to pay for the activities.

4 Fewer students have been participating in intramural sports recently.

5 They can organize their own teams and play sports.

■ **Listening**

`Script` 🎧 02-25

W Student: Did you see the news about the school canceling intramural sports?

M Student: It's no big deal. Not many students play them.

W: You can't be serious. I play intramural softball, and there are more than twenty teams. There were only fourteen teams last year, so participation is increasing. Each team has fifteen players, so that's a lot of students participating in softball.

M: But the announcement pointed out that fewer students are playing sports, which is one reason the activities are being canceled.

W: That's simply not true. Whoever wrote that announcement isn't correct.

M: Huh. That's strange. I wonder how the school made such a big mistake.

W: You know, uh, I'm surprised you don't play intramural sports.

M: Why is that?

W: Well, playing intramural sports is a great way to get in shape and to lose weight. I'm in the best shape of my life since I play various sports throughout the school year. I might not be able to do that anymore.

M: Maybe some students should complain about this to the administration.

해석

W Student: 학교측이 교내 스포츠 행사를 취소한다는 소식을 봤니?

M Student: 대단한 일은 아닌걸. 그다지 많은 학생들이 참여하지도 않잖아.

W: 설마 진심인 건 아니겠지. 나는 교내 소프트볼 경기에 참여하는데, 팀이 20개 이상 존재해. 작년에는 14개의 팀만 있었기 때문에 참가율이 증가하고 있어. 각각의 팀에는 15명의 선수가 있으니 많은 학생들이 소프트볼을 하고 있는 셈이야.

M: 하지만 공지에는 스포츠 행사에 참여하는 학생이 줄고 있고, 그것이 바로 스포츠 행사가 취소되는 한 가지 이유라고 나와 있는 걸.

W: 사실이 아니야. 공지를 작성한 사람이 틀렸어.

M: 허. 이상하네. 학교측이 어떻게 그처럼 큰 실수를 했는지 궁금하군.

W: 알다시피, 어, 나는 네가 교내 스포츠 행사에 참여하지 않는다는 점이 놀라워.

M: 어째서?

W: 음, 교내 스포츠 행사는 체력을 기르고 체중을 줄일 수 있는 좋은 방법이지. 나는 학기 내내 다양한 스포츠를 하기 때문에 지금이 내 인생에서 가장 체력이 좋은 때야. 이제 더 이상은 그럴 수 없을지도 모르겠네.

M: 아마도 그러한 점 때문에 일부 학생들이 학교 당국에 불만을 가질 수도 있겠군.

■ **Organization**

1 The woman opposes the school's decision to cancel intramural sports.

2 She plays intramural softball, and there are more teams this year than there were last year.

3 It is not true that fewer students are playing intramural sports these days.

4 She is surprised that the man does not play intramural sports.

5 She is in the best shape of her life since she plays intramural sports.

■ **Comparing**

Sample Response

`Script` 🎧 02-26

According to the announcement, all intramural sports at the school, including football, soccer, and volleyball, are canceled. The announcement states that the school cannot afford to pay for the activities since it is undergoing a funding crisis. It also points out that the number of students playing intramural sports has been going down for five years. The woman expresses her unhappiness with this decision by the school. First of all, she mentions that there are twenty teams playing in her intramural softball league, but there were only fourteen teams last year. She claims it is not true that the number of participants in intramural sports is declining. Next, she says that she is in excellent shape because she plays intramural sports throughout the year. She tells the man that she will probably get out of shape if she is unable to play intramural sports anymore.

해석

공지에 따르면 미식축구, 축구, 그리고 배구를 포함하여 교내의 모든 스포츠 행사가 취소된다. 공지에는 학교측이 금전적인 위기를 겪고 있어서 그러한 활동에 대해 비용 지출을 감당할 수 없다고 나와 있다. 또한 교내 스포츠 행사에 참여하는 학생수가 5년 동안 줄어들었다는 점을 지적한다. 여자는 학교측의 이러한 결정에 불만을 나타낸다. 먼저 그녀는 교내 소프트볼 리그에 20개의 팀이 있는데, 작년에는 14개의 팀만 있었다고 언급한다. 그녀는 교내 스포츠 행사의 참가 인원이 줄고 있다는 것은 사실이 아니라고 주장한다. 다음으로 그녀는 자신이 1년 내내 교내 스포츠 경기에 참여함으로써 우수한 체력을 길렀다고 말한다. 그녀는 남자에게 자신이 더 이상 교내 스포츠 경기에 참여하지 못한다면 아마도 체력이 떨어질 수도 있을 것이라고 말한다.

Unit 28　Course Requirements

Exercise ·· p.86

Reading

해석

새로운 졸업 요건

학생들에게 새로운 졸업 요건이 생겼습니다. 모든 1학년 및 2학년생들이 졸업을 하기 위해서는 체육학과 수업을 반드시 한 차례 들어야 합니다. 또한 입학 예정인 모든 학생들도 한 번은 수업을 들어야 할 것입니다. 3학년과 4학년생들은 이러한 요건에서 면제됩니다. 대학은 학생들의 정신뿐만 아니라 신체도 훈련시켜야 하는데, 주로 이러한 이유 때문에 이번 요건이 신설되었습니다. 체육학과에는 학생들이 선택할 수 있는 많은 과정이 존재하며 이들은 다양한 낮 시간대에 개설될 것입니다. 더 많은 정보가 필요하시면 594-2938로 전화하셔서 내선 번호 42를 눌러 주십시오.

Comprehension

1 It mentions that all incoming students, freshmen, and sophomores must take one course in the Physical Education Department to graduate.
2 Juniors and seniors are exempt.
3 The university should train the minds and bodies of students.
4 There are many courses to choose from, and they take place throughout the day.
5 They can call a telephone number for more information.

Listening

Script 🎧 02-27

M Student: Another course requirement? I can't believe it.

W Student: It's just one extra course. And many students here could use the exercise. I like this decision.

M: That's easy for you to say. You're a junior, so you're exempt. I'm a sophomore, so it's required for me.

W: Why do you dislike this decision?

M: Hmm . . . First of all, we already have too many required classes. I would prefer to take more classes in my major to learn it better. But now I'll have to take one less economics class because of this requirement.

W: I see. Do you have any other reasons?

M: Sure. I already work out a lot. I jog three miles a day and visit the gym four times a week. I'm in outstanding shape and have no need to take a P.E. class to exercise.

W: I wonder if the school would make an exception for you.

M: What do you mean?

W: Because you exercise so much, maybe you might not have to take a class. Why don't you call that number and ask?

해석

M Student: 졸업 요건이 또 생긴다고? 믿을 수가 없네.

W Student: 단 한 개만 추가된 거잖아. 그리고 이곳의 많은 학생들이 운동을 할 수 있을 거야. 나는 이번 결정이 마음에 들어.

M: 쉽게 말을 하는군. 너는 3학년이라서 면제가 되지. 나는 2학년이라서 나한테는 필수 사항이야.

W: 왜 이번 결정을 싫어하는 거니?

M: 흠… 무엇보다 이미 필수 과목들이 너무 많아. 나는 전공을 더 많이 배우기 위해 오히려 전공 수업을 더 듣고 싶어. 하지만 이번 졸업 요건 때문에 이제 경제학 수업을 하나 덜 들어야만 해.

W: 알겠어. 다른 이유도 있니?

M: 그럼. 나는 운동을 많이 하는 편이야. 하루에 조깅으로 3마일을 뛰고 일주일에 네 번 체육관에 가고 있지. 나는 체력도 뛰어나서 운동을 하기 위해 체육 수업을 들을 필요가 없다고.

W: 학교측이 너는 예외로 둘 수 있는지 궁금한데.

M: 무슨 말이니?

W: 네가 그렇게 운동을 많이 하니까 아마도 수업을 들을 필요가 없을지도 모르겠어. 저 번호로 전화를 해서 물어보는 것이 어떨까?

Organization

1 The man is upset about the new course requirement.
2 He thinks the students already have too many required classes.
3 He would rather take more classes in his major in order to become better at it.
4 He is in great shape and does not need to take a P.E. class.
5 She suggests that he ask that the school make an exception for him.

Comparing

Sample Response
Script 🎧 02-28

The announcement declares that all freshmen, sophomores, and incoming students have an additional course requirement. They must all take a class in the Physical Education Department. According to the announcement, it is the duty of the university not only to improve the minds of students but also to make their bodies better. The man is upset about this announcement by the school. First, he remarks that students already have too many required courses to take. He was hoping to take more classes in his major, economics, but now he will have to take one less class because of the new requirement. He also notes that he jogs every day and goes to the gym to work out frequently. As a result, he is in excellent physical condition, so there is no need for him to take a P.E. class like other students may need to.

해석

공지는 모든 신입생, 2학년생, 그리고 추후의 입학생들에게 졸업 요건이 추가되었다는 점을 알리고 있다. 이들 모두 체육학과 수업을 들어야 한다. 공지에 따르면 학생들의 정신뿐만 아니라 신체적인 능력을 향상시키는 것도 대학의 의무이다. 남자는 학교측의 이러한 공지 내용에 반발한다. 먼저 그는 학생들이 수강해야 할 필수 과목들이 너무 많다는 점을 언급한다. 그는 자신의 전공인 경제학 수업을 더 듣고 싶었지만 이제 새로운 졸업 요건 때문에 하나의 수업을 덜 들어야만 할 것이다. 그는 또한 자신이 매일 조깅을 하며 자주 체육관에 가서 운동을 한다고 말한다. 따라서 체력이 뛰어나기 때문에 그가 다른 학생들에게는 필요할 수도 있는 체육 수업을 꼭 들을 필요는 없다.

Unit 29 Hiring More Professors

Exercise p.89

Reading

해석

공과 대학 확장

화학 공학과, 토목 공학과, 전기 공학과, 그리고 기계 공학과를 포함하고 있는 공과 대학이 올해 확장될 예정입니다. 이들 학과에 최대 20명의 전임 교수님들을 채용할 계획입니다. 학교측은 공학과의 규모가 확장되기를 간절히 바라고 있습니다. 최근 공과 대학의 학생수가 30% 정도 증가했기 때문에 교수님들이 더 필요합니다. 학교측은 또한 과학 및 첨단 기술 분야의 수업에 중점을 두고자 합니다. 채용 예정인 첫 번째 교수님들은 봄 학기부터 수업을 하시게 될 것입니다.

Comprehension

1 The announcement is about a plan to expand the School of Engineering.

2 It will hire up to twenty new full-time professors.

3 It is eager to make the school's engineering departments bigger.

4 The number of students in the School of Engineering has increased by thirty percent.

5 It wants to stress science and technology classes.

Listening

Script 🎧 02-29

W Student: This is great news. I'm really pleased that the school will be hiring more engineering professors.

M Student: Are you in the School of Engineering?

W: I'm not, but my roommate is, and she tells me about the need for more instructors all the time.

M: Why are they necessary?

W: First, because there are so many students, class sizes are too big. This makes it difficult for students to get individual instruction. Hiring more professors will let class sizes decrease. Then, the professors will be able to work with more students one on one.

M: Yeah, I can see how that works.

W: It sure does. I wish the school would employ more professors in my major for the same reason.

M: What else does your roommate say?

W: She hopes that getting more professors will let the school introduce new classes. She thinks the school ought to offer more specialized engineering classes. That way, engineering students can get better educations during their time here.

M: That makes a lot of sense. I hope that happens.

해석

W Student: 좋은 소식이네. 학교측이 공과대 교수님들을 더 고용할 것이라니 정말 마음에 드는걸.

M Student: 너 공과대 소속이야?

W: 그건 아니고 내 룸메이트가 공과대 소속인데, 그녀가 나한테 항상 선생님들이 더 필요하다고 말을 하거든.

M: 왜 필요한 거지?

W: 우선 학생들이 너무 많아서 수업 규모가 너무 커. 그래서 학생들이 개별적인 지도를 받는 것이 힘들지. 교수님들을 더 채용하면 수업 규모가 줄어들 거야. 그러면 교수님들이 더 많은 학생들을 일대일로 지도할 수 있을 테고.

M: 그래, 어떤 식인지 알겠어.

W: 분명 그럴 거야. 나는 학교측이 같은 이유로 우리 전공 과목 교수님들도 더 채용하면 좋겠어.

M: 네 룸메이트가 말한 또 다른 점도 있어?

W: 학교측이 더 많은 교수님들을 채용해서 새로운 수업을 개설하기를 바라고 있어. 학교측이 보다 전문적인 공학 수업을 더 많이 개설해야 한다고 생각하던데. 그렇게 되면 공과대 학생들이 이곳에 있는 동안 더 좋은 교육을 받을 수가 있지.

M: 말이 되는군. 그렇게 되면 좋겠네.

Organization

1 The woman is pleased with the university's plan.

2 She says that the class sizes in the School of Engineering are too big.

3 Professors will be able to work with more students one on one.
4 The school will be able to offer new classes.
5 More specialized engineering classes will be offered, so students will get better educations.

Comparing

Sample Response

Script 🎧 02-30

The announcement concerns a decision by the university regarding the School of Engineering. It intends to hire as many as twenty new full-time professors in the school's various engineering departments. The School of Engineering has increased almost by one-third, so more professors are needed. Additionally, the school wants to stress science and technology classes. The woman supports this decision for a couple of reasons. She says that while she is not an engineer, her roommate is. The woman believes that the classes have too many students in them, so professors cannot focus on individual students. However, if the school hires more professors, that will allow the class sizes to shrink. In addition, where there are new professors, they will teach new classes. This, in turn, will enable students to get better educations since they will be able to take various specialized classes.

해석

공지는 공과 대학과 관련된 대학측의 결정에 관한 것이다. 교내의 다양한 공학과들에서 20명 가량의 전임 교수들이 새로 채용될 예정이다. 공과 대학은 거의 1/3 정도 증원되었기 때문에 더 많은 교수가 필요하다. 또한 학교측은 과학 및 첨단 과학 기술 수업에 중점을 두고자 한다. 여자는 두 가지 이유로 이러한 결정을 지지한다. 그녀는 자신이 공과대 학생은 아니지만 자신의 룸메이트가 공과대 학생이라고 말한다. 여자는 수업에 학생들이 너무 많기 때문에 교수가 각각의 학생들에게 집중할 수 없다고 생각한다. 하지만 학교측이 교수를 새로 채용한다면 수업 규모가 줄어들 것이다. 게다가 교수들이 새로 오면 그들이 새로운 수업을 담당하게 될 것이다. 이로 인해 학생들이 다양한 전문적인 수업을 들을 수 있게 됨으로써, 결국 학생들에게 더 좋은 교육이 제공될 것이다.

Unit 30 Cafeteria Policies

Exercise p.92

Reading

해석

교내 식당의 새로운 결제 규정

8월 29일을 시작으로 대학의 4개 구내 식당에서 학생, 교수진, 그리고 교직원들의 현금 결제가 더 이상 가능하지 않게 됩니다. 대신 모든 결제는 학생증, 직불

카드, 혹은 신용카드로 이루어져야 합니다. 많은 학생들이 최근 구내 식당에 들어오기 위해 긴 줄을 서는 것에 대한 불만을 제기했습니다. 현금 거래는 카드 거래보다 서너 배의 시간이 더 걸릴 수 있기 때문에 현금 사용을 금지함으로써 처리 속도가 빨라질 것입니다. 또한 현금 거래를 차단함으로써 거래상 불균형이 나타나지 않을 것이며 현금이 때때로 사라지는 일도 없어질 것입니다.

Comprehension

1 The university's four cafeterias will no longer accept cash payments from students, faculty, and staff members.
2 All payments must be made by student ID card, debit card, or credit card.
3 Many students have complained about long lines to get into the cafeteria recently.
4 Banning cash will speed up the process of paying for meals.
5 Eliminating cash transactions will ensure that there are no imbalances in transactions and that cash does not go missing at times.

Listening

Script 🎧 02-31

M Student: Have you seen the notice about not being able to use cash at the cafeterias anymore?

W Student: Sure. I saw it. I think it's a great idea because the lines are too long.

M: I disagree.

W: Why is that?

M: I always use cash when I eat at one of the cafeterias. I don't have a meal plan, so I can't use my student ID, and I don't like using credit cards and debit cards. For me, cash is king.

W: Wow, you're not like most students. I don't think I know anyone else who uses cash.

M: For me, it's very convenient, so I prefer to pay for most of my purchases with cash.

W: I guess I can see your point.

M: There's something else I should mention. It's not right for the school to discriminate against people who use cash. It would be easy for the school to add another cash register. That would make the lines move faster than banning cash.

W: Hmm . . . That argument makes a lot of sense.

해석

M Student: 더 이상 구내 식당에서 현금을 사용할 수 없다는 공지 봤어?

W Student: 물론이지. 봤어. 줄이 너무 길기 때문에 좋은 아이디어라고 생각해.

M: 나는 동의할 수 없어.

W: 어째서?

M: 나는 교내 식당 중 한 곳에서 식사를 할 때 항상 현금을 사용해. 밀플랜이 없어서 학생증을 사용할 수도 없고, 신용카드와 직불카드를 사용하는 것은 좋아하지 않아. 나로서는 현금이 최고야.

W: 와, 대부분의 학생들과는 다르네. 너 말고 현금을 사용하는 사람은 없는 것 같아.

M: 나로서는 현금이 편하기 때문에 대부분의 경우 현금으로 구입하는 것을 선호하는 편이지.

W: 무슨 말인지 알 것 같아.

M: 언급해야 할 점이 또 하나 있어. 학교측이 현금을 사용하는 사람들을 차별하는 것은 옳지 않아. 학교측이 금전 등록기를 한 대 더 마련하면 일이 쉬워질 텐데. 그러면 현금을 금지하는 경우보다 줄이 더 빠르게 줄어들 거야.

W: 흠… 그러한 주장도 일리가 있네.

Organization

1 The man disagrees with the decision to ban cash.

2 The man always uses cash.

3 He says that cash is king and that he doesn't like using credit cards and debit cards.

4 He thinks that the school should not discriminate against people who use cash.

5 He suggests that the school set up another cash register to make the lines move faster.

Comparing

Sample Response

Script 🎧 02-32

The notice mentions that none of the cafeterias on the university campus will accept cash payments in the future. They will only accept electronic payment methods. According to the notice, the purposes are to make the long lines shorter and to make sure that no money goes missing when cash payments are made. The man disagrees with the decision to ban cash as a payment method. The first reason he gives is that he prefers to use cash for all of his payments. He notes that he doesn't have a meal plan and dislikes using credit cards and debit cards, so cash is much more convenient for him. The next point he makes is that the school is engaging in discriminating behavior by refusing to accept cash. He states that another cash register should be added so that the lines can go faster.

해석

공지는 대학교 내의 어떤 구내 식당에서도 앞으로는 현금 결제가 허용되지 않을 것이라고 안내한다. 전자 결제 수단만 받아들여질 것이다. 공지에 따르면 그 목적은 긴 줄을 짧게 만들고 현금 결제 시 현금이 분실되는 일을 막기 위해서이다. 남자는 결제 수단으로서 현금을 금지하는 결정에 반대한다. 그가 제시하는 첫 번째 이유는 그가 모든 결제에 있어서 현금 사용을 선호하기 때문이다. 그는 자신이 밀플랜을 가지고 있지 않으며 신용카드 및 직불카드 사용을 싫어하기 때문에 자신에게는 현금이 훨씬 더 편리하다고 말한다. 그가 제시하는 다음 논점은 학교 측이 현금 결제를 거부함으로써 차별적인 행동을 하고 있다는 점이다. 그는 금전 등록기를 하나 더 추가하면 줄이 더 빨리 줄어들 수 있다고 주장한다.

Unit 31 Psychology I

Exercise p.100

Reading

해석

구체화

부모들은 보통 아이가 긍정적인 방식으로 행동하기를 바란다. 그렇게 하기 위해 부모들은 종종 구체화를 이용하여 아이들의 행동을 조절한다. 구체화 방법을 사용할 때 부모는 아이에게 목표를 설정해 준다. 아이가 목적을 달성하면, 일반적으로 매우 작은 단계의 목표를 달성하면, 부모는 아이를 칭찬한 후 아이가 다음 목표로 나아가도록 격려한다. 만약 아이가 성공하지 못하는 경우에는 부모가 아이를 칭찬하지 않는다. 아이들은 보통 칭찬을 갈망하기 때문에 부모가 구체화시킨 행동을 함으로써 더 많은 칭찬을 받으려고 하는 경우가 많다.

Comprehension

1 Parents use shaping to get their children to act positively and to help control their children's behavior.

2 To use shaping, a parent must set small goals for a child.

3 When the child succeeds at one of the goals, the parent praises the child.

4 If the child fails to do something properly, the parent will not say anything to the child.

5 Shaping is often successful with children because children want to be praised by their parents, so they will work hard to get more compliments.

Listening

Script 🎧 03-03

W Professor: Raising a child isn't the easiest thing in the world. However, there are certain methods you can use to, uh, mold your child's behavior. Allow me to explain.

One day, my young daughter asked for some coloring books. But she'd never even held a marker or a crayon before. Simply doing that was hard for her. So I decided to use shaping to help her. First, whenever she made any kind of mark in the proper place, I'd praise her loudly. I'd say, "Wow! Look at that. That's great." I'd pay her lots of compliments. That would encourage her to continue coloring. But there were some times when she'd make a mark outside the drawing. Then, I wouldn't say anything. I wouldn't praise her at all. My daughter would realize she was drawing improperly. So she'd work harder to draw inside the lines.

Later, I'd make sure to praise her when she got the colors right. For example, if she drew a tree trunk brown, I'd praise her a lot. If she colored it, uh, pink, I wouldn't say a thing. That got my daughter to focus more, so she'd even try to get the colors right. You should see her pictures now. No, don't worry. I'm not going to show you them. Anyway, that's how shaping works.

해석

W Professor: 아이를 키우는 일은 전 세계 어디에서도 쉬운 일이 아니에요. 하지만 아이의 행동에, 어, 영향을 미치기 위해 사용할 수 있는 방법들이 있습니다. 설명해 드리죠.

하루는 제 어린 딸이 색칠 공부 책을 사 달라고 조르더군요. 하지만 딸은 한 번도 마커나 크레용을 쥐어본 적이 없었어요. 그렇게 하는 것도 딸에게는 힘든 일이었죠. 그래서 저는 딸애를 도와 주기 위해 구체화를 사용하기로 했습니다. 먼저, 딸애가 적절한 곳에 표시를 할 때마다 저는 큰 소리로 칭찬을 해 주었어요. "와! 저것 좀 봐. 대단한데."라고 말을 했죠. 칭찬을 많이 해 주었습니다. 그 덕분에 딸은 계속 색칠을 했어요. 하지만 선 바깥에 색칠을 하는 경우도 몇 번 있었습니다. 그러면 저는 아무 말도 하지 않았어요. 칭찬은 전혀 하지 않았고요. 제 딸은 자기가 그림을 잘못 그리고 있다는 것을 깨달았습니다. 그래서 선 안쪽에 그림을 그리려고 더 열심히 노력했어요.

나중에 저는 제 딸이 색을 제대로 칠할 때마다 칭찬을 해 주었습니다. 예를 들어 그녀가 나무줄기를 갈색으로 칠하면 칭찬을 많이 해 주었어요. 만약 분홍색으로 칠했다면 아무 말도 하지 않았을 테죠. 그래서 제 딸은 더 집중해서 색을 제대로 칠하려고 노력을 했습니다. 이제 딸애가 그린 그림을 보시죠. 아니에요, 걱정하지 마세요. 보여 드리지 않을 거예요. 어쨌든 이것이 바로 구체화가 작동하는 방식입니다.

Organization

1 The professor's daughter was trying to learn how to draw properly.

2 Any time her daughter made a mark where she was supposed to, the professor praised her daughter.

3 The professor would not say anything when her daughter drew something in an improper location.

4 The second step set by the professor was to have her child use the proper colors.

5 She praised her daughter when she made something the right color and did not say anything if she made it the wrong color.

Comparing

Sample Response
Script 🎧 03-04

The professor lectures on the methods she used to teach her daughter to draw properly. She states that at first, her daughter could barely even hold the markers or crayons. So any time her daughter made a mark where she was supposed to, the professor praised her. However, she wouldn't say anything when her daughter drew something in an improper location. The daughter, realizing she wasn't drawing properly, tried to draw better. The professor was using shaping, a psychological approach that sets small goals for children. When the child accomplishes a goal, the parent praises the child. When the child fails, the parent says nothing. The professor did this. She also set higher goals for her child by then having her use proper colors. For example, when her daughter drew a tree trunk the right color, the professor praised her. If her daughter colored it improperly, she'd say nothing.

해석

교수는 자신이 딸에게 그림 그리는 법을 가르치기 위해 사용했던 방법에 관해 강의를 하고 있다. 그녀는 처음에 자신의 딸이 마커나 크레용을 거의 잡지도 못했다고 말한다. 그래서 딸이 표시를 해야 할 곳에 표시를 할 때마다 교수는 딸을 칭찬해 주었다. 하지만 잘못된 곳에 무언가를 그리는 경우에는 아무 말도 하지 않았다. 딸은 자신이 제대로 그리지 못 하고 있다는 점을 깨닫고서 더 잘 그리기 위해 노력했다. 교수는 아이들에게 작은 목표를 설정해 주는 심리학적 방법인 구체화를 사용하고 있었다. 아이가 목표를 달성하면 부모는 아이를 칭찬한다. 아이가 잘못할 경우에는 부모가 아무 말도 하지 않는다. 교수도 그렇게 했다. 또한 그녀는 이후 아이가 적절한 색을 칠하게 함으로써 아이에게 더 높은 목표를 설정해 주었다. 예를 들어 딸이 나무줄기에 적합한 색을 칠했을 때에는 딸을 칭찬해 주었다. 잘못된 색깔을 칠했다면 아무 말도 해 주지 않았을 것이다.

Unit 32 Psychology II

Exercise ··· p.103

Reading

해석

기억

과학자들은 무엇이 기억력을 향상시키는지에 관한 수많은 연구를 진행해 왔다. 그들은 사람의 환경이 기억력에 극적인 영향을 미친다는 점을 알아냈다. 실제로 연구자들은 몇 가지 요인들이 사람들의 사실 기억 능력에 영향을 끼친다는 점을 알게 되었다. 이러한 요인에는 물리적 환경, 주변 인물, 그리고 시간대도 포함된다. 사람들을 대상으로 장기 연구를 진행하면서 과학자들은 사람들이 유사하거나 익숙한 환경에 처하면 기억력이 크게 향상된다는 점을 발견했다. 간단히 말해서 편안한 환경에 있는 것이 큰 도움이 된다.

Comprehension

1 Researchers have conducted studies on trying to find out why some people memorize better than others.

2 The researchers concluded that a person's environment affects how well that person can memorize something.

3 Some of the factors affecting people's abilities to memorize are the location, the people nearby, and the time of day.

4 The long-term studies showed that people can memorize better when they are in familiar or similar circumstances.

5 According to the passage, a comfortable environment greatly helps people memorize better.

Listening

Script 🎧 03-05

M Professor: What makes people memorize facts better? This should interest you all since, of course, as students you have to memorize tons of facts lest you fail your exams. I once conducted an experiment on memorization. Let me tell you how it went.

I had two classes on the same topic. I assigned both of them work memorizing facts about the rainforest. The first class had to memorize them while just sitting at their desks. I gave them ten minutes to try to memorize the facts and then quizzed them on the facts. These students did somewhat poorly. Afterward, many claimed they felt uncomfortable trying to memorize everything while the other students were around them. In short, they felt that their environment hindered them in their attempts at memorization.

As for the second class, I let them split up into small groups composed of their friends in the class. They spread out through the classroom and worked together. When I tested them, their performance was much better. Upon questioning, most said they had felt very comfortable working together with their partners. They were also able to ignore the other students since they weren't sitting nearby, and they could focus on the task at hand without any outside hindrances.

해석

M Professor: 어떻게 하면 사람들이 사실을 더 잘 기억하게 될까요? 학생인 여러분들은 시험에 낙제하지 않기 위해 엄청난 사실들을 암기해야 하기 때문에, 당연하게도, 여러분 모두 이 문제에 관심이 있을 거예요. 저는 예전에 기억에 관한 실험을 했습니다. 어떻게 진행되었는지 설명해 드리죠.

동일한 주제로 두 개의 수업을 진행했습니다. 두 수업 모두에서 열대 우림에 관한 사실들을 암기하는 과제를 내 주었어요. 첫 번째 반은 책상에 앉아 있는 상태로 암기를 해야 했습니다. 10분을 주고 사실을 암기하게 한 다음 그러한 사실에 대해 간단한 시험을 보았죠. 이 학생들의 성적은 다소 저조했어요. 그 후 많은 학생들이 주위에 다른 학생들이 있으면 암기하는 것이 불편하게 느껴진다고 말을 했습니다. 간단히 말해서 환경이 암기하려는 노력에 방해가 된다고 느꼈던 것이죠.

두 번째 반에 대해 말을 하자면, 저는 학생들을 친한 친구들로 구성된 소그룹으로 나누었어요. 그 학생들은 강의실에 흩어져 함께 암기를 했죠. 시험을 보니 이들의 성적이 훨씬 더 높았습니다. 질문을 하자 대부분이 파트너들과 함께 암기를 할 때 매우 편안한 느낌을 받았다고 하더군요. 또한 다른 학생들이 가까이 앉아 있지 않았기 때문에 이들을 무시할 수 있었고, 어떠한 외부적인 방해물도 없어서 과제에 집중할 수가 있었습니다.

Exercise ··· p.106

Reading

해석

주기적 개체수 변화

일반적인 생각과는 반대로 생태계는 정적인 환경이 아니라 항상 변화를 겪는다. 가장 큰 변화 중 일부는 생태계에 서식하는 종의 개체수에서 일어난다. 종의 개체수는 항상 불균형 상태에 있다. 예를 들어 몇 년 동안 많은 수의 먹이가 있다고 가정하자. 이로써 포식자의 수가 증가하는데, 그 이유는 생태계가 이들의 증가를 감당할 수 있기 때문이다. 하지만 결국 포식자의 수가 너무 많아질 것이며 먹이는 부족하게 될 것이다. 그 결과 먹이가 부족해져서 많은 수의 포식자가 죽게 된다. 이러한 개체수 변화는 사실상 모든 생태계에서 주기적으로 일어난다.

Comprehension

1 Most people mistakenly believe that ecosystems never change.
2 The populations of species in an ecosystem often change.
3 Species' populations tend to increase and decrease as they are constantly in states of imbalance.
4 When there is a large amount of prey available, the number of predators will increase.
5 When there is not enough prey to feed all of the predators, the number of predators will begin to decrease.

Listening

Script 🎧 03-07

W Professor: You've all seen that news report about how we've got a record number of deer in the forests this year, right? Well, what has made the numbers of deer increase dramatically? It's called cyclic population change. Let me give you an explanation so that you can understand it easily.

Now, this usually happens in three separate phases. Imagine a forest with a large number of mice yet a small number of wolves. What happens? Well, the wolves have an enormous food source, so their numbers increase rapidly since they can feast on all of the mice. This is what we refer to as phase one in cyclic population change.

However, pretty soon, you've got a massive wolf population yet a miniscule mouse population. The wolves have simply overfed and increased their numbers rapidly. This is phase two.

Organization

1 During his lecture, the professor mentions an experiment on memorization that he conducted on two separate classes one year.
2 According to the lecturer, the first class had to sit at their desks and memorize some facts.
3 These students claimed to have felt uncomfortable when trying to work alongside the other students.
4 The second group of students was allowed to divide into groups of friends and work together.
5 These students commented that they had felt comfortable working together with their friends and had not been bothered by the other students nearby.

Comparing

Sample Response

Script 🎧 03-06

During his lecture, the professor mentions an experiment on memorization that he conducted on two separate classes one year. He had both his classes memorize some facts, but he put them into two separate situations. According to the professor, the first class had to sit at their desks and memorize some facts. Unfortunately, these students did poorly and claimed to have felt uncomfortable when trying to work alongside the other students. The second group of students was allowed to divide into groups of friends and work together. These students did much better and commented that they had felt comfortable working together with their friends. They also hadn't been bothered by the other students nearby. In both cases, the students confirmed previous research done on memorization. This research noted that the location and the people nearby can affect a person's ability to memorize, which is exactly what happened.

해석

강의에서 교수는 어느 해 각기 다른 두 반을 대상으로 진행했던 암기에 대한 실험을 언급한다. 그는 두 반 모두에게 사실을 암기하게 시켰지만 이들을 서로 다른 두 가지 상황에 처하도록 했다. 교수에 따르면 첫 번째 반은 책상에 앉아 암기를 해야 했다. 안타깝게도 이 학생들은 성적이 저조했고 다른 학생들과 함께 있는 상태에서 외우느라 불편함을 느꼈다고 주장했다. 두 번째 그룹은 친구들끼리 모여서 함께 외우는 것이 허용되었다. 이 학생들의 성적이 훨씬 좋았는데, 그들은 친구들과 함께 외워서 편안함을 느꼈다고 언급했다. 또한 근처의 다른 학생들로부터 방해도 받지 않았다. 두 경우 모두에서 학생들은 암기와 관련해 진행되었던 이전의 연구 결과를 확인시켜 주었다. 이 연구는 장소 및 근처에 있는 사람들이 암기력에 영향을 미칠 수 있다고 설명했는데, 정확히 그대로였다.

Next, the number of wolves begins to decrease even more rapidly than it had increased. The mice, not having to worry about looking behind their backs for wolves everywhere, begin to recover their numbers. This is phase three. Of course, once the mice numbers totally recover, we're back at phase one again, and the cycle starts anew.

해석

W Professor: 여러분 모두 올해 숲에 사는 사슴의 수가 기록적이라는 뉴스를 보았을 거예요. 그렇죠? 음, 왜 사슴의 수가 급증하게 되었을까요? 이는 주기적 개체수 변화라고 불립니다. 이해하기 쉽도록 설명을 할게요.

자, 이러한 일은 보통 각기 다른 세 가지 단계로 일어납니다. 어떤 숲에 쥐는 많은데 늑대는 적다고 가정해 보죠. 어떤 일이 일어날까요? 음, 늑대의 먹이가 넘쳐나서 이들이 쥐들을 마음껏 잡아먹을 수 있기 때문에 늑대의 수가 빠르게 증가합니다. 이를 주기적 개체수 변화의 1단계라고 부릅니다.

하지만 곧 늑대의 개체수는 엄청나게 많은 반면 쥐의 개체수는 크게 적어집니다. 늑대는 먹이를 마음껏 먹고 그 수가 빠르게 증가했어요. 이것이 2단계입니다.

다음으로 늑대의 수는 증가했을 때보다 훨씬 더 빠른 속도로 감소하기 시작합니다. 쥐는, 어디에서건 뒤를 쫓아오곤 하던 늑대에 대해 걱정할 필요가 없어지자, 그 숫자를 회복하기 시작합니다. 이것이 3단계예요. 물론 쥐의 수가 완전히 회복되면 다시 1단계로 돌아가서 주기가 새로 시작됩니다.

Organization

1 In the lecture, the professor declares that cyclic population change has three separate phases.
2 In phase one, the wolves feed upon the large mice population, which rapidly increases the wolf population.
3 In phase two, there are too many wolves with a very small population of mice.
4 In phase three, the number of wolves starts dropping very quickly while the mice population begins recovering.
5 The professor notes that when the mice recover, the cycle promptly begins again with a return to phase one.

Comparing

Sample Response
Script 🎧 03-08

In the lecture, the professor focuses on cyclic population change and declares it has three separate phases. First, the professor sets up a scenario in which there are many mice yet few wolves in the forest. In phase one, the wolves feed upon the mice, which rapidly increases the wolf population. This leads to phase two, which is the state of having too many wolves with a very small population of mice. Finally, in phase three, the number of wolves starts dropping very quickly while the mice

population begins recovering. The professor notes that the cycle promptly begins again with a return to phase one. The reading passage describes this exact same situation. It notes that ecosystems aren't static but are constantly changing. This is a mirror image of the changes in the wolf and mice populations, which are never constant but are constantly in states of imbalance.

해석

강의에서 교수는 주기적 개체수 변화에 초점을 맞추고 그것에 각기 다른 세 단계가 존재한다고 말한다. 먼저 교수는 숲에 쥐는 많지만 늑대는 거의 없는 시나리오를 설정한다. 1단계에서는 늑대가 쥐를 잡아먹고 늑대의 수가 급증한다. 이로써 2단계가 시작되는데, 이때 늑대의 수는 너무 많아지고 쥐의 개체수는 매우 적어진다. 마지막으로 3단계에서는 늑대의 수가 매우 빠르게 줄어들며 쥐의 개체수는 회복되기 시작한다. 교수는 곧바로 주기가 다시 시작되어 1단계로 되돌아가게 된다고 말한다. 읽기 지문은 이와 정확하게 똑같은 상황을 설명하고 있다. 생태계는 정적이지 않고 끊임없이 변한다고 나와 있다. 이는, 정적이지 않고 항상 불균형 상태에 있는, 늑대와 쥐의 개체수 변화에 대한 내용을 그대로 보여 준다.

Unit 34 Psychology III

Exercise ·· p.109

Reading

해석

단기 기억

매일 사람들은 수천 가지의 정보를 단기 기억으로 저장한다. 안타깝게도 많은 기억들이 잠깐 동안만 기억되다가 곧 잊혀진다. 심리학자들은 사람들이 단기 기억을 잃어버리는 두 가지 이유를 알아냈다. 첫 번째 이유는 감퇴이다. 기억은 그 사람이 사용하지 않으면 감퇴, 즉 소멸된다. 두 번째 이유는 간섭이다. 이는 새로운 기억이 뇌에 입력되어 다른 기억이 빠져나가는 경우이다. 이 두 가지 요인 때문에 사람들은 자신의 단기 기억을 전부 가지고 있을 수가 없다.

Comprehension

1 People develop thousands of short-term memories every day.
2 Many people forget their memories after a short period of time.
3 Decay, which is the slow fading away of memories, is the first reason why short-term memories disappear.
4 The second reason short-term memories disappear is interference, which occurs when a new memory entering the brain makes an old one disappear.
5 Because of decay and interference, people cannot keep every single short-term memory in their minds.

Script 🎧 03-09

M Professor: Do you have a good short-term memory? You probably do for some things yet don't for others. So what makes people suddenly forget their short-term memories? There are a couple of reasons.

I'm sure you've all been told something only, much to your chagrin, to forget it a couple of hours later. Perhaps your friend tells you his phone number, but you don't write it down. You might repeat it a couple of times and remember it with no problem, but an hour or two later, you can't even recall the first digit. Why did this happen? You didn't use that knowledge, so the memory simply decayed. It went away from disuse.

Here's a personal example. I went to a bookstore last week to purchase two books I wanted. I had the list with me, but when I got into the bookstore, I realized I'd forgotten the list in the car. Yet I still remembered the books' titles. However, before I could grab them, I ran into an old friend. We talked about a different book for a few minutes, and then my friend left. However, the only title I could remember was the book my friend and I had conversed about. This new memory was interfering with my ability to recall the titles of the other two books.

해석

M Professor: 여러분은 단기 기억이 좋은 편가요? 아마도 그런 경우도 있고 그렇지 않은 경우도 있을 거예요. 그러면 왜 단기 기억을 갑자기 잊어버리게 될까요? 두 가지 이유가 있습니다.

여러분 모두 어떤 이야기를 들었는데, 정말 안타깝게도, 한두 시간 후에 분명 잊어버린 적이 있었을 것입니다. 아마 친구가 자신의 전화번호를 알려 주는데 적어두지 않을 수도 있어요. 몇 번 되뇌인 후 아무런 문제없이 기억하지만 한두 시간이 지난 다음에는 첫 번째 숫자조차 기억하지 못할 수도 있습니다. 왜 이런 일이 일어났을까요? 그러한 지식을 사용하지 않기 때문에 기억이 감퇴한 것입니다. 사용되지 않아 사라진 것이었죠.

개인적인 사례를 들어 드릴게요. 저는 지난주에 원하는 두 권의 책을 사러 서점에 갔습니다. 리스트를 지니고 있었지만 서점에 들어갔을 때 리스트를 차에 두고 내렸다는 점을 깨달았어요. 그래도 책 제목들은 여전히 기억이 났어요. 하지만 책을 찾기 전에 우연히 옛 친구를 만나게 되었습니다. 우리는 몇 분 동안 다른 책에 대해 이야기를 했고, 그 후 친구는 자리를 떠났습니다. 하지만 제가 기억할 수 있는 책 제목은 친구와 얘기를 나누던 책뿐이었어요. 이 새로운 기억이 다른 두 권의 책 제목을 기억하려는 제 능력을 간섭한 것이었습니다.

Organization

1 The professor notes there is more than one way for a person suddenly to forget a short-term memory.

2 His first example is of a person who is given a phone number to remember yet neglects to write it down.

3 He forgets the number because it is an example of decay, which is when a memory slowly fades away from disuse.

4 The professor's second example involves going to a bookstore for two books.

5 He cannot remember the other books' titles because of interference, which is when new memories push old ones out of people's minds.

Comparing

Sample Response

Script 🎧 03-10

The professor notes there is more than one way for a person suddenly to forget a short-term memory. His first example is of a person who's given a phone number to remember yet neglects to write it down. Even though the person repeats the number at first, within a couple of hours, he has forgotten it. This relates to the reading passage in that it's an example of decay, which is when a memory slowly fades away from disuse. The professor's second example is a personal one. He discusses going to a bookstore for two books. At first, he remembered their titles, but he met a friend there, and they started chatting about a different book. After the friend left, he couldn't remember the other books' titles. This represents the idea of interference as described in the reading passage. In interference, new memories push old ones out of people's minds.

해석

교수는 사람들이 단기 기억을 갑자기 잃을 수 있는 한 가지 이상의 방법이 있다고 말한다. 첫 번째 예는 기억해야 할 전화번호를 듣고 이를 적어 두지 않은 사람이다. 처음에는 번호를 되뇌지만 한두 시간 내에 번호를 잊어버린다. 이는 기억이 사용되지 않을 경우 서서히 사라진다는 감퇴의 예라는 점에서 읽기 지문과 관련이 있다. 교수의 두 번째 예는 개인적인 사례이다. 그는 두 권의 책을 사기 위해 서점에 간 이야기를 한다. 처음에 그는 제목을 기억하고 있었지만, 서점에서 친구를 만나 또 다른 책에 관해 이야기를 나누기 시작했다. 친구가 떠난 후 그는 다른 책들의 제목을 기억할 수 없었다. 이는 지문에 설명되어 있는 간섭의 개념을 보여 준다. 간섭이 일어나면 새로운 기억이 기존 기억을 생각 밖으로 밀어낸다.

Unit 35   Marketing I

Exercise p.112

Reading

해석

향기 마케팅

매장들은 일반적으로 쇼핑객이 방문하면 보다 많은 제품을 구입하도록 유도할 수 있는 방법을 모색한다. 그들이 알아낸 한 가지 효과적인 방법은 향기 마케팅이다. 판매자들은 쇼핑객들이 종종 향기와 특정한 기억 혹은 심지어 느낌을 연관시킨다는 점을 알아냈다. 연구에 따르면 향기는 사람들로 하여금 편안함, 나른함, 긴장감, 혹은 기타 여러 감정들을 느끼도록 만들 수 있다. 즐거운 기억을 떠올리게 만드는 향기가 특히 효과적이다. 매장 내의 다양한 구역에서 이러한 향기가 나게 함으로써 매장 소유주들은 쇼핑객들이 무의식적으로 평소에 구매하던 것보다 많은 제품을 구매하도록 유도할 수 있다.

Comprehension

1 Stores often try to find ways to encourage shoppers to buy more of their products.
2 Scent marketing is usually successful at getting people to purchase more items.
3 People typically associate various feelings and memories with certain scents.
4 A scent might make someone feel comfortable, relaxed, or tense.
5 When a scent reminds the shopper of some feeling, the shopper is being subconsciously encouraged to purchase a product.

Listening

Script 🎧 03-11

W Professor: You've all probably visited the local department store only to be besieged by all of the different scents. Have you ever wondered why there are so many different scents? It's called scent marketing, and it's the concept that various scents actually encourage people to shop more.

There was a study conducted a while back about the scents used in a department store. One store scented its entire women's clothing section with fragrances which were appealing to women. It also sprayed its men's clothing section with aromas that men found to be pleasing. Interestingly, it doubled the number of clothes that it sold. In a nutshell, both men and women, since they were attracted to those smells, associated the clothes with those fragrances and made more purchases than they normally would have.

There was also a survey about running shoes that was conducted recently. I think you'll find the results fascinating. Well, more often than not, people preferred for the running shoes they purchased to have some kind of fragrance. Furthermore, they actually expected to pay more money—around ten dollars in most cases—for the shoes that smelled nicer. So not only do smells encourage people to spend more, but they also get people to pay more for the same products.

해석

W Professor: 아마도 여러분 모두 인근에 있는 백화점에 갔다가 온갖 종류의 향기에 둘러싸인 적이 있었을 거예요. 왜 그렇게 많은 향기가 나는지 궁금했던 적이 있나요? 이는 향기 마케팅이라고 불리는 것으로, 다양한 향기가 사람들로 하여금 실제로 쇼핑을 더 많이 하도록 만든다는 개념입니다.

얼마 전에 백화점에서 사용되는 향기에 관한 연구가 진행되었습니다. 한 백화점이 여성복 코너 전체를 여성들이 좋아하는 향기로 채웠어요. 또한 남성복 코너에는 남성들이 좋아한다고 알려진 향기를 뿌렸습니다. 흥미롭게도 의류 매출이 두 배가 되었습니다. 한 마디로 그러한 향기에 끌려서 남성들과 여성들 모두 의류와 향기와 연관시키고 평소보다 더 많은 제품을 구입한 것이었죠.

또한 최근에 운동화와 관련된 조사도 이루어졌습니다. 결과가 흥미롭게 생각될 것 같군요. 음, 종종 사람들은 자신이 구매한 운동화에서 어떤 향기가 나는 것을 좋아했습니다. 뿐만 아니라 실제로 더 좋은 향기가 나는 신발에 대해서는, 대부분의 경우 10달러 정도, 값을 더 낼 용의도 나타냈어요. 따라서 향기는 사람들로 하여금 더 많은 지출을 유도할 뿐만 아니라 동일한 제품에 대해 더 많은 돈을 쓰도록 만들기도 합니다.

Organization

1 The professor mentions that department stores often overwhelm their customers with smells because of a concept known as scent marketing.
2 A department store once spayed fragrances attractive to men and women in the men's and women's clothing sections, respectively.
3 The end result was that clothing sales at the store doubled.
4 The professor relates that many people actually want their running shoes to have some kind of a fragrance.
5 She also notes that customers are willing to pay more money for the privilege of having scented running shoes.

Comparing

Sample Response
Script 🎧 03-12

The professor mentions that department stores often overwhelm their customers with smells because of a concept known as scent marketing. According to the reading, scent marketing recognizes that people associate certain feelings with different smells. Therefore, by using the proper smells, stores can entice their customers to make more purchases. This is exactly what the professor describes. In the first example, she notes that a department store once spayed fragrances attractive to men and women in the men's and women's clothing sections, respectively. The end result was that clothing sales at the store doubled. The second example concerns a survey on running shoes. The professor relates that many people actually want their running shoes to have some kind of a fragrance. She also notes that they are willing to pay more money for this privilege. This once again shows the importance of scent marketing in shopping.

해석

교수는 향기 마케팅이라고 알려진 개념 때문에 백화점에서 종종 고객들이 향기에 휩싸인다고 말한다. 읽기 지문에 따르면 향기 마케팅은 사람들이 특정 감정과 다양한 향기들을 연관시킨다는 점을 알고 있다. 따라서 적절한 향기를 이용함으로써 백화점들은 고객들로 하여금 보다 많은 제품을 구매하도록 유인할 수 있다. 교수가 설명하는 것도 바로 이러한 점이다. 첫 번째 예에서 교수는 한 백화점이 남성복과 여성복 코너에 각각 남성과 여성이 선호하는 향기를 뿌렸다고 말한다. 그 결과 백화점의 의류 매출이 두 배로 증가했다. 두 번째 예는 운동화에 관한 조사와 관련된 것이다. 교수는 많은 사람들이 실제로 자신의 운동화에서 어떤 향기가 나는 것을 바란다고 언급한다. 또한 이러한 이점을 누리기 위해 사람들이 기꺼이 더 많은 돈을 지불하려고 한다는 점에 주목한다. 이 역시 쇼핑에 있어서 향기 마케팅의 중요성을 보여 준다.

Unit **36** Zoology

Exercise ·· p.115

해석

고정 행동 양식

동물과 인간은 때때로 한번 시작하면 사실상 그만둘 수 없는 행동을 하게 된다. 예를 들어 어떤 동물이 예상 가능한 방식으로 의식적이고 자동적으로 반응하게 만드는 자극을 받을 수 있다. 이러한 반응이 고정 행동 양식이다. 그 예가 짝짓기 춤이다. 종종 암컷이 있기만 하면 수컷이 짝짓기 춤을 추는데, 그러면 춤을 끝까지 추어야 한다. 고정 행동 양식은 동물에게서 더 흔하게 나타나지만 인간이 이러한 행동을 하는 경우도 있다. 예를 들어 하품하는 사람을 보면 근처에 있는 다른 사람들 또한 종종 하품을 하게 된다.

Comprehension

1 The passage notes that some actions cannot be stopped by animals once they have begun.

2 A fixed action pattern is a predictable, yet automatic, response to a specific stimulus.

3 A mating dance is an example of a fixed action pattern.

4 Fixed action patterns are more common in animals than in humans.

5 Yawning is an example of a human fixed action pattern.

Script 🎧 03-13

W Professor: Sometimes we have no choice in how we respond to something. Like yawning. If I talk about it . . . See. Look how many of you yawned just now. That's called a fixed action response. It's more common in animals of, well, lower intelligence, than in humans though. Let me illustrate it with a couple of examples.

The male stickleback fish gets a bright red and blue belly during its breeding season. It's a very aggressive fish, so if it sees another male with a red stomach, it'll attack that male. However, if you put a red ball near a stickleback, it'll attack the red ball, too. You see, uh, it automatically responds to the presence of anything red by attacking. That action is fixed for the stickleback.

The graylag goose provides another example of a fixed action response. Graylag geese sit on their eggs before they hatch. However, sometimes an egg might roll out of the nest. The mother goose simply rolls the egg back into the nest with her long neck and beak. Now, if someone takes the egg away, the goose will continue trying to push an imaginary egg back into her nest. Additionally, if there are any egg-like objects nearby—marbles, stones, or whatever—the goose will try rolling them into her nest as well.

해석

W Professor: 때때로 무언가에 달리 반응하지 못하는 경우가 있습니다. 하품처럼요. 하품에 대해 이야기를 하면… 보세요. 방금 몇 명이나 하품을 했는지 보세요. 이를 고정 행동 반응이라고 부릅니다. 하지만 이는, 음, 인간보다 지능이 낮은 동물들에게 보다 일반적이에요. 두 가지 예를 들어 설명해 드리죠.

짝짓기 기간에 가시고기 수컷의 배는 선명한 붉은색과 파란색을 띕니다. 이들은 공격성이 대단히 높은 물고기라서 배가 빨간 다른 수컷을 보면 그 수컷을 공격할 거예요. 하지만 가시고기 근처에 빨간색 공을 놓아도 빨간색 공을 공격할 것입니다. 아시겠지만, 어, 빨간색이 보이면 자동적으로 반응을 해서 공격을 하는 것이죠. 이것이 가시고기의 고정 행동입니다.

회색기러기는 또 다른 고정 행동 양식의 예를 보여 주죠. 회색기러기는 알이 부화하기까지 알을 품습니다. 하지만 때때로 알이 둥지 바깥으로 굴러 나올 수도 있어요. 어미 기러기는 긴 목과 부리를 이용해 알을 다시 둥지로 굴려 넣습니다. 자, 누군가가 알을 빼앗아가면 기러기는 상상 속의 알을 둥지 안으로 굴려 넣으려고 계속 애를 쓸 거예요. 또한 근처에 알처럼 생긴 것이 있으면, 구슬, 돌, 혹은 그 무엇이든, 기러기는 그것을 둥지 안으로 굴려 넣으려고 할 것입니다.

Organization

1 The professor begins her lecture by mentioning that fixed action responses are more common in animals than in humans.

2 The male stickleback fish's stomach turns red during its breeding season.

3 The male stickleback fish will attack anything red it sees.

4 The graylag goose uses its long neck and beak to roll any eggs out of its nest back into it.

5 Should an egg disappear, the goose will pretend to roll an imaginary egg into the nest, and if it sees something egg shaped, it will roll that into its nest, too.

Comparing

Sample Response

Script 🎧 03-14

The professor begins her lecture by mentioning that fixed action responses are more common in animals than in humans. She reinforces this by providing two examples of this behavior. She states that the male stickleback fish's stomach turns red during its breeding season and that it'll attack other red-bellied males upon sight. However, it'll also attack a red ball and anything else red it sees. Likewise, the graylag goose uses its long neck and beak to roll any eggs out of its nest back into it. But should an egg disappear, the goose will pretend to roll an imaginary egg into the nest. In addition, if it sees something egg shaped, it'll roll that into its nest. These are both examples of fixed action responses. They are actions done in response to certain stimulations. The animals have no control over how they act but simply do so automatically.

해석

교수는 고정 행동 양식이 인간보다 동물에게서 더 흔하다는 말로 강의를 시작한다. 그녀는 이러한 점을 고정 행동의 두 가지 예를 제시함으로써 뒷받침한다. 그녀는 수컷 가시고기의 경우 짝짓기 기간에 배가 빨갛게 되며 배가 빨간 다른 수컷을 보면 즉시 공격할 것이라고 말한다. 하지만 빨간색 공 및 기타 빨간 물체가 보이는 경우에도 공격을 할 것이다. 마찬가지로 회색기러기는 긴 목과 부리를 이용해 둥지 바깥에 있는 알을 전부 안으로 굴려 넣는다. 하지만 알이 사라지면 상상 속의 알을 둥지 안으로 굴려 넣는 식으로 행동할 것이다. 또한 알처럼 생긴 것을 보는 경우에도 이를 둥지 안으로 굴려 넣을 것이다. 이 둘 모두 고정 행동 양식의 사례이다. 고정 행동 양식은 특정 자극에 대한 반응으로 행해지는 행동이다. 동물들은 자신의 행동을 통제하지 못하고 자동적으로 그렇게 한다.

Unit 37 Marketing II

Exercise ·· p.118

Reading

해석

창조적 범주화

마케팅 전문가들은 최선을 다해 고객들이 제품을 구매하도록 유도한다. 대다수 사람들에게, 그 이유가 무엇이든, 매력적이지 못한 제품과 종종 마주하는 경우 마케터들은 제품이 속해 있는 범주를 바꾸어 놓는다. 이러한 과정을 창조적 범주화라고 부른다. 이렇게 함으로써 마케터들은 제품의 매력을 높일 수 있다. 창조적 범주화의 가장 일반적인 두 가지 방법은 제품 가격이나 디자인을 바꾸는 것이다. 그렇게 하면 소수의 사람들만 구입하던 제품이 커다란 매력을 지닌 제품으로 바뀔 수 있다.

Comprehension

1 Marketers attempt to get people to buy their products.

2 Marketers change the category of their products in these cases.

3 Creative categorization is making a product more appealing by changing the category in which it is included.

4 Marketers often alter either the price of design of a product to change its category.

5 The end result of creative categorization is that the product often develops mass appeal.

Listening

Script 🎧 03-15

M Professor: Imagine you're a marketing executive and you have some products to sell. There may even be a huge section of society which doesn't purchase your products. Well, there are a couple of ways to break into that market.

You might try changing the price of your product. Did you know, for example, that watches were once regarded as expensive pieces of jewelry? Timepieces used to cost too much for most people. But many of you have watches, right? What happened? Well, one brilliant marketer started touting watches as fashion accessories. Sales of watches leaped dramatically. You can get watches for less than ten dollars nowadays, and they come in all kinds of styles. By changing the category into which watches fell, they began appealing to a greater number of people.

Here's another. Think about mobile phones. At first, their use was limited, and only rich people or businessmen used them. However, companies began marketing them to the masses. Now you've got kids and grandparents with mobile phones these days. Does a six-year-old kid need a phone? Not at all. But marketers have made it so that phones are no longer outrageously expensive. Likewise, they aren't considered tools only for the rich or for businessmen anymore. They're fashion devices now, almost like accessories for many people.

M Professor: 여러분이 마케팅 담당 직원인데 판매해야 할 제품이 있다고 가정해 보죠. 아마도 매우 많은 사람들이 여러분의 제품을 구매하지 않을 수도 있습니다. 음, 그러한 시장에 침투해 들어갈 수 있는 두 가지 방법이 있습니다.

제품의 가격을 바꾸려고 할 수도 있겠네요. 예를 들어 손목 시계가 한때는 값비싼 귀금속으로 간주되었다는 점을 아셨나요? 대부분의 사람들에게 시계는 너무 비싼 것이었습니다. 하지만 여러분 중 다수가 손목 시계를 차고 있어요, 그렇죠? 어떤 일이 일어났던 걸까요? 음, 한 탁월한 마케터가 시계를 패션 액세서리로 홍보하기 시작했습니다. 손목 시계의 판매가 급증했어요. 요즘에는 10달러 미만의 시계를 구입할 수도 있고, 온갖 스타일의 시계가 나와 있죠. 손목 시계가 속해 있는 범주를 바꿈으로써 시계가 훨씬 더 많은 사람들에게 매력적으로 보이기 시작했습니다.

또 다른 예가 있습니다. 휴대 전화를 생각해 보세요. 처음에는 사용이 상당히 제한적이어서 부유층이나 사업가들만 사용을 했죠. 하지만 기업들이 대중을 상대로 마케팅을 하기 시작했습니다. 요즘에는 아이들과 할머니 및 할아버지들도 휴대 전화를 가지고 있어요. 6살짜리 아이에게 휴대 전화가 필요할까요? 전혀 그렇지 않죠. 하지만 마케터들의 활약으로 휴대 전화는 더 이상 엄청나게 비싸지가 않습니다. 마찬가지로 더 이상 부유층이나 사업가들의 전유물로 간주되지도 않고요. 이제는 패션용품으로서, 많은 사람들에게 거의 액세서리와 같은 존재입니다.

marketing them to the masses, now even young children and the elderly have them, often as fashion accessories. As described in the reading, these are both examples of creative categorization. The reading mentions that this is putting an existing product into a new category, typically by changing its price or design, in order to make it attractive to more people.

강의 주제는 어떻게 마케팅 담당 직원이 매력적이지 않은 제품을 매우 매력적인 제품으로 변화시킬 수 있는지에 관한 것이다. 교수는 과거에 손목 시계가 실제로 매우 비쌌기 때문에 귀금속으로 간주되었다고 말한다. 하지만 마케터들이 이를 패션 액세서리로 홍보하기 시작하자 상황이 바뀌어서 지금은 시계가 값도 저렴하고 널리 사용되고 있다. 두 번째로 제시된 예는 휴대 전화이다. 교수는 한때 휴대 전화가 비쌌으며 부유층 및 사업가들의 전유물로 간주되었다고 말한다. 하지만 기업들이 대중을 상대로 이들을 마케팅하기 시작하자 지금은 종종 패션 액세서리로서 어린 아이들 및 노년층도 휴대 전화를 가지고 있다. 읽기 지문에서 설명된 것과 같이 이 두 가지 모두 창조적 범주화의 사례이다. 읽기 지문에는 창조적 범주화가 기존 제품을 보다 많은 사람들에게 매력적으로 보이도록 만들기 위해, 주로 그 가격이나 디자인을 변경함으로써, 해당 제품을 새로운 범주에 넣는 것이라고 나와 있다.

Organization

1 The subject of the talk is how marketing executives can transform a product with low appeal to one that has mass appeal.
2 The professor states that watches actually used to be very expensive and were considered jewelry.
3 This changed when marketers began promoting them as fashion accessories, so now they are both cheap and prevalent.
4 The professor declares that mobile phones were once used exclusively by rich people and businessmen.
5 Now even young children and the elderly have mobile phones, often as fashion accessories.

Comparing

Sample Response

Script 🎧 03-16

The subject of the talk is how marketing executives can transform a product with low appeal to one that has mass appeal. The professor states that watches actually used to be very expensive and were considered jewelry. However, this changed when marketers began promoting them as fashion accessories, so now they're both cheap and prevalent. The second example given is that of mobile phones. The professor declares that they were once expensive and used exclusively by rich people and businessmen. However, once companies began

Unit 38 Psychology IV

Exercise p.121

Reading

과정 설명

누군가에게 어떤 것이 작동되거나 운영되는 방식을 말해 주는 것을 과정 설명이라고 부른다. 과정 설명은 각기 다른 두 가지 방식으로 이루어질 수 있다. 두 가지 중 첫 번째는 지시적 과정 설명이다. 이 방법을 사용하는 사람은 어떻게 하는지를 단계별로 설명한다. 이는 종종 말이나 글로 된 지시를 통해 이루어질 수 있다. 두 번째 방법은 정보 과정 설명이다. 이러한 유형의 설명은 일반적으로 주제에 대한 정보만 제공하고 실제로 그것을 어떻게 하는지는 설명하지 않는다.

Comprehension

1 Process explanation is telling a person how something works or runs.
2 Directive process explanation is giving a person step-by-step instructions on how to do something.
3 Directive process explanation can be accomplished with either spoken or written instructions.
4 The second kind mentioned is information process explanation.

5 In information process explanation, the person merely gives some information on the topic but does not explain how to do anything.

Listening

Script 🎧 03-17

M Professor: We all have things we don't comprehend or know how to do. In these cases, we require explanations to learn the steps involved in doing them. When people provide explanations, they can do so in a couple of different ways.

For example, I bought a smartphone the other day. I'm somewhat, uh, technologically challenged, so I had no clue as to how to use it. I could make and receive calls, but that was about it. I wanted to save some numbers on my telephone so that I wouldn't have to remember them, but I didn't know what to do. One of my friends then showed me exactly how to do it. He took me through it step by step and made sure that I could do it by myself before he took off.

Later that night, I was watching an educational channel on television. There was a program about smartphone technology and how it's improving our lives. That show imparted a whole lot of knowledge about smartphones; however, by the end of the program, I still had no idea how to operate my phone. Sure, I knew all about the theory in how they work. I had the information. But the program never explained the process of actually using a smartphone.

해석

M Professor: 우리 모두에게는 이해하지 못하거나 어떻게 하는지 모르는 것들이 있죠. 이러한 경우 그것을 하는데 필요한 단계를 익히기 위해서는 설명이 필요합니다. 사람들이 설명을 하는 경우, 각기 다른 두 가지 방법으로 설명을 할 수가 있습니다.

예를 들면 저는 며칠 전에 스마트폰을 구입했어요. 제가 약간, 어, 기계치라서 어떻게 사용하는지 전혀 알 수가 없었죠. 전화를 걸고 받을 수는 있었지만 그게 다였어요. 전화번호를 외울 필요가 없도록 전화기에 전화번호를 저장하고 싶은데 어떻게 하는지 몰랐죠. 제 친구 중 한 명이 제게 방법을 알려 주었습니다. 친구는 단계별로 알려 주고서 자리를 떠나기 전에 제가 혼자서 할 수 있는지를 확인했어요.

그날 밤 저는 텔레비전에서 교육 방송을 보고 있었습니다. 스마트폰 기술과 그 기술이 우리의 삶을 어떻게 발전시키고 있는지에 관한 프로그램이었죠. 그 프로그램은 스마트폰에 대한 온갖 정보를 보여 주었어요. 하지만 프로그램이 끝날 때쯤 저는 제 전화기 사용법을 여전히 모르고 있었습니다. 물론 작동 방식에 관한 이론은 모두 알고 있었어요. 그러한 정보를 받았으니까요. 하지만 그 프로그램에서는 실제 스마트폰을 사용하는 방법이 전혀 설명되지 않았습니다.

Organization

1 According to the professor, people often need an explanation when they do not understand something.

2 The professor wanted to save some numbers on his smartphone but did not know how.

3 The professor's friend showed him how to save numbers on his smartphone step by step.

4 The show talked about smartphones; however, ultimately, the professor still had no idea how to use his phone.

5 He knew the theory behind how smartphones work but could not put it into practice.

Comparing

Sample Response

Script 🎧 03-18

During the lecture, the professor talks about what people typically do when they don't understand something. The professor's first example is of a smartphone he recently bought. He wanted to save some numbers on it but didn't know how. His friend showed him how to do it step by step. The professor's example is connected to the reading in that it's an example of directive process explanation. When using this method of explanation, a person explains all the steps involved in doing something. The second example concerns a program on smartphones the professor watched. The show talked about smartphones; however, ultimately, he still had no idea how to use his phone. He knew the theory behind it but couldn't put it into practice. This relates to the reading in that it's an example of information process explanation, which talks about a topic but does not actually explain it.

해석

강의에서 교수는 사람들이 이해하지 못하는 것이 있는 경우 보통 어떻게 하는지에 대해 이야기한다. 교수가 든 첫 번째 예는 자신이 최근에 구입한 스마트폰에 관한 것이다. 그는 전화에 번호를 저장하고 싶었지만 방법을 몰랐다. 교수의 친구가 어떻게 하는지 단계별로 설명해 주었다. 교수의 사례는 지시적 과정 설명의 예에 해당된다는 점에서 읽기 지문과 관련이 있다. 이 설명 방법을 사용하면 행동과 관련된 모든 단계를 설명하게 된다. 두 번째 예는 교수가 시청했던 스마트폰에 관한 프로그램과 관련이 있다. 그 방송은 스마트폰을 다루었다. 하지만 결국 교수는 자신의 전화를 어떻게 사용하는지 알 수 없었다. 그 이면에 존재하는 이론은 알게 되었지만 그것을 실행에 옮길 수는 없었다. 이러한 점은 정보 과정 설명의 예에 해당된다는 점에서 읽기 지문과 관련이 있는데, 이러한 방법은 어떤 주제에 대해 이야기하지만 실제로 그것을 설명하지는 않는다.

Exercise p.124

Reading

해석

능력 단계

사람들은 서로 다른 기술에 대한 다양한 능력 수준을 갖추고 있다. 개인의 기술 수준은 종종 두 가지 단계, 즉 의식적 능력과 무의식적 능력으로 구분될 수 있다. 의식적 능력 단계에서는 무엇인가를 하는 방법을 알거나 적어도 그 이론을 이해한다. 하지만 이러한 행동을 할 때에는 실수를 하지 않도록 매우 집중해야 한다. 무의식적 자질 수준에서는 사람들이 일반적으로 어떤 행동을 하는데 매우 능숙하다. 실제로 행동을 할 때 그러한 행동에 대해 생각을 하거나 집중할 필요가 없는 경우도 있다.

Comprehension

1 People have different skill levels depending upon what they are doing.
2 The two stages of skill levels are conscious and unconscious competence.
3 Conscious competence is knowing how to do something but having to focus on doing it.
4 Unconscious competence is having a high skill level at doing something.
5 A person with a conscious competence at something must pay close attention while doing it, but a person with unconscious competence can do it almost automatically.

Listening

Script 🎧 03-19

W Professor: All of you have got activities you're good at and others that you don't perform so well. You have, therefore, reached varying levels of competence at these activities. So are you consciously or unconsciously competent at them? Let's find out.

I'll use some personal examples to illustrate what I mean. Yesterday, I was typing up a manuscript in my office when the phone rang. I was in a hurry because of a deadline, but this phone call was important. So I kept typing away as I talked. Unfortunately, I'm not a good typist. I need to focus a lot when typing. After chatting for ten minutes, I looked at the computer screen. It was filled with errors. You see, I'm at the conscious competence stage for typing. I can't do it well unless I concentrate.

While driving home that same day, I got another phone call. I've been driving for years, so I'm pretty good. As I was on the phone, someone cut into my lane, but

without even thinking, I swerved away and avoided the car. Then, a kid ran into the middle of the road. Without thinking, I slammed on the brakes, so I didn't hit him. All this happened while I was on the phone. Driving has become second nature to me, so I'm at the unconscious competence stage of it.

해석

W Professor: 여러분 모두에게 자신이 잘하는 활동도 있고 그다지 잘하지 못하는 활동도 있습니다. 따라서 이러한 활동들에 있어서 각자 다양한 능력 수준을 가지고 있는 것이죠. 그러면 여러분은 그러한 일에 대한 의식적인 능력을 가지고 있는 걸까요, 아니면 무의식적인 능력을 가지고 있는 걸까요? 한번 알아보죠.

개인적인 사례를 들어 제 말이 무슨 뜻인지 설명해 드리겠습니다. 어제 저는 사무실에서 원고를 타이핑하고 있었는데 전화벨이 울렸어요. 저는 마감 시간 때문에 서두르고 있었지만 이 전화는 중요한 전화였어요. 그래서 저는 통화를 하면서 타이핑을 계속 했죠. 안타깝게도 제 타이핑 실력은 좋지가 않습니다. 타이핑을 할 때 매우 집중을 해야 하죠. 10분 동안 통화를 한 뒤 컴퓨터 화면을 보았습니다. 오타 투성이었죠. 알겠지만 저는 타이핑에 있어서 의식적 능력 단계에 있습니다. 집중을 하지 않으면 잘 할 수가 없죠.

같은 날 운전을 해서 집에 도는 도중에 또 다른 전화를 받았어요. 저는 여러 해 동안 운전을 해 왔기 때문에 운전에 꽤 능숙합니다. 통화 도중 누군가 제 앞으로 끼어들었는데, 저는 생각도 하지 않고 방향을 틀어 그 차를 피했어요. 그러자 한 아이가 도로 한가운데로 뛰어들어 왔어요. 저는 아무 생각 없이 브레이크를 밟아서 아이를 치지 않았습니다. 이 모든 일들이 제가 통화를 하던 중에 일어났어요. 제게 운전은 제2의 천성이기 때문에 운전에 있어서는 제가 무의식적 자질 단계에 있습니다.

Organization

1 The professor tells the class she was typing on a manuscript in her office.
2 The phone rang, so she tried talking and typing simultaneously.
3 She is not a competent typist, so she made many mistakes.
4 While driving home, a car swerved in front of her, yet she avoided it, and then a child ran into the street, but she stopped before hitting him.
5 She failed to have an accident because, in the professor's words, "Driving has become second nature."

Comparing

Sample Response
Script 🎧 03-20

The topic of the lecture is the different stages of competence people possess. The professor tells the class she was typing on a manuscript in her office. However, the phone rang, so she tried talking and typing simultaneously. Unfortunately, she's not a competent typist, so she made many mistakes. She next describes her drive home while talking on her phone. A car swerved in front of her, yet she avoided it. Then, a child ran into the street, but she stopped before hitting him. She failed to have an accident because, in the professor's words, "Driving has become second nature." Both of the professor's examples relate to the reading because they describe stages of competence. She has a conscious competence at typing; therefore, she must pay attention lest she do it poorly. But she has an unconscious competence at driving, so she can do it without even thinking.

해석

강의의 주제는 사람들이 가진 서로 다른 두 가지 단계이다. 교수는 학생들에게 자신이 사무실에서 원고를 타이핑하고 있었다고 말한다. 그런데 전화가 와서 교수는 통화를 하면서 동시에 타이핑을 하려고 했다. 안타깝게도 그녀는 타이핑을 잘 하는 편이 아니었기 때문에 오타가 많이 나왔다. 그 다음으로 그녀는 전화 통화를 하면서 집까지 운전했던 일을 설명한다. 차 한 대가 그녀 앞으로 끼어들었지만 그녀는 차를 피했다. 그런 다음 한 아이가 도로로 뛰어들자 그녀는 아이를 치기 전에 차를 멈추었다. 본인의 말을 빌리자면 그녀는 "운전이 제2의 천성"이었기 때문에 사고를 피할 수 있었다. 교수가 든 예는 모두 능력 단계를 설명하기 때문에 읽기 지문과 관련이 있다. 그녀는 타이핑에 있어서 의식적 능력을 가지고 있으므로 타이핑을 잘하려면 주의를 기울여야 한다. 하지만 운전에 있어서는 무의식적 능력을 가지고 있기 때문에 생각을 하지 않고서도 운전을 할 수 있다.

Unit 40   Psychology VI

Exercise p.127

Reading

해석

선택의 역설

역설은 맞는 것처럼 보이지만 그 안에 명백한 모순이 있는 진술이다. 다양한 종류의 역설이 존재한다. 그중 하나가 선택의 역설이다. 이 역설에서는 종종 사람들이 선택할 수 있는 옵션은 많지만 실제로 선택을 하는 과정이 자유롭지 못하고 사실상 스트레스를 주는 경우가 많다. 일반적으로 사람들은 선택의 여지가 많아서 좋다고 말하는 경우가 많지만 실은 무언가를 선택해야 함으로써 무언가는 선택할 수 없다는 점에 불만을 갖는다. 이 경우 너무 많은 선택권이 있다는 것이 자유를 주기보다 부담스러운 일이 된다.

Comprehension

1 A paradox is something that appears to be true yet has some aspect that makes it seem false.

2 A paradox of choice is being pleased to have many choices yet ultimately being unable to make a choice because of the sheer number of them.

3 People often act happy to have a large number of choices.

4 When people must make a choice, they often complain about having to do so.

5 The result of having to choose is that the process becomes a burden to them.

Listening

Script 🎧 03-21

M Professor: Nowadays, everyone talks about how they have more choices than ever before. But . . . Is this a good thing? It may seem like a paradox, but having so many choices is not necessarily positive.

Many people talk about the freedom having so many choices gives them. They say it's so nice to get to choose from a wide range of selections. But do you know what? That's not always true. Last night, I took my daughter down to the mall to buy some blue jeans. Apparently, there are tons of different brands and styles of blue jeans out there. At first, my daughter thought all those choices were great. However, soon she realized it was something of a burden. She had so many options that she couldn't make up her mind. That's quite the paradox, isn't it?

Here's another. My wife and I were trying to decide what to order for dinner last night. Our town has so many different kinds of restaurants that deliver. Unfortunately, that makes choosing difficult at times. We talked for about thirty minutes but couldn't decide on anything. In the end, it caused us so much stress that we just ordered the simplest thing and got a pizza. Of course, neither one of us was happy, but that's how paradoxes work sometimes.

해석

M Professor: 요즘에는 모두들 예전보다 더 많은 선택권이 생겼다고 말을 해요. 하지만… 이것이 좋은 일일까요? 역설적으로 들릴지 모르겠지만 선택권이 많다는 것이 반드시 긍정적인 것은 아닙니다.

많은 사람들이 선택할 수 있는 것이 많아서 비롯되는 자유에 대해 이야기합니다. 다양한 선택지 중에서 하나를 고르는 것은 좋은 일이라고 말을 하죠. 하지만 아시나요? 항상 그런 것은 아닙니다. 어젯밤에 저는 청바지를 사 주기 위해 딸을 데리고 쇼핑몰에 갔습니다. 보아하니 그곳에는 수많은 브랜드와 스타일의 청바지들이 있더군요. 처음에 제 딸은 그처럼 고를 수 있는 것이 많아서 좋다고 생각했어요. 하지만 곧 그것이 일종의 부담이라는 것을 깨달았죠. 선택의 여지가 너무 많아서 결정을 내릴 수가 없었습니다. 이것이 바로 역설인 것이죠, 그렇지 않나요?

또 다른 예도 있습니다. 제 아내와 저는 지난밤에 저녁으로 무엇을 시켜 먹을까 고민하고 있었어요. 우리 동네에는 배달이 가능한 식당이 정말 많거든요. 안타깝게도 그러한 점 때문에 때때로 선택이 힘들어집니다. 우리는 약 30분 동안 이야기를 했는데도 결정을 내릴 수 없었어요. 결국 그로 인해 너무 스트레스를 받아서 저희는 가장 간단한 피자를 주문했습니다. 당연하게도 저희 둘 모두 기분이 좋지 않았는데, 바로 이런 식으로 가끔 역설이 일어나기도 합니다.

1 The professor claims people are often happy to have so many choices, but they soon discover that making them is difficult.

2 The professor says he and his daughter went shopping for jeans the previous night.

3 His daughter was initially pleased by all the choices; however, having to choose became burdensome, so she was unable to make up her mind.

4 The professor and his wife were trying to decide what to eat for dinner.

5 Because of all the choices, they could not decide after much discussion, so they settled on something that made neither of them happy.

Comparing

Sample Response

Script 🎧 03-22

The professor gives a talk on paradoxes. He claims people are often happy to have so many choices, but they soon discover that making them is difficult. The professor says he and his daughter went shopping for jeans the previous night. She was initially pleased by all the choices; however, having to choose became burdensome, so she was unable to make up her mind. The second story related is of the professor and his wife trying to decide what to eat for dinner. Because of all the choices, they couldn't decide after much discussion, so they settled on something that made neither happy. Both instances are examples of paradoxes of choice. The reading states that this is a situation where a person is at first pleased to have many choices but then becomes frustrated or stressed out by having to make a definite choice.

해석

교수는 역설에 관해 이야기한다. 그의 주장으로는 선택의 여지가 많으면 종종 사람들이 좋아하지만 곧 선택을 하는 일이 어렵다는 것을 깨닫게 된다. 교수는 전날 밤 딸과 함께 청바지를 사러 갔다. 처음에 그녀는 선택의 여지가 많아서 좋아했다. 하지만 선택을 해야 한다는 점이 부담스러워져서 결정을 내릴 수가 없었다. 그와 관련된 두 번째 이야기는 교수와 교수의 아내가 저녁 식사로 무엇을 주문할지 고민을 했던 일이다. 선택의 여지가 너무 많아서 오랜 토론 후에도 결정을 내릴 수가 없었기 때문에 결국 두 사람 다 만족스럽지 못한 선택을 하게 되었다. 두 경우 모두 선택의 역설에 관한 예이다. 읽기 지문은 이를 어떤 사람이 처음에는 선택지가 많아서 좋아하다가 이후 확실한 선택을 해야 한다는 점에서 좌절하거나 스트레스를 받는 상황이라고 설명한다.

Unit 41 Biology I

Exercise p.130

Reading

해석

자원 배분 원리

지구의 모든 생물에게 다양한 목적으로 활용될 수 있는 자원은 한정적이다. 그러한 목적에는 채집이나 사냥을 통해 먹이를 구하는 것, 포식자들에게 잡혀서 죽지 않는 것, 짝짓기 상대를 찾는 것, 번식하는 것, 몸집을 키우는 것, 그리고 거처를 찾거나 만드는 것이 포함된다. 생물들이 예컨대 먹이와 같은 자원을 활용하여 이러한 일 중 하나를 하고자 할 때 이 자원을 다른 목적으로는 사용할 수 없다. 이는 생물이 모든 측면에서 결코 최대 잠재력을 달성할 수 없다는 점을 의미한다. 따라서 생물은, 거처를 마련하는 대신 먹이를 찾은 일에 자원을 배분하는 것과 같이, 절충안을 찾게 된다.

Comprehension

1 They have a limited number of resources that they can utilize for various purposes.

2 They can use resources to acquire food either through foraging or hunting, to avoid being caught and killed by predators, to find a mate and reproduce, to grow larger, and to find or build shelter.

3 They cannot use those resources for other tasks.

4 One result is that organisms will never achieve their maximum potential in all aspects.

5 One example of a trade-off is that organisms allocate resources to finding food at the expense of acquiring shelter.

Listening

Script 🎧 03-23

M Professor: There are only twenty-four hours in a day, and during that time, you have to do a number of different tasks. For instance, you have to sleep several hours a day. You have to spend time eating as well. You're students, so you spend time studying, but you might also have jobs, so you have to spend a few hours working, too. There are other activities that you do on a daily basis as well, right?

How do you decide which activities to do and which ones not to do? Well, you have to allocate your resources wisely if you want to be successful. When I was younger, I often spent my time poorly. At school, I frequently neglected my studies in favor of hanging out with my friends and playing video games. Unsurprisingly, my grades began to decline since I was utilizing my resources poorly.

Fortunately, I wised up and began spending my time better. I quit playing games, met my friends less often, and focused on my studies. My grades improved enough that I was able to get hired as a professor. That provided me with more resources in the form of money, which I used to acquire a house, a car, and other things. I don't have everything I want, but I've learned to allocate my resources much better nowadays.

해석

M Professor: 하루는 24시간뿐이고 그 시간 동안 여러분은 여러 가지 일을 해야 합니다. 예를 들어 하루에 몇 시간은 잠을 자야 하죠. 또한 식사에도 시간을 써야 합니다. 학생이기 때문에 공부에도 시간을 써야 하지만, 아르바이트를 할 수도 있으니 아르바이트에도 몇 시간을 써야 해요. 매일 하는 기타 활동들도 있을 것이고요, 그렇죠?

어떤 일을 하고 어떤 일은 하지 않을지 어떻게 결정할까요? 음, 성공하고 싶다면 자원을 현명하게 배분해야 합니다. 저는 젊었을 때 시간을 제대로 활용하지 못하는 경우가 많았어요. 학생일 때에는 친구들과 어울리고 비디오 게임하는 것을 좋아해서 학업은 소홀히 했죠. 당연히 자원을 제대로 활용하지 못했기 때문에 성적은 떨어지기 시작했습니다.

다행히도 저는 정신을 차리고 시간을 더 잘 활용하기 시작했어요. 게임을 그만두고, 친구들과 만나는 횟수를 줄이고, 그리고 학업에 집중했습니다. 성적이 크게 올라서 교수로 채용될 수 있었어요. 그래서 돈이라는 형태의 자원을 더 얻게 되었고, 이를 사용해 집, 자동차, 그리고 기타의 것들을 구입했습니다. 제가 원하는 모든 것을 가지고 있는 것은 아니지만, 지금은 자원을 훨씬 더 효과적으로 배분하는 법을 알고 있죠.

Organization

1 Every day, students sleep, eat, study, work, and do other activities.
2 They have to allocate their resources.
3 He spent his time poorly by neglecting his studies and by playing video games and by meeting his friends.
4 His grades began to decline.
5 He spent his time better, so his grades improved, and he was hired as a professor.

Comparing

Sample Response

Script 🎧 03-24

In his lecture, the professor talks about his activities in the past. He states that when he was young, he didn't spend his time well. Instead, he ignored his schoolwork and just met his friends and played video games with them. Because of his actions, his grades declined. However, the professor started spending his time more wisely, so his grades improved enough that he was able to be hired as a professor. He states that he has a lot of resources

now and that he can use his resources smarter these days. The professor's actions are related to the principle of allocation. This refers to the fact that organisms have a limited number of resources to use. They use these resources for actions such as food and shelter acquisition, protection, and finding a mate. When organisms use resources on one thing, they cannot use those resources on another one.

해석

강의에서 교수는 과거의 자신의 행동에 대해 이야기한다. 그는 젊었을 때 자신이 시간을 잘 쓰지 못했다고 말한다. 대신 학업을 소홀히 했으며 친구들과 만나 함께 비디오 게임을 했다. 자신의 행동 때문에 성적은 떨어졌다. 하지만 교수는 시간을 보다 현명하게 사용하기 시작했고, 성적이 올라 교수로 채용될 수 있었다. 그는 자신이 지금은 많은 자원을 가지고 있으며 현재에는 자원을 보다 더 현명하게 사용할 수 있다고 말한다. 교수의 행동은 자원 배분 원리와 관련이 있다. 이는 생물이 사용할 수 있는 자원이 한정되어 있다는 사실을 가리킨다. 생물은 먹이 및 거처 마련, 보호, 그리고 짝짓기 상대 찾기와 같은 활동에 그러한 자원을 사용한다. 생물이 한 가지 일에 자원을 사용하면 다른 일에는 그러한 자원을 사용할 수 없다.

Unit 42 Psychology VII

Exercise ·· p.133

Reading

해석

강박

일부 사람들은 어떤 면에서 문제가 되거나 부정적일 수 있는 행동을 반복적으로 그리고 일관적으로 한다. 이는 강박 혹은 강박 행동으로 알려져 있다. 매우 다양한 행동이 강박 행동이 될 수 있다. 어떤 사람들은 쇼핑 중독에 빠져서 너무 많은 돈을 쓰거나 불필요한 제품을 구입하기도 한다. 물건들을 절대 버리지 못하고 보관하는 사람들도 있다. 음식, 도박, 그리고 심지어 운동과 관련된 강박을 느끼는 사람들도 있을 수 있다. 이러한 강박에 시달리는 사람들은 불안 문제를 겪는 경향이 있다. 불안은 강박 행동을 함으로써 완화될 수 있으나 안도감은 오래 지속되지 못한다.

Comprehension

1 They are behaviors that people repeatedly and consistently engage in that can be troubling and negative.
2 They spend too much money and buy unneeded items.
3 They never throw away items but keep them.
4 Other people have compulsions concerning food, gambling, and exercise.
5 They tend to have anxiety issues.

W Professor: I'd like to talk to you about something that affects a lot of people, yet they typically don't want to discuss it. I'm referring to hoarding. My parents were hoarders. They wouldn't throw anything away, so their home was cluttered with all kinds of things. Let me see . . . There were piles of newspapers and magazines from the floor to the ceiling. There were all kinds of boxes, plastic containers, and other similar items.

They simply couldn't help it. It was almost literally painful for them to throw things away. They both had a severe compulsion to save everything that they could. It was awful to go to their home because you could barely even move around in it. I have no idea how they could live like that.

Fortunately, my brother and I had a solution. First, we sent our parents away on a weeklong cruise, and while they were gone, we cleaned the entire house out. We threw out tons of stuff, but we got their house cleaned out. When my parents returned, they were upset at what we had done, but then we got them help from a medical professional. Through therapy and some medication, they were able to overcome their compulsions and could then lead better lives.

해석

W Professor: 많은 사람들에게 영향을 미치지만 사람들이 보통 논의하고 싶어하지 않는 일에 대해 이야기를 하고자 해요. 저장 장애를 말씀드리는 것입니다. 제 부모님께 저장 장애가 있었죠. 어떤 것도 버리지 못하셨기 때문에 집이 온갖 물건들로 어질러져 있었습니다. 생각해 보면… 바닥에서 천장까지 신문과 잡지들이 쌓여 있었어요. 온갖 종류의 상자, 플라스틱 용기, 그리고 그와 비슷한 물건들이 있었습니다.

그분들도 어쩔 수 없으셨어요. 물건을 내다 버리는 것이 말그대로 고통스러운 일이었죠. 두 분 모두 심각한 강박을 가지고 있어서 가능한 모든 것을 보관해 두셨어요. 그 안에서 거의 돌아다닐 수가 없기 때문에 그분들 집에 가는 것은 끔찍한 일이었습니다. 어떻게 그처럼 사실 수 있었는지 모르겠어요.

다행히도 제 남동생과 저는 해결책을 찾았습니다. 먼저 부모님께 일주일간 크루즈 여행을 시켜드렸고 그분들이 없는 동안 저희는 집 전체를 청소했어요. 수많은 물건을 버렸고 집은 깨끗해졌죠. 부모님들께서는 돌아오셔서 저희가 한 일에 대해 언짢아 하셨지만, 그 후 저희는 그분들이 의료진의 도움을 받도록 해 드렸어요. 치료와 약물을 통해 부모님들은 강박을 극복할 수 있었고 이후에는 더 나은 삶을 사실 수 있었죠.

Organization

1 She says that they were hoarders who would not throw anything away.

2 It was cluttered with all kinds of things, including piles of newspapers and magazines from the floor to the ceiling.

3 It was painful for them to throw anything away.

4 They sent their parents away and then they cleaned up their parents' house and threw everything away.

5 They recovered through therapy and medication.

Comparing

Sample Response

Script 🎧 03-26

In her lecture, the professor tells the students about her parents. She remarks that they were hoarders, so they saved everything and would not throw anything away. She notes that their home was cluttered with all kinds of things and that it was awful to go there. She then adds that her parents couldn't throw things away because it was painful for them to do that. To solve the problem, the professor and her brother sent her parents on a trip. Then, they cleaned their parents' home and threw everything away. When their parents returned, they received therapy and took medication, which helped them improve. The professor's parents suffered from a compulsion. This happens when a person repeatedly engages in an activity that can be harmful. Hoarding and shopping too much are examples of compulsions. Compulsions often give people anxiety issues, which can create problems for them.

해석

강의에서 교수는 학생들에게 자신의 부모에 대한 이야기를 한다. 그녀는 부모들이 저장 장애를 겪고 있었기 때문에 모든 것을 보관해 두고 버리지 않으려 했다고 언급한다. 그녀는 부모의 집이 온갖 물건들로 어질러져 있었고 그곳에 가는 일이 끔찍했다고 말한다. 이어서 물건을 버리는 일이 그들에게 고통스러운 것이었기 때문에 부모가 물건을 버릴 수 없었다고 말한다. 문제를 해결하기 위해 교수와 교수의 남동생은 부모가 여행을 떠나도록 했다. 그 후 부모의 집을 청소하고 모든 것을 버렸다. 부모가 돌아온 후 그들은 치료를 받고 약물을 복용함으로써 증상이 나아졌다. 교수의 부모는 강박을 겪고 있었다. 이는 어떤 사람이 해로울 수 있는 행동을 반복할 때 나타난다. 저장 장애와 쇼핑 중독이 강박의 예이다. 강박은 종종 사람들에게 불안감을 가져다 주며 이로 인해 그들에게 문제가 발생할 수 있다.

Unit 43   Marketing III

Exercise p.136

Reading

해석

리텐션 마케팅

많은 업체들이 새로운 고객을 유치하기 위해 초점을 맞춘다. 하지만 업체들은 현재 그 어느 때보다 이미 확보한 고객들을 계속 유지시키기 위해 최선을 다하고 있다. 또한 이러한 고객들이 구입하는 각 제품의 수익성을 높이려고 한다. 이는 리텐션 마케팅으로 알려져 있다. 이는 전자 상거래를 하는 기업들에게 특히 인기가 있는 마케팅 방식이지만 기타 업체들도 이를 이용한다. 기업들은 특정한 방식으로 고객들의 입맛을 맞춤으로써 이를 실행한다. 예로는 세일, 빠르고 저렴한 배송, 정기적인 피드백 요청, 그리고 쇼핑 경험에 대한 고객 만족 서비스를 들 수 있다.

Comprehension

1 They are focusing on retaining the customers they already have.
2 They are attempting to increase the profitability of each purchase by their existing customers.
3 Companies doing e-commerce often practice retention marketing.
4 They cater to their customers in certain ways.
5 Some examples are having sales, providing fast, cheap shipping, requesting regular feedback, and helping make customers satisfied with their shopping experiences.

Listening

Script 🎧 03-27

M Professor: Jackson Airlines is a fairly new regional airline. It serves several states here in the southeastern part of the country. It has only been around for about five years, but the company is highly profitable and is starting to expand its fleet. What's the secret of its success? Let me tell you . . .

First, Jackson Airlines puts the customer first. Now, uh, all businesses claim to do that, but many actually take their customers for granted once they acquire new customers. Jackson Airlines, however, is focused on its existing customers. It wants those customers to keep flying on it. After all, a customer who flies on the airline several times a year is more valuable than several customers who fly once but then never return.

Here is what Jackson Airlines does. First, repeat customers get discounts on ticket prices. That is one way the company encourages people to keep taking flights on it. In addition, the company constantly asks its customers how it can upgrade its services. I've flown on Jackson Airlines before, and I've filled out multiple surveys. Even better, the company listens to its customers. When customers request a change or something new, they often get it. That is a wonderful way to retain customers.

해석

M Professor: Jackson 항공은 상당히 최근에 생긴 지역 항공사입니다. 남동부 지역에 있는 이곳 몇몇 주들이 서비스 대상이죠. 약 5년밖에 되지 않았지만 이 기업은 매우 높은 수익을 올리고 있으며 항공기들도 추가하기 시작했어요. 성

공 비결이 무엇일까요? 제가 말씀을 드리죠…

먼저 Jackson 항공은 고객들을 우선시합니다. 자, 어, 모든 업체들이 그렇게 한다고 주장하지만 사실 다수는 신규 고객을 유치한 후 고객을 당연한 것으로 생각하죠. 하지만 Jackson 항공은 기존 고객에게 초점을 맞춥니다. 이 고객들이 계속해서 자기 항공사를 이용하기를 바라죠. 어쨌거나 자신의 항공사를 1년에 몇 차례 이용하는 한 명이 고객이 한 차례만 이용하고 다시는 찾지 않는 몇 명의 고객보다 더 소중합니다.

Jackson 항공이 하고 있는 일을 알려 드리죠. 먼저 반복 구매 고객은 항공권 구매 시 할인을 받습니다. 사람들이 계속해서 자신을 이용하도록 장려하기 위한 한 가지 방법이죠. 또한 이 기업은 항상 고객들에게 서비스를 업그레이드 할 수 있는 법을 묻습니다. 저도 전에 Jackson 항공을 이용했는데 여러 차례 설문 조사지를 작성했어요. 훨씬 더 좋은 것은 이 기업이 고객들의 말에 귀를 기울인다는 점입니다. 고객들이 변화나 새로운 것을 요청하는 경우 종종 요청이 받아들여집니다. 이것이 바로 고객을 계속 유지할 수 있는 훌륭한 방법이죠.

Organization

1 It is a highly profitable regional airline that is expanding its fleet.
2 It puts the customer first.
3 The airline focuses on its existing customers.
4 Repeat customers get discounts on ticket prices.
5 He has filled out many surveys.

Comparing

Sample Response
Script 🎧 03-28

In his lecture, the professor talks about Jackson Airlines, a regional airline that is highly profitable and that is currently expanding its fleet. The professor notes that the airline puts its customers first. In addition, the airline focuses on its existing customers because it wants them to fly on the airline again and again. The airline provides a few benefits for repeat customers. For instance, they receive discounts on their tickets. They are also asked to complete surveys on how the company can improve its services. Then, the airline listens to its customers and implements the requested changes. This is an example of retention marketing. This refers to actions that companies take in order to get existing customers to continue making purchases with them and to spend more money than before. While companies engaged in e-commerce often use this technique, other companies may practice retention marketing as well.

해석

강의에서 교수는 수익성이 높고 현재 항공편을 확대하고 있는 지역 항공사인 Jackson 항공에 대해 이야기한다. 교수는 이 항공사가 고객들을 우선시한다는 점에 주목한다. 또한 이 항공사는 기존 고객들이 자신을 계속해서 이용하기를 바라기 때문에 기존 고객들에게 초점을 맞춘다. 이 항공사는 반복 구매 고객에게

몇 가지 혜택을 제공한다. 예를 들어 항공권 구입 시 할인을 받는다. 또한 이 기업이 어떻게 자사 서비스를 향상시킬 수 있는지에 대한 설문 조사를 요청받는다. 그런 다음 항공사는 고객의 말에 귀를 기울여 요청 사항을 반영한다. 이는 리텐션 마케팅의 예이다. 이는 기존 고객들이 계속해서 자신의 제품을 구입하고 전보다 더 많은 돈을 소비하도록 만들기 위해 기업이 취하는 행동을 가리킨다. 전자상거래를 하는 기업들이 종종 이러한 기법을 사용하지만 기타 기업들 또한 리텐션 마케팅을 이용할 수 있다.

Unit 44 Psychology VIII

Exercise p.139

Reading

해석

오정보 효과

모든 기억이 똑같이 유지되는 것은 아니다. 때때로 외부의 영향 때문에 기억이 바뀔 수도 있다. 예를 들어 사람들이 특정한 사건을 목격하고 그에 대한 기억을 가질 수 있다. 하지만 이후 사건에 대한, 옳거나 옳지 않은, 새로운 점을 알거나 들을 수 있는데, 이로 인해 어떤 일이 일어났는지에 대한 기억이 바뀔 수 있다. 이러한 오정보 효과는 다른 사람의 행동을 통해 기억을 변화시킴으로써 과거에 일어났던 일을 사람들이 잘못 생각하도록 만드는 일이 얼마나 쉬운 것인지 보여 준다.

Comprehension

1 They may not remain the same.
2 They can change due to outside influences.
3 When people learn something new about a past event, it can make their memories change.
4 People can be misled about what happened in the past.
5 Their memories are changed due to the actions of others.

Listening

Script 🎧 03-29

W Professor: In the late 1970s, American psychologist Elizabeth Loftus conducted a fascinating study on how people's memories of events can be changed through the introduction of incorrect information.

A group of people were shown a video of two cars involved in an accident. After they saw the video, the people were asked questions as if they had been witnesses to the actual event. Among the many questions they were asked was this one: How fast were the cars traveling when they hit each other? However, not everyone was asked that exact question. In some cases, the word "hit" was changed to "smashed into."

So the new question became this: How fast were the cars traveling when they smashed into each other?

A few days later, the people were once again asked about the accident to test their memories of what had occurred. One of the questions asked the people if they saw the broken glass. There had been no broken glass, so most of the people responded correctly and said no. However, some of the people who had been asked if the cars had smashed into each other incorrectly recalled the accident and said that they had seen the broken glass. In this way, their memories were changed by incorrect information.

해석

W Professor: 1970년대 후반 미국인 심리학자 엘리자베스 로프터스는 사건에 관한 사람들의 기억이 부정확한 정보에 의해 어떻게 바뀔 수 있는지에 관한 흥미로운 연구를 진행했습니다.

한 무리의 사람들에게 두 대의 자동차가 교통 사고를 내는 비디오를 보여 주었습니다. 비디오를 본 후 사람들에게는 마치 그들이 실제 사고를 목격했던 것처럼 질문이 주어졌습니다. 그들에게 물어본 여러 질문 중에는 이런 것도 있었어요: 자동차가 부딪쳤을 때 속도가 얼마나 빨랐나요? 하지만 모두에게 정확히 같은 질문이 주어지지는 않았습니다. 일부 경우에는 "부딪히다"라는 단어가 "크게 충돌하다"로 바뀌었죠. 그래서 새로운 질문은 다음과 같았습니다: 자동차가 크게 충돌했을 때 속도가 얼마나 빨랐나요?

며칠 뒤 사람들에게 다시 한 번 사고에 관한 질문을 해서 어떤 일이 일어났는지에 대한 이들의 기억을 테스트했습니다. 질문 중 하나는 그들이 깨진 유리를 보았는지 물어보는 것이었어요. 깨진 유리가 없었기 때문에 대부분의 사람들은 올바로 대답을 해서 보지 못했다고 말을 했습니다. 하지만 자동차가 크게 충돌했는지 물어보는 질문을 받았던 사람들 중 일부는 사고를 제대로 기억해 내지 못하고 자신들이 깨진 유리를 보았다고 말을 했어요. 이런 식으로 그들의 기억이 부정확한 정보에 의해 바뀌었습니다.

Organization

1 She was an American psychologist who conducted a study on how people's memories of past events can be changed.
2 They were shown a video of a car accident.
3 They were asked how fast the cars were traveling when they hit each other.
4 The word "hit" was replaced with "smashed into."
5 People were asked if they saw the broken glass a few days later.

Comparing

Sample Response

Script 🎧 03-30

The professor lectures about an experiment which was conducted by an American psychologist named

Elizabeth Loftus. The study involved showing a group of people a video of two cars involved in an accident. After the people saw the video, they were asked about it. One question asked how fast the cars were going when they hit each other. However, some people were instead asked how fast the cars were going when they smashed into each other. A few days later, the people were asked if they saw the broken glass. There had been no broken glass, so most people answered correctly. But those who had been asked about the cars smashing into each other sometimes developed false memories and said they had seen the glass. This is an instance of the misinformation effect, which shows how information introduced after an event can make people develop false memories.

해석

교수는 엘리자베스 로프터스라는 미국인 심리학자가 수행한 실험에 대해 강의하고 있다. 이 연구에서는 한 무리의 사람들에게 두 대의 자동차가 교통 사고를 내는 비디오를 보여 주었다. 비디오 시청 후 사람들에게는 그에 관한 질문이 주어졌다. 한 가지 질문은 자동차들이 부딪쳤을 때 자동차의 속도를 묻는 것이었다. 하지만 몇몇 사람들은 그 대신 자동차들이 서로 크게 충돌했을 때 자동차의 속도를 묻는 질문이 주어졌다. 며칠 뒤 사람들에게 깨진 유리를 보았는지 물었다. 깨진 유리는 없었기 때문에 대부분의 사람은 올바르게 대답했다. 하지만 크게 충돌한 자동차에 관한 질문을 받았던 사람들은 때때로 잘못된 기억을 떠올려서 자신이 유리를 보았다고 말했다. 이는 오정보 효과의 사례인데, 이는 사건 이후에 주어진 정보가 어떻게 사람들로 하여금 잘못된 기억을 갖도록 만들 수 있는지를 보여 준다.

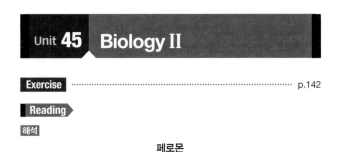

Unit 45 Biology II

Exercise ·· p.142

Reading

해석

페로몬

모든 커뮤니케이션이 구두로 혹은 시각으로 이루어지는 것은 아니다. 다양한 생물들이 동일한 종의 다른 개체에게 메시지를 전달할 수 있는 화학 물질을 분비한다. 페로몬은 곤충류, 갑각류, 그리고 척추 동물에 의해 사용된다. 이는 보통 분비선에서 분비되지만 신체에서 빠져나가는 소변과 같은 물질에서도 발견될 수 있다. 페로몬은 다양한 목적을 지닌다. 곤충과 같은 동물들은 종종 페로몬을 이용해 복잡한 행동을 하기도 하는데, 이로써 서로가 한 마음으로 협동할 수 있다. 이는 또한 경고나 매력 발산의 수단으로서 사용될 수도 있다.

Comprehension

1 It can be done orally and visually.

2 They are chemicals secreted by various organisms which are capable of transmitting messages to others of the same species.

3 Insects, crustaceans, and vertebrates use pheromones.

4 They are secreted by glands.

5 They use pheromones to conduct complex activities enabling them to work together as a single mind.

Listening

Script 🎧 03-31

M Professor: Have you ever wondered how bees can have some complex societies? I mean, thousands can live in a single colony, and each bee has specific jobs to do to keep the colony running smoothly. So . . . how do they manage to do this? One reason is that bees rely on pheromones to communicate with one another.

For instance, there are several animals that attack beehives to attempt to get the honey the bees make. Bears, of course, do this. So do badgers, humans, and many other animals. When a colony is under attack, bees release alarm pheromones into the air. These chemical secretions are detected by other members of the colony, which rush to its defense. If enough bees can sting the attacker or chase it away, then they can successfully defend the hive.

Bees also require varying amounts of food depending upon how many adult bees, young bees, and bee larvae there are at any certain time. When the colony is in need of more food, certain bees, including the queen, may release pheromones that stimulate the urge to forage. Due to the influence of these forager pheromones, worker bees then search for food in order to guarantee that the colony has enough for all of its members.

해석

M Professor: 벌들이 어떻게 복잡한 사회를 유지할 수 있는지 궁금해 본 적이 있나요? 제 말은 수천 마리의 벌들 하나의 군락에서 생활할 수 있고, 각각의 벌은 특정한 일을 맡아서 군락이 원활하게 돌아가도록 한다는 것이에요. 그러면⋯ 어떻게 그럴 수가 있을까요? 한 가지 이유는 벌들이 페로몬을 이용해 서로 커뮤니케이션을 하기 때문입니다.

예를 들어서 벌들이 만든 꿀을 가져가기 위해 벌집을 공격하는 몇몇 동물들이 있습니다. 물론 곰이 그렇게 하죠. 오소리, 인간, 그리고 기타 많은 동물들도 마찬가지입니다. 군락이 공격을 받으면 벌들은 경고성 페로몬을 공중에 분사합니다. 이처럼 화학 물질이 분비되면 군락의 다른 구성원들이 이를 감지해서 신속히 방어 태세를 갖추게 됩니다. 충분한 수의 벌들이 공격자에게 침을 쏘거나 이들을 쫓아내면 성공적으로 벌집을 방어할 수가 있죠.

벌들은 또한 특정 시간에 성체 꿀벌, 어린 꿀벌, 그리고 꿀벌 애벌레의 수에 따라 다양한 양의 먹이를 필요로 합니다. 군락에 먹이가 더 필요한 경우 여왕벌을 포함하여 특정 벌들이 먹이를 찾아 나서도록 자극하는 페로몬을 분비할 수 있어요. 이러한 먹이 찾기 페로몬의 영향 때문에 일벌들은 군락의 모든 구성원들에게 충분한 양의 먹이가 마련될 수 있도록 먹이를 찾아 나섭니다.

1 They use pheromones to communicate with one another.

2 They want to get the honey that bees make.

3 They release alarm pheromones, which encourage bees to attack an invader.

4 The queen and other bees release pheromones that stimulate the need to forage.

5 Worker bees search for food to make sure that all of the members of the colony have enough to eat.

Comparing

Sample Response

Script 🎧 03-32

In his lecture, the professor points out that bees have complex societies. He says they can function together well because they use pheromones. According to the reading passage, pheromones are chemical secretions released by insects, crustaceans, and vertebrates. They let animals function together as a single unit and can be used as warnings and signs of attraction. The first example the professor uses is when animals such as bears attack a beehive to get the bees' honey. Some bees release alarm pheromones, which are detected by other colony members. Bees hurry to defend the colony by attacking the invader. The second example cited concerns bees' food supply. The professor states that bees need varying amounts of food at times. When more food is needed, the queen and other bees release forager pheromones. These induce bees to search for food so that there is enough for the colony.

해석

강의에서 교수는 벌들이 복잡한 사회를 가지고 있다고 지적한다. 그는 벌들이 페로몬을 사용하기 때문에 함께 잘 활동할 수 있다고 말한다. 읽기 지문에 따르면 페로몬은 곤충류, 갑각류, 그리고 척추 동물들이 분비하는 화학 물질이다. 이는 동물들로 하여금 하나의 단위로서 활동할 수 있게 하고, 경고 및 매력 발산 수단으로서 사용될 수도 있다. 교수가 제시하는 첫 번째 예는 곰 같은 동물들이 벌꿀을 얻기 위해 벌집을 공격하는 경우이다. 몇몇 벌들이 경고성 페로몬을 분비하면 군락의 다른 구성원들이 이를 감지한다. 벌들은 침입자를 공격함으로써 신속히 군락을 방어한다. 언급된 두 번째 예는 벌의 먹이와 관련된 것이다. 교수는 벌들이 때때로 다양한 양의 먹이를 필요로 한다고 말한다. 더 많은 먹이가 필요한 경우 여왕벌 및 기타 벌들이 먹이 찾기 페로몬을 분비한다. 이로 인해 벌들은 군락에 충분한 먹이가 있을 수 있도록 먹이를 찾아 나선다.

Unit 46 Biology I

Exercise p.150

Listening

Script 🎧 04-03

M Professor: Most animals have ways to protect themselves. They require defenses since virtually every animal is potential prey for another animal higher on the food chain. Over countless generations, animals have developed various ways to protect themselves. Interestingly, some are categorized as defensive while others are considered offensive adaptations.

　Let's look at the defensive adaptations first. Look at the picture in your book on page, uh, page 242. It's a turtle, right? You've all seen them. Some of you may have even had pet turtles. But do you know they've actually developed two defensive methods? The first is the most obvious. It's the shell. The shell covers the turtle's entire body, including its vital organs. The shell is very hard. Most predators give up trying to bite through it. Now, uh, take a look at the neck. It's really long. Oh, a weak point, right? Wrong. The turtle has a flexible neck, so it can easily fold its neck back into its shell when danger comes along.

　But remember that some adaptations are offensive. Look at the picture on the opposite page. You may not be familiar with this animal. It's a hedgehog. Now, look at those spines on its back. Nasty looking, aren't they? These spines are an offensive weapon the hedgehog can use against much larger animals. First, it wraps itself up in a ball. This makes it hard to attack. Sometimes the hedgehog might even ram its attacker. And those spines hurt. Oh, but there's more. Those spines, unlike the porcupine's, are hard to remove. So the attacking animal suffers twice—when it gets stuck with the spines and when it tries to remove them.

해석

M Professor: 대부분의 동물들은 스스로를 보호하는 방법을 가지고 있어요. 사실상 모든 동물들이 먹이 사슬 상 보다 위쪽에 있는 동물의 먹이이기 때문에 방어 수단을 필요로 합니다. 수없이 많은 세대에 걸쳐 동물들은 스스로를 보호하는 다양한 방법을 발전시켰습니다. 흥미롭게도 방어적 적응으로 분류되는 것도 있고 공격적 적응으로 생각되는 것들도 있습니다.

　먼저 방어적 적응을 살펴보죠. 여러분 책에서, 어, 242페이지에 있는 사진을 보세요. 거북입니다, 그렇죠? 여러분 모두 거북을 본 적이 있습니다. 여러분 중 일부는 애완용 거북을 기를 수도 있겠네요. 그런데 거북들이 실제로 두 개의 방어 수단을 발전시켰다는 점을 아시나요? 첫 번째는 가장 눈에 띄는 것입니다. 바로 등껍질이죠. 등껍질은 중요 기관을 포함해 거북의 신체를 전체적으로 덮어 줍니다. 등껍질은 매우 단단합니다. 대부분의 포식자들은 등껍질을 물어뜯는 걸 포기하죠. 이제, 어, 목을 보세요. 정말 깁니다. 오, 약점일까요, 그런가요? 아닙니다. 거북은 유연한 목을 가지고 있어서 위험이 닥치면 쉽게 목을 접어 등껍질 속으로 넣을 수 있습니다.

하지만 공격적 적응도 있다는 점을 기억하세요. 반대편 페이지에 있는 사진을 보세요. 이 동물은 친숙하지 않을 수도 있겠군요. 바로 호저입니다. 자, 등에 있는 가시를 보세요. 무시무시하게 보입니다, 그렇죠? 이 가시들은 호저가 훨씬 덩치가 큰 동물을 상대로 사용할 수 있는 공격성 무기입니다. 먼저 호저는 공 모양으로 몸을 맙니다. 이러면 공격하기가 어려워지죠. 때때로 호저가 공격자를 들이받는 경우도 있어요. 그러면 가시가 고통을 주죠. 오, 하지만 더 있어요. 고슴도치와는 달리 호저의 가시는 빼내기가 힘듭니다. 그래서 공격을 했던 동물은 가시에 찔려서 고생을 하고 그걸 빼내느라 고생을 해서 이중고를 겪게 되죠.

Organization ▶

1 The topic of the lecture is physical variations animals use to protect themselves from animals which are attacking them.
2 The first kind of adaptation the professor discusses is defensive variations.
3 The professor mentions the turtle and its two kinds of defensive adaptations.
4 The second example the professor cited is animals with offensive protective adaptations.
5 The professor cites the hedgehog as an example of an animal that uses its physical adaptations offensively.

Comparing ▶

Sample Response
Script 🎧 04-04

The topic of the lecture is physical adaptations animals use to protect themselves from animals which are attacking them. During the lecture, the professor mentions two different adaptations. The first one he discusses is defensive adaptations, for which he cites the turtle. The professor states that the turtle uses two different defensive mechanisms. The first is its hard shell, which protects the turtle's body since animals can't bite through it. The other is its flexible neck, which it can fold up and hide under its shell. The second example the professor cites is animals with offensive adaptations. He names the hedgehog as an example. First, the hedgehog has spines on its back. So when an animal attacks, the hedgehog rolls into a ball and then attacks its assailant with its harmful spines. Second, the spines are difficult to remove, so the animal suffers again later when extracting them.

해석
강의의 주제는 동물들이 자신을 공격하는 동물로부터 스스로를 보호하기 위해

사용하는 신체적 적응이다. 강의에서 교수는 각기 다른 두 가지 적응을 언급한다. 교수가 논의하는 첫 번째 적응은 방어적 적응으로, 그는 거북을 그 예로 든다. 교수는 거북이 두 가지 방어 기전을 사용한다고 말한다. 첫 번째는 딱딱한 등껍질로, 이는 다른 동물들이 물어뜯을 수가 없기 때문에 거북의 몸을 보호해 준다. 다른 하나는 유연한 목인데, 거북은 이를 접어서 등껍질 안에 넣을 수 있다. 교수가 든 두 번째 예는 공격적 적응을 한 동물이다. 그는 그에 대한 예로 호저를 든다. 첫째, 호저의 등에는 가시가 있다. 그래서 공격을 받으면 호저는 공 모양으로 몸을 만 후에 해로운 가시로 공격자를 공격한다. 둘째, 가시는 빼내기가 힘들기 때문에 나중에 가시를 뺄 때 공격자는 또 한 번 고통을 겪는다.

Unit 47 Marketing I

Exercise ·· p.152

Listening ▶
Script 🎧 04-05

M Professor: Advertisers are always searching for new, effective ways to pitch their products to consumers. They try many approaches, but the most important one is building name recognition. If consumers can easily recognize a product's name, then they are much more likely to purchase it.

How do advertisers build name recognition? One way to do this in their commercials and print ads is to, well, reiterate the name of the product as often as possible. Think of some of the ads you've seen on TV. The most effective ones undoubtedly mention the product's name multiple times. This kind of reinforcement helps consumers recall the product's name when they go to purchase it. Think about some of the most popular brand names . . . Let's see. Coca Cola is one. You often say, "I want a Coke," when you mean any cola in general. Or how about Xerox, the copier company? People often say, "I need a Xerox," to mean they need a copy. It's no surprise both companies are leaders in their industries.

On the other hand, let's consider products with low name recognition. Unfortunately, if a product has low name recognition, people are less likely to purchase it. One simple reason is that they can't remember its name when they're at the store. You've probably had this happen to you in the past, right? You visited a store intending to buy a product, but you simply couldn't remember its name. You might have wound up buying a different, more popular, but less-effective, product instead. So you see, this is how name recognition is integral to the economic welfare of companies. Without it, they have trouble selling their products.

M Professor: 광고 제작자들은 항상 제품을 소비자에게 광고할 수 있는 새롭고 효과적인 방법을 찾습니다. 여러 가지 방법을 시도하지만 가장 중요한 것은 제품의 인지도를 높이는 것이에요. 소비자들이 쉽게 제품명을 알아차릴 수 있으면 구매할 가능성이 훨씬 더 높아지겠죠.

　어떻게 광고 제작자들이 제품의 인지도를 높일까요? TV 광고나 인쇄물 광고에서 그럴 수 있는 한 가지 방법은, 음, 제품명을 최대한 자주 반복하는 것입니다. TV에서 본 몇몇 광고들을 생각해 보세요. 가장 효과적인 광고에서는 틀림없이 제품명이 수차례 언급됩니다. 이러한 강화 작용으로 소비자는 제품을 사러 갈 때 그 제품명을 떠올리게 되죠. 가장 유명한 브랜드를 떠올려 보시면… 봅시다. 코카콜라가 있군요. 일반적인 콜라를 의미할 때에도 종종 "코카콜라 주세요,"라고 말을 합니다. 아니면 복사기 회사인 제록스는 어떨까요? 사람들은 복사가 필요하다는 점을 의미할 때에도 종종 "제록스가 필요해,"라고 말합니다. 당연하게도 두 회사 모두 해당 분야에서 선도적인 기업입니다.

　반면에 인지도가 낮은 제품을 생각해 보죠. 안타깝지만 제품의 인지도가 낮으면 사람들이 이를 구매할 가능성이 낮습니다. 한 가지 단순한 이유는 제품이 매장에 있어도 이름을 기억할 수 없기 때문이에요. 아마 여러분들도 전에 그런 적이 있었을 거예요, 그렇죠? 어떤 제품을 사기 위해 매장에 갔는데 이름이 기억나지 않았습니다. 결국 그 대신 다른 제품, 더 잘 팔리지만 덜 효과적인 제품을 구매하게 되었죠. 따라서 알겠지만 바로 이러한 점 때문에 제품 인지도가 기업의 경제적 후생에 필수적인 것입니다. 인지도가 없으면 제품 판매에 어려움을 겪게 되죠.

professor declares that this is why they are leaders in their fields. The professor's second explanation focuses on low name recognition. He asserts that products with low name recognition do not sell well. An example he gives is that people might go to a store wanting to buy a product but can't remember its name. They therefore buy another more popular product instead because they recognize that product's name.

강의는 제품 인지도 및 제품을 판매하려는 기업에게 제품 인지도가 얼마나 중요한 것인지 다룬다. 먼저 교수는 높은 인지도를 가지고 있는 제품의 가치를 언급한다. 이에 대한 첫 번째 예는 광고의 효율성이다. 교수에 따르면 가장 효과적인 광고에서는 제품명이 반복된다. 그는 또한 코카콜라와 제록스와 같은 기업들을 언급하는데, 이 회사들의 이름은 콜라 및 복사기의 동의어가 되었다. 교수는 이들이 자신의 분야에서 선도 기업이기 때문에 그러한 일이 가능하다고 주장한다. 교수가 든 두 번째 예는 낮은 인지도와 관련이 있다. 그는 인지도가 낮은 제품은 잘 팔리지 않는다고 주장한다. 그가 제시한 예는 사람들이 어떤 제품을 사기 위해 매장에 가지만 그 이름을 기억할 수 없는 경우이다. 따라서 사람들은 결국 자신이 이름을 알고 있는, 더 잘 알려진 제품을 구입하게 된다.

Organization

1 The entire lecture covered name recognition and how important it is to a company that wants to sell its products.

2 First, the professor mentions the value of a product having high name recognition.

3 According to the professor, the most effective advertisements state the product's name repeatedly.

4 The professor's second explanation focuses on low name recognition.

5 He asserts that products with low name recognition do not sell well.

Comparing

Sample Response

Script 🎧 04-06

The entire lecture covered name recognition and how important it is to a company that wants to sell its products. First, the professor mentions the value of a product having high name recognition. His first example of this is the effectiveness of advertisements. According to the professor, the most effective advertisements state the product's name repeatedly. He also refers to companies like Coca Cola and Xerox, whose names have become synonymous with cola and copies. The

Unit 48　Art History I

Exercise p.154

Listening

Script 🎧 04-07

W Professor: I'd like to point out something about art from the past. In previous eras, making art was expensive. Most artists required patrons merely to afford the paint, the canvas, and everything else they needed, and these patrons, naturally, kept most of the artwork in their homes for their own personal viewing. This made art inaccessible to most people. The artists, quite understandably, didn't appreciate this, so they came up with two ways to enable the public to admire their work.

For one, many artists began using cheaper materials. This let them work without a sponsor. This way, they could produce the art they wanted to and also retain possession of their art. They were then free to display it wherever they wanted to. This, naturally, permitted many more people to see their work. Of course, one drawback to this approach was that the lower quality of the paint and other materials meant their work often faded quickly. Fortunately, many of these works can now be restored by using modern methods.

Another thing artists did was to display their art both outdoors and in public places. Remember that artists didn't just make paintings. They created statues, sculptures, and many other kinds of art. Take a look at any cathedral. There is art everywhere. Look at the statues and the stained-glass windows in them. They're all works of art. And consider one of the greatest examples of art anywhere: Michelangelo's work in the Sistine Chapel. How many millions of people have seen his artwork? He attained what most artists strive for: for the greatest number of people to admire his work.

해석

W Professor: 과거의 미술에서 대해 지적하고 싶은 점이 있습니다. 과거에는 미술품을 만드는 비용이 높았어요. 대부분의 화가들은 물감, 캔버스, 그리고 기타 필요한 모든 것을 사기 위해 후원자를 필요로 했으며, 이들 후원자들은 당연하게도 대부분의 미술품들을 자신만 감상할 수 있는 그들의 집에 보관했습니다. 이로써 미술은 대다수의 사람들이 접할 수 없는 것이 되었어요. 화가들은 당연히 이러한 점을 좋게 생각하지 않았기 때문에 대중도 작품을 감상할 수 있는 두 가지 방법을 생각해 냈습니다.

먼저 많은 화가들이 보다 저렴한 재료를 사용하기 시작했어요. 그래서 후원자가 없어도 작업을 할 수 있었죠. 이런 식으로 자신이 원하는 작품을 만들어서 작품을 소장하기도 했어요. 그런 다음에는 어디든 자신이 원하는 곳에서 무료로 전시를 하기도 했습니다. 이로써 자연스럽게 많은 사람들이 작품을 볼 수 있게 되었습니다. 물론 이러한 방법의 한 가지 단점은 물감과 기타 재료들의 질이 나빴기 때문에 종종 작품의 색이 쉽게 바란다는 것이었죠. 다행스럽게도 이러한 작품 중 다수는 현대적인 기술에 의해 현재 복원이 가능합니다.

화가들이 사용했던 또 한 가지 방법은 야외 및 공공 장소에 작품을 전시하는 것이었어요. 화가들이 그림만 그린 것은 아니라는 점을 기억하세요. 조각상, 조각품, 그리고 기타 많은 종류의 작품들도 만들었습니다. 아무 대성당이나 살펴보세요. 사방에 예술 작품이 있습니다. 그 안에 들어 있는 조각상과 스테인드글라스 창문을 보세요. 모두 예술 작품이죠. 그리고 모든 예술 작품 중에서 가장 뛰어난 작품 중 하나인 미켈란젤로의 시스틴 성당 그림을 생각해 보세요. 얼마나 많은 사람들이 그의 작품을 보았을까요? 그는 대부분의 화가들이 갈망하는 바를 얻었습니다. 바로 엄청난 수의 사람들이 자신의 작품을 감상하는 일이죠.

Organization

1 The main idea of the lecture is that artists did not want their work to be viewed by a limited number of people but instead desired for as many people as possible to see it.

2 Artists utilized cheaper materials to avoid having patrons, who would keep the artists' works for themselves.

3 What happened is that artists owned their own works, so they were at liberty to display them anywhere they wanted.

4 The professor discusses how artists made sure their works were displayed outdoors or in public places.

5 She states that cathedrals are full of art like statues and stained-glass windows, and she also mentions Michelangelo's work in the Sistine Chapel.

Comparing

Sample Response

Script 🎧 04-08

The main idea of the lecture is that artists didn't want their work to be viewed by a limited number of people but instead desired for as many people as possible to see it. The professor covers a couple of steps artists took to ensure that this happened. In her first example, she says that artists utilized cheaper materials to avoid having patrons, who would keep the artists' works for themselves. What happened is that artists owned their own works, so they were at liberty to display them anywhere they wanted. The professor then discusses how artists made sure their works were displayed outdoors or in public places. She states that cathedrals are full of art like statues and stained-glass windows, and she also mentions Michelangelo's work in the Sistine Chapel. In her view, doing art like this enabled the greatest number of people to see the artists' works.

해석

강의의 주제는 화가들이 자신의 작품을 제한된 사람들만 감상하는 것을 원하지 않고 대신 최대한 많은 사람들이 작품을 보는 것을 원했다는 것이다. 교수는 그러한 일이 일어나도록 만들기 위해 화가들이 취했던 두 가지 방법을 다룬다. 첫 번째 예에서 그녀는 화가들이 자신의 작품을 집에 보관하는 후원자들이 필요 없도록 보다 저렴한 재료를 사용했다고 말한다. 그 결과 화가들은 자신의 작품을 소장하게 되었고 원하는 곳이면 어디에서나 자유롭게 작품을 전시할 수 있었다. 그리고 나서 교수는 화가들이 자신의 작품을 야외나 공공 장소에 전시한 방법에 대해 논의한다. 그녀는 성당에 조각상 및 스테인드글라스 창문과 같은 예술 작품이 가득하다고 말하고 시스틴 성당의 미켈란젤로의 작품 또한 언급한다. 그녀는 이런 식의 미술 활동을 통해 최대한 많은 사람들이 화가의 작품을 감상할 수 있었다고 생각한다.

Unit 49 Biology II

Exercise ·· p.156

Listening

Script 🎧 04-09

W Professor: While we often point out how humans benefit by cooperating with one another, we should also note that many animals act in concert, too. In fact, without cooperating with one another, many animals would be much less well off. For example, many animals cooperate to maximize their protection from predators while others work together in order to locate and exploit new food sources.

Let's think about deer first. With their antlers, you'd imagine they wouldn't need any protection. But what about does, fawns, and older deer? Wolves and other predators can take down a deer easily, especially by hunting in packs. So what do deer do? One defensive measure they use is to feed in groups. This helps keep them safe from predators. How? For one, they can alert one another more quickly when predators are nearby, which allows younger, older, and weaker deer to hide or escape. Second, there's safety in numbers. Predators are far more likely to attack a single animal than a large group of them.

Now, how about honeybees? They work together, too. You've heard of the honeybee dance, right? That's a textbook case of animal cooperation. When looking for food, honeybees all head in different directions. When they find a potential food source, they return to the hive. Then, they perform a complicated dance, which, scientists believe, actually gives the direction, the distance, and the amount of food located. This allows bees to abandon unpromising searches and to move on to food sources that are closer and that will be able to provide more food for the hive.

해석

W Professor: 우리는 종종 인간이 협동을 통해 어떻게 이익을 얻는지 이야기하지만 많은 동물들도 협력을 한다는 점에 주목해야 합니다. 실제로 많은 동물들이 협동을 하지 않는다면 훨씬 더 힘들게 지낼 것입니다. 예를 들어 많은 동물들이 협동을 해서 포식자로부터 스스로를 최대한 보호하며, 새로운 먹이를 찾아 이를 먹기 위해 협력을 하는 동물들도 있습니다.

먼저 사슴에 대해 생각해 보죠. 사슴은 뿔을 가지고 있으니 다른 보호 장치가 필요 없을 것으로 생각할 수도 있겠군요. 하지만 새끼 사슴이나 늙은 사슴은 어떨까요? 늑대 및 다른 포식자들은, 특히 무리를 지어 사냥함으로써, 사슴 한 마리를 쉽게 쓰러뜨릴 수 있습니다. 그러면 사슴은 어떻게 할까요? 그들이 사용하는 한 가지 방어 조치는 무리를 지어서 먹이를 먹는 것입니다. 이렇게 하면 포식자들로부터 안전할 수 있어요. 어떻게요? 우선, 포식자들이 근처에 있으면 보다 빠르게 서로에게 경고를 해 줄 수가 있는데, 이로써 어린 사슴과 약한 사슴이 숨거나 달아날 수가 있습니다. 둘째, 여럿이 있으면 안전합니다. 포식자들은 대규모 무리의 동물보다 혼자 있는 동물을 공격할 가능성이 훨씬 더 큽니다.

자, 꿀벌은 어떨까요? 꿀벌 역시 협동을 합니다. 아마도 꿀벌의 춤에 대해 들어본 적이 있을 것 같군요, 그렇죠? 이는 동물의 협동을 보여 주는 교과서적인 사례입니다. 꿀벌은 먹이를 찾을 때 각기 다른 방향으로 나아갑니다. 먹이라고 생각되는 것이 발견되면 벌집으로 돌아갑니다. 이때 복잡한 춤을 추는데, 이는 과학자들의 생각에 의하면 먹이의 방향, 거리, 그리고 양을 알려 줍니다. 이로써 벌들은 가망이 없는 먹이 탐사를 그만 두고 더 가깝고 더 많은 먹이를 벌집에 가져다 줄 수 있는 식량원으로 이동하게 됩니다.

2 In her first example, she discusses deer and how they protect themselves from predators.

3 This lets various young, old, and sick deer hide while others stay close together to attempt to ward off the attackers.

4 On the same topic, the professor then cites the example of the honeybee.

5 By doing this dance, they share their knowledge of the location of the food source with other bees, which enables them better to provide for the needs of the entire hive.

▌Comparing▐

Sample Response
Script 🎧 04-10

The professor looks into two different ways in which animals cooperate with one another. She emphasizes that cooperation is not solely a human trait but that animals do it as well. In her first example, she discusses deer and how they protect themselves from predators. By feeding together, deer can alert one another quickly when predators come. This lets various young, old, and sick deer hide while others stay close together to help dissuade predators from attacking. On the same topic, the professor then cites the example of the honeybee. Honeybees go in different directions in search of food and upon locating it, return to their hives to perform a dance. By doing this dance, they share their knowledge of the location of the food source with other bees, which enables them more effectively to provide for the needs of the entire hive.

해석

교수는 동물들이 협력을 하는 각기 다른 두 가지 방법을 논의한다. 그녀는 협동이 인간의 전유물이 아니며 동물들 또한 협동을 한다는 점을 강조한다. 첫 번째 예에서 그녀는 사슴과 이들이 어떻게 포식자로부터 스스로를 보호하는지 이야기한다. 사슴은 함께 먹이를 먹음으로써 포식자가 다가오면 서로에게 신속히 경고를 보낼 수 있다. 이로써 다른 사슴들이 가까이 붙어서 포식자들의 공격을 주저하게 만드는 동안 어리고, 늙고, 그리고 아픈 사슴들은 몸을 숨길 수 있다. 동일한 주제에 대해 교수는 꿀벌의 예를 든다. 꿀벌들은 먹이를 찾아 각기 다른 방향으로 이동하다가 먹이를 발견하면 벌집으로 돌아와 꿀벌의 춤을 춘다. 이러한 춤을 춤으로써 꿀벌은 식량원의 위치에 대한 정보를 다른 꿀벌과 공유하게 되는데, 이로써 꿀벌들은 벌집 전체에 필요한 먹이를 보다 효과적으로 공급할 수 있다.

▌Organization▐

1 The professor looks into two different ways in which animals cooperate with one another.

Exercise ··· p.158

Listening

Script 🎧 04-11

M Professor: Let's move on to pollination and how flowers attract pollinators. Most flowers get pollinated by insects, so let's focus on them. You've probably noticed that flowers have their own distinct appearances and smells. Don't think those are for your benefit. Okay? They actually look and smell those ways in order to attract insects to pollinate them. Allow me to explain in detail.

One major attractor, unsurprisingly, is appearance. It's the most important one of all. Some insects can see colors well. So there are some colors that, depending upon the insect, make it just want to stop and sit down on the flower. For example, many butterflies are attracted to the colors red and yellow, two of the three primary colors. Think of the painted daisy. Here's a picture . . . It has red petals and a yellow center. Butterflies simply won't miss being attracted to that flower. It's irresistible. So remember . . . that's why we see so many different colors of flowers. They are attracting various kinds of insects to pollinate them.

Odor is the second most common attractor used. Unfortunately for flowers, most insects can't differentiate colors. They're essentially colorblind. But they can recognize different scents, that is, smells. Take the moth. You know, those insects that look like butterflies but which always appear at night. Well, they're attracted to, um, sweet smells. Jasmine is one example. Now, get a load of this. Jasmine produces a strong, sweet smell . . . but only at night, which is the perfect time to attract moths. Amazing, huh? So the moths, having been attracted, will be able to pollinate the jasmine plants. And that's nature at work.

해석

M Professor: 다음으로 수분과 꽃이 어떻게 수분 매개체를 유인하는지 살펴보도록 하죠. 대부분의 꽃은 곤충에 의해 수분이 되기 때문에 이들에게 초점을 맞춥시다. 여러분은 아마도 꽃들이 각각 고유한 생김새와 냄새를 가지고 있다는 점을 알고 계실 거예요. 이것이 여러분을 위한 것이라고 생각하지는 마세요. 아시겠죠? 실은 수분을 해 줄 곤충을 유인하기 위해 그런 형태와 냄새를 지니고 있는 것입니다. 자세히 설명을 해 드리죠.

가장 중요한 유인 요소는, 당연하겠지만, 생김새입니다. 가장 중요한 것 중 하나이죠. 일부 곤충들은 색깔을 잘 구별할 수 있어요. 그래서 곤충에 따라 가던 길을 멈추고 앉아서 쉬게 만드는 색깔이 존재합니다. 예를 들어 다수의 나비는 대부분 삼원색 중 두 개인 빨간색과 노란색에 이끌립니다. 페인티드 데이지 꽃을 생각해 보세요. 여기에 사진이 있는데… 꽃잎은 빨간색이고 중심부는 노랗습니다. 나비는 그 꽃을 그냥 지나치지 않을 거예요. 거부할 수가 없는 것이죠. 그래서

기억하셔야 할 점은… 바로 그러한 점 때문에 그렇게 많은 색깔의 꽃이 존재한다는 점이에요. 이들은 다양한 종류의 곤충을 유인해서 수분을 합니다.

향기는 두 번째로 흔히 사용되는 유인 요소입니다. 꽃으로서는 안타까운 일이지만 대부분의 곤충들은 색깔을 구별하지 못해요. 기본적으로 색맹입니다. 하지만 여러 가지 향기, 즉 냄새는 구별할 수 있어요. 나방을 예로 들어보죠. 아시다시피 나방은 나비처럼 보이지만 항상 밤에 나타납니다. 그러니까, 나방은, 음, 달콤한 냄새에 이끌려요. 재스민이 한 가지 예입니다. 자, 들어보세요. 재스민은 강하고 달콤한 냄새를 발산하지만… 나방을 유인하기에 최적의 시간인 밤에만 그렇게 합니다. 놀랍지 않나요? 그래서 재스민으로 이끌려 날아온 나방 덕분에 재스민의 수분이 이루어질 수 있습니다. 이것이 바로 자연의 원리이죠.

Organization

1 The professor discusses two of the ways that flowers attract insects so that the insects will pollinate them.

2 First of all, he covers the importance of the flower's colors to attracting insects.

3 Since some insects can see colors well, flowers use this fact to their advantage.

4 The professor then points out that most insects are in fact colorblind, so flowers must resort to using scents to attract insects for the purpose of pollination.

5 Since the moth, which is active at that time, is attracted to sweet scents, jasmine can be pollinated by moths.

Comparing

Sample Response

Script 🎧 04-12

The professor discusses two of the ways that flowers attract insects so that the insects will pollinate them. First of all, he covers the importance of the flower's colors to attracting insects. Since some insects can see colors well, flowers use this fact to their advantage. The professor brings up the point that butterflies are attracted to red and yellow colors. So some flowers, like the painted daisy, which is yellow and red, use these colors to entice insects to come and pollinate them. The professor then points out that most insects are in fact colorblind, so flowers must resort to using scents to attract insects for the purpose of pollination. The example cited by the professor is jasmine, which emits a sweet scent only at night. Since the moth, which is active at that time, is attracted to sweet scents, jasmine can be pollinated by moths.

해석

교수는 수분이 이루어질 수 있도록 꽃이 곤충을 유인하는 두 가지 방법에 대해 논의한다. 먼저 그는 곤충을 유인하는데 있어서 꽃의 색깔의 중요성을 이야기한다. 일부 곤충은 색깔을 잘 볼 수 있기 때문에 꽃은 이러한 사실을 잘 이용한다. 교수는 나비가 빨간색과 노란색에 이끌린다는 점을 지적한다. 따라서 빨간색과

노란색을 띄는 페인티드 데이지와 같은 일부 꽃들은 그러한 색깔을 이용해 곤충을 유인해서 수분을 한다. 그 후 교수는 대부분의 곤충들이 사실 색맹이기 때문에 꽃이 곤충의 수분을 유도하기 위해서는 향기를 사용해야 한다고 말한다. 교수가 든 예는 재스민으로, 이 꽃은 밤에만 달콤한 냄새를 발산한다. 야행성인 나방은 달콤한 향기에 이끌리기 때문에 나방에 의해서 재스민의 수분이 이루어질 수 있다.

Unit 51 | Art History II

Exercise p.160

Listening
Script 🎧 04-13

M Professor: We all know the saying that a picture's worth a thousand words. That's probably why many of you are into photography. And you should all know that, depending upon how a photographer frames, er, takes his picture, he can make his subject look sympathetic or make it appear dark and ominous. Think about how photographers in different centuries portrayed industrialization. Their attitudes in the nineteenth and twentieth centuries were almost completely different, which is reflected in their work.

Photography as we know it was invented in the nineteenth century. And this is important, for this was the century when industrialism was really starting to take off. But do you know what? These advances frightened people. They thought the world was changing too quickly. So photographers were often quite critical of industrialism. They took more photographs of nature and people instead. They focused mostly on humanity at the expense of industrialism. Those pictures that did show industrialism often emphasized people's dirty, worn, and hopeless faces after they'd worked in factories all day or other such negative representations.

The twentieth century, however, saw a dramatic change in attitudes. People began to, uh, celebrate industrialism. Photographers therefore started taking more pictures of machines and other tools of industrialization. Not only did they increase the numbers of pictures they took, but they also made sure the pictures showed machines in the best possible light. Here . . . See this picture inside an automobile factory. Notice how clean everything is and how the people are smiling as they do their jobs. This picture is typical of twentieth-century attitudes toward industrialization. It meant to honor industrialization, not to demonize it.

M Professor: 우리 모두 사진은 천 마디 말의 가치가 있다는 속담을 알고 있어요. 아마도 그러한 점 때문에 여러분 중 상당수가 사진을 좋아할 것입니다. 그리고 여러분 모두가 아셔야 할 점은, 사진 작가가 배치를 어떻게 하느냐에 따라, 어, 사진을 찍느냐에 따라 대상을 호감이 가도록 만들 수도 있고 아니면 어둡고 암울해 보이도록 만들 수도 있다는 것이에요. 각기 다른 세기에 사진 작가들이 산업화를 어떻게 묘사했는지 생각해 보세요. 20세기와 21세기의 이들의 태도는 거의 완전히 다른데, 이러한 점은 그들의 작품에 반영되어 있습니다.

아시다시피 사진은 19세기에 발명되었어요. 그리고 이러한 점이 중요한 것은 산업주의가 실제로 시작된 것도 바로 19세기였기 때문이죠. 하지만 알고 계시나요? 이러한 발전들은 사람들을 두렵게 만들었습니다. 세상이 너무 빨리 변하고 있다고 생각했어요. 그래서 사진 작가들은 종종 산업주의를 비판했습니다. 풍경 사진과 인물 사진을 더 많이 찍었어요. 산업주의 대신 인간성에 주로 초점을 맞추었죠. 산업주의를 나타내는 사진들은 종종 하루 종일 공장에서 일을 한 사람들의 지저분하고, 지치고, 그리고 무기력한 표정이나 기타 부정적인 장면들을 강조했습니다.

하지만 20세기가 되자 그러한 태도에 급격한 변화가 일어났어요. 사람들은 산업주의를, 어, 숭배하기 시작했죠. 따라서 사진 작가들은 기계 및 기타 산업화와 관련된 다른 도구들의 사진을 더 많이 찍기 시작했습니다. 사진을 더 많이 찍은 것만이 아니라 사진에서 기계가 최대한 좋게 보이도록 만들었죠. 여기를 보시면… 자동차 공장 내부의 사진을 보세요. 모든 것이 깨끗하고 일을 하는 사람들이 미소를 짓고 있다는 점에 주목하세요. 이 사진은 산업화에 대한 20세기의 태도를 보여 주는 전형적인 사진입니다. 산업화를 악마로 나타내는 대신 숭배했던 것이죠.

Organization

1 During the course of the talk, the professor focuses upon how photographers represented industrialization in the nineteenth and twentieth centuries.
2 He first discusses the way industrialization was portrayed in the nineteenth century.
3 According to the professor, many people during this time were afraid of technology and feared it was taking over their lives.
4 The twentieth century saw people starting to appreciate industrialization, so photographers began showing pictures of machines that made them look good.
5 The professor shows a picture of a clean automobile factory with smiling, happy workers.

Comparing

Sample Response
Script 🎧 04-14

During the course of the talk, the professor focuses upon how photographers represented industrialization in the nineteenth and twentieth centuries. He first discusses the way it was portrayed in the nineteenth century. According to the professor, many people during this time were afraid of technology and feared it was changing the world too quickly. So photographers spent most of their time snapping shots of nature and people. When they did photograph industrialization, they portrayed it in a negative light, such as by showing people all worn out from working in factories. On the other hand, the twentieth century saw people starting to appreciate industrialization, so photographers began showing pictures of machines that made them look good. As an example, the professor shows a picture of a clean automobile factory with smiling, happy workers. He notes this as an example of how photographers honored industrialization in the twentieth century.

해석

강의에서 교수는 19세기와 20세기의 사진 작가들이 산업화를 표현한 방식에 초점을 맞춘다. 그는 먼저 19세기의 표현 방식에 대해 이야기한다. 교수에 따르면 이 시기에는 많은 사람들이 과학 기술을 두려워했고 과학 기술이 세상을 너무 빠르게 변화시킨다는 점을 무서워했다. 따라서 사진 작가들은 주로 풍경 사진과 인물 사진을 찍었다. 산업화 사진을 찍는 경우, 공장 업무로 녹초가 된 사람들을 보여 주는 사진과 같이 산업화를 부정적인 시각에서 묘사했다. 반면에 20세기에는 사람들이 산업화를 긍정적으로 평가하기 시작했기 때문에 사진 작가들도 멋지게 보이는 기계를 찍기 시작했다. 그러한 예로서 교수는 미소를 띤 행복한 노동자들이 있는 깨끗한 자동차 공장의 사진을 보여 준다. 그는 이 사진을 20세기의 사진 작가들이 어떻게 산업화를 숭배했는지에 대한 예로 언급한다.

Unit 52 Advertising

Exercise ·· p.162

Listening

Script 🎧 04-15

M Professor: Did everyone do their reading last night? Excellent. Then I'd like quickly to review a couple of the advertising techniques you read about. As you should recall, two techniques were primarily focused on. They are the direct and indirect methods of persuasion. I'd like to give a couple of examples of them now.

All ads try to persuade people to purchase the products which they're promoting. The direct method of persuasion is one popular way. When using this, advertisers note the features of their products that make them extraordinary and different from other similar products. They may cite various facts and statistics that will tell viewers exactly why they should go out and purchase that particular product. For example, a car manufacturer using direct persuasion advertising techniques might stress how safe the car is according to recent statistics. Or it might mention the car's gas mileage and note how it's much more economical than its competitors.

On the other hand, there is also the indirect method of persuasion. Here, advertisers attempt to persuade customers by using association. They might show the results of using or purchasing their product. For example, let's go back to car ads. Perhaps the car being sold is rather ordinary. Well, the manufacturer is going to show people smiling while they're driving. The mom and the dad will be in the front listening to music while the kids in the back will be playing games or looking out the window to admire the scenery. That's an example of indirect persuasion. The company's trying to make potential buyers think they'll be as happy as the people in the ad if they purchase that company's product.

해석

M Professor: 어젯밤에 읽기 과제를 모두 하셨나요? 좋아요. 그러면 여러분이 읽은 두 가지 광고 기법을 간단히 확인하고 넘어가죠. 기억하시겠지만 두 가지 기법이 주로 논의되어 있었어요. 바로 직접적 설득 방법과 간접적 설득 방법입니다. 이제 이들에 대한 두 가지 예를 들어 드리죠.

모든 광고는 자신들이 홍보하는 제품을 사람들이 구매하도록 설득하려고 합니다. 직접적인 설득의 방법은 흔히 사용되는 방법이에요. 이 방법을 사용하는 경우 광고 제작자들은 제품을 특별하게 만들고 이를 다른 유사 제품들과 다르게 보이도록 만드는 제품의 특성에 주목합니다. 광고를 보는 사람들에게 왜 가서 해당 특정 제품을 사야 하는지 정확하게 알려 주는 다양한 사실과 통계 자료를 인용할 수도 있어요. 예를 들어 직접적 설득 방법을 사용해서 기술을 광고하는 자동차 제조업체는 최근 통계 자료에 따라 자사의 자동차가 얼마나 안전한지 강조할 수도 있습니다. 또는 연비를 언급하면서 그 차가 경쟁 자동차에 비해 훨씬 더 경제적이라고 말할 수도 있어요.

반면에 간접적 설득 방법도 있습니다. 이 경우 광고 제작자들은 연상을 이용해 소비자를 설득하려고 합니다. 자사 제품의 사용 및 구매 결과를 보여 줄 수 있어요. 예를 들어 자동차 광고로 다시 돌아가 보죠. 판매되는 자동차가 다소 평범한 차라고 할게요. 음, 제조업체에서는 운전을 하면서 미소를 짓고 있는 사람들의 모습을 보여줄 것입니다. 엄마와 아빠는 앞좌석에서 음악을 듣고 있고 아이들은 뒤쪽에서 게임을 하거나 창 밖 풍경을 감상할 거예요. 이것은 간접적 설득의 예입니다. 기업은 잠재 고객들로 하여금 만약 자사 제품을 구매한다면 광고 속의 사람들만큼 행복해질 것이라고 생각하도록 만들려는 것이죠.

Organization

1 The professor focuses on two different methods of persuasion that companies like using when trying to sell their products.

2 He first mentions direct persuasion as one popular method of advertising.

3 Ads may discuss a car's excellent gas mileage or mention how economical it is.

4 Another approach that is commonly used is indirect persuasion.

5 Instead of citing facts, the advertisement will try to convince people to want to be in the situation in which the car riders are in.

Sample Response
Script 🎧 04-16

The professor focuses on two different methods of persuasion that companies like using when trying to sell their products. He first mentions direct persuasion as one popular method of advertising. When an advertiser utilizes direct persuasion, it emphasizes facts and statistics. The example given by the professor involves the direct advertising of a car. In using this approach, the ad may discuss a car's excellent gas mileage or mention how economical it is. Meanwhile, another approach that is commonly used is indirect persuasion. Here, companies utilize association to convince people to buy their products. Again, the example used is that of selling a car. However, instead of citing facts, the advertisement will try to convince people to want to be in the situation in which the car riders are. Everyone riding will be happy and having a good time, so potential customers will associate that car with having fun.

해석

교수는 제품을 판매하고자 할 때 광고 회사들이 즐겨 사용하는 서로 다른 두 가지 설득 방법에 초점을 맞춘다. 그는 먼저 널리 사용되는 광고 기법으로서 직접적 설득을 언급한다. 광고 제작자가 직접적 설득을 사용하는 경우에는 사실과 통계 자료가 강조된다. 교수가 든 예는 자동차의 직접적 광고이다. 이 방법을 사용하면 광고에서는 자동차의 뛰어난 연비나 차가 얼마나 경제적인지 언급될 수 있다. 반면에 흔히 사용되는 또 다른 방법으로 간접적 설득이 있다. 이 방법에서는 기업들이 연상을 이용해 사람들이 제품을 구입하도록 만든다. 또 다시 자동차 광고의 예가 설명된다. 하지만, 사실을 언급하는 대신, 이 광고는 사람들이 그 차를 탄 사람들의 상황에 놓이고 싶어하도록 만들 것이다. 차를 타는 모든 사람이 행복해지고 즐거워할 것이기 때문에 잠재 고객들은 그 차를 즐거움과 연상시킬 것이다.

Unit 53 Psychology I

Exercise p.164

Listening
Script 🎧 04-17

M Professor: I'm sure you all have certain things you absolutely loathe doing. I have a few myself. So . . . how do you convince yourself to do them? Are you the kind of person who uses positive reinforcement, or do you rely upon negative reinforcement to get yourself to do these undesirable activities?

I'm sure many of you aren't morning people, right? Then consider a worker who hates getting up early in the morning. Unfortunately, his job starts at 7:30, so he's got to wake up by 6:00. Now, how does he convince himself to get out of bed? One way is to use positive reinforcement. This is when you add some kind of behavior or reward to get yourself to do something. Our worker loves doughnuts, but he doesn't eat them very often. However, as a reward for getting up early, he eats a doughnut for breakfast each morning prior to leaving home for work. That's positive reinforcement at work.

Now shall we consider negative reinforcement? This is the process of removing some kind of behavior or punishment in order to convince yourself or another to do something. What does that mean? Here's an example. Let's say that another worker who must get up early hates showering in the morning. He simply can't stand it. He feels like he's punishing himself by getting in the shower at 6:00 AM, which makes him dread getting up that early. By using negative reinforcement, he takes a shower at night before going to bed. That removes a behavior he dislikes in the morning, thereby making it more likely that he'll get up out of bed and go to work.

해석

M Professor: 분명 여러분 모두에게 절대로 하기 싫은 일들이 있을 거예요. 저도 몇 가지 있습니다. 그런 경우에... 어떻게 스스로를 설득해서 하게 되나요? 이런 원치 않는 일들을 해야 하기 위해서 정적 강화를 사용하는 편인가요, 아니면 부적 강화를 사용하는 편인가요?

여러분 중 다수는 아침형 인간이 아닐 거예요, 그렇죠? 그러면 아침 일찍 일어나는 것을 정말 싫어하는 직장인을 생각해 보세요. 불행하게도 그 사람의 업무는 7시 30분에 시작되기 때문에 6시까지는 일어나야 해요. 자, 그가 어떻게 자신을 잠자리에서 빠져 나오도록 설득할까요? 한 가지 방법은 정적 강화를 사용하는 것입니다. 이것은 어떤 종류의 행동이나 보상을 추가함으로써 스스로가 무엇을 하도록 만들 때 이루어집니다. 이 직장인은 도넛을 너무 좋아하지만 그리 자주 먹지는 못해요. 그런데 일찍 일어나는 대가로 그는 출근을 하기 전에 매일 아침 식사로 도넛을 먹습니다. 정적 강화가 효과를 내는 것이죠.

자 부적 강화를 살펴볼까요? 이것은 어떤 일을 하도록 스스로를 설득하기 위해 어떤 행동이나 처벌을 없애는 과정이에요. 이게 무슨 뜻일까요? 한 가지 예를 들어 드리죠. 또 다른 직장인이 있는데, 이 사람은 일찍 일어나야 하지만 아침에 샤워하는 것을 매우 싫어합니다. 끔찍하게 싫어하죠. 오전 6시에 샤워를 하면 스스로에게 벌을 내리고 있는 것처럼 느끼기 때문에 그는 그처럼 일찍 일어나는 것을 끔찍하게 여기게 됩니다. 부적 강화를 사용함으로써 그는 잠자리에 들기 전밤에 샤워를 합니다. 이로써 아침에 하기 싫어하는 행동이 사라지고 그 결과 그가 잠자리에서 빠져 나와 출근할 가능성이 높아집니다.

Organization

1 The professor tells his class about two different methods people often resort to when they need to do something they do not enjoy.

2 The first one he mentions is positive reinforcement.

3 This is adding a behavior or reward to get oneself to do the displeasing activity.

4 The second explanation deals with negative reinforcement, the opposite of positive reinforcement.

5 When using this method, the person removes an activity or behavior he dislikes.

Comparing

Sample Response

Script 🎧 04-18

The professor tells his class about two different methods people often resort to when they need to do something they don't enjoy. The first one he mentions is positive reinforcement, which is adding a behavior or reward to get oneself to do the displeasing activity. The professor talks about a worker who hates waking up early in the morning. In an example of positive reinforcement, he gives himself a doughnut, which he loves, for breakfast every morning. He therefore rewards himself for getting up. The second explanation deals with negative reinforcement, the opposite of positive reinforcement. When using this method, the person removes an activity or behavior he dislikes. The example given is that a worker who hates showering in the morning will instead shower at night. Therefore, since he doesn't have to shower once he wakes up, that will encourage him to get up every morning.

해석

교수는 학생들에게 사람들이 하기 싫은 일을 해야 할 때 종종 사용하는 두 가지 방법에 대해 이야기한다. 그가 말한 첫 번째 방법은 정적 강화로, 이는 스스로에게 하기 싫은 일을 시키기 위해 어떤 행동이나 보상을 추가하는 것을 말한다. 교수는 아침 일찍 일어나기 싫어하는 직장인을 예로 든다. 정적 강화의 예로서 그는 자기가 매우 좋아하는 도넛을 자신에게 아침 식사로 준다. 따라서 일찍 일어난 것에 대한 보상을 받는 것이다. 두 번째 설명은 부적 강화와 관련된 것으로, 이는 정적 강화와 반대이다. 이 방법을 사용할 경우 자신이 싫어하는 활동이나 행동을 제거하게 된다. 교수가 든 예는 아침에 샤워하는 것을 싫어하는 직장인이 그 대신 밤에 샤워를 하려고 한다는 것이다. 따라서 일어났을 때 샤워를 할 필요가 없기 때문에 그는 매일 아침 일찍 일어날 것이다.

Exercise ·· p.166

Listening

Script 🎧 04-19

W Professor: Movie directors have many techniques to convey various messages to their audiences. Messages can be passed to the audience without actual dialog. In other words, performers don't need words to say everything. Even camera shots can get across various meanings. Some directors use the angle of the camera— called a shot—to strengthen various feelings or to add more significance to a scene.

For example, one common method that directors use is to angle up the camera. That means you're looking upward at the person from below. What kind of image would this convey? Think about it . . . If you're looking up at someone, you're typically admiring a powerful person or at least someone very important. So these low-angle shots give an impression of power. A director filming, say, the queen of England might use this method. She's not the tallest woman, yet the impression one would get from a low-angle shot of her is of a woman looking down on her subjects as she stands above them.

So if there are low-angle shots, then naturally, there are high-angle shots, right? Of course there are. What's the message here? Well, how do you normally feel if you're looking down? Let me give you an example first. Say you're filming a man lost in the desert. He feels helpless, and he's all alone. You'd film him from a down angle. In other words, you'd be elevated above him. This would help to show the utter hopelessness of his situation because you'd show not only him but the vast wasteland of the desert all around him. Everyone got that?

해석

W Professor: 영화 감독은 여러 가지 기법을 사용해서 관객들에게 다양한 메시지를 전달합니다. 실제 대화가 없어도 관객들에게 메시지를 전달할 수도 있어요. 배우들이 꼭 단어를 이용해서 모든 것을 말할 필요는 없다는 뜻이에요. 심지어 카메라 샷도 다양한 의미를 전달할 수 있습니다. 일부 감독들은 다양한 감정을 강조하거나 한 장면에 더 많은 의미를 부여하기 위해 샷이라고 불리는 카메라 앵글을 사용하기도 하죠.

예를 들어 감독들이 사용하는 한 가지 흔한 방법은 카메라 앵글을 위로 향하는 것입니다. 아래쪽에서 위쪽으로 인물을 보게 된다는 뜻입니다. 이로써 어떤 이미지가 전달될까요? 생각해 보세요… 만약 어떤 사람을 올려다 본다면 일반적으로 존경받는 권력자이거나 적어도 매우 중요한 사람을 보고 있을 거예요. 그래서 이러한 로우 앵글 샷은 권력의 인상을 남깁니다. 가령 영국 여왕의 영화를 찍고 있는 감독이 이러한 방법을 사용할 수도 있을 거예요. 가장 키가 큰 여성은 아니지만 그녀를 로우 앵글 샷으로 찍어서 얻을 수 있는 인상은 백성들 위에서 백성들을 내려다보는 여성의 인상입니다.

이렇듯 로우 앵글 샷이 있다면 당연하게도 하이 앵글 샷도 있겠죠? 물론 그렇습니다. 어떤 메시지를 전달할까요? 음, 여러분은 내려다볼 때 보통 어떤 느낌을 받나요? 먼저 한 가지 예를 들어 드릴게요. 여러분이 사막에서 길을 잃은 남자의 영화를 찍고 있다고 해 보죠. 그는 무력하고 완전히 혼자입니다. 여러분은 그를 다운 앵글로 찍을 거예요. 다시 말해서 여러분이 그보다 위에 있는 것이죠. 그러면 그 사람뿐만 아니라 주변의 광활한 황무지 같은 사막까지 보여 줄 수 있기 때문에 그가 처한 완전히 절망적인 상황을 나타내는데 도움이 됩니다. 모두 이해가 가나요?

Organization

1 The professor tells her students about film shots and how directors use them to transmit messages to their audiences.
2 The first example given is that of low-angle shots.
3 Low-angle shots send a message of power since they make the person appear to be looking down at people.
4 Something else similar is high-angle shots, which are taken from above the subject so are thus looking downward.
5 The professor describes a person stranded in the desert.

Comparing

Sample Response
Script 🎧 04-20

The professor tells her students about film shots and how directors use them to transmit messages to their audiences. The first example given is that of low-angle shots. These are shots taken with the camera aiming up toward a person or object. Low-angle shots send a message of power since they make the person appear to be looking down at people. The professor mentions that one would take a low-angle shot of the queen of England to stress her power as she looks down at her subjects. Something else similar is high-angle shots, which are taken from above the subject so are thus looking downward. The professor describes a person stranded in the desert. By looking down at him, the camera conveys a message of hopelessness. The reason is that the shot not only shows the person but also the surrounding area, which further emphasizes the person's bad situation.

해석
교수는 학생들에게 영화의 샷과 감독들이 샷을 이용해 관객들에게 메시지를 전달하는 방법에 대해 이야기한다. 첫 번째 예는 로우 앵글 샷이다. 이는 카메라를 위쪽에 있는 사람이나 사물에게 향해 찍는 것이다. 로우 앵글 샷은 그 사람이 다른 사람들을 내려다보고 있는 것처럼 보이게 하기 때문에 권력의 메시지를 전달한다. 교수는 로우 앵글 샷을 이용해 영국 여왕을 촬영하면 그녀가 백성들을 내려다보는 식이 되기 때문에 그녀의 권력이 강조될 것이라고 언급한다. 이와 유사한 것이 하이 앵글 샷으로, 이는 대상을 위쪽에서 아래쪽으로 내려다보면서 찍는 것이다. 교수는 사막에서 꼼짝 못하는 사람의 예를 든다. 그를 아래로 내려다봄으

로써 카메라는 절망감의 메시지를 전달하게 된다. 그 이유는 샷에서 사람만 보이는 것이 아니라 주변 지역까지 보이기 때문인데, 이로써 그 사람의 절박한 상황이 더욱 강조된다.

Unit 55 Psychology II

Exercise p.168

Listening
Script 🎧 04-21

M Professor: Thinking positively is one of the most important things people can do. Positive thinking, as opposed to negative thinking, can drastically affect the way people react to various situations. You might find these examples rather interesting.

Everyone watches the weather forecast, right? Well, I watched it this morning, and the meteorologist said there was a fifty-percent chance of sunny weather today. That, of course, means there is also a fifty-percent chance of cloudy or rainy weather. But he didn't say anything about clouds or rain, did he? No, he only said the word "sunny." Now, how many of you saw today's weather report? Okay, a few. And how many of you brought umbrellas with you? None. Just as I expected. When the weatherman says there's a fifty-percent chance of cloudy weather, most people will take umbrellas with them. However, if he says there's a fifty-percent chance of sunny weather, very few people will carry umbrellas. That's positive thinking at work.

Here's another example. It's flu season these days, so perhaps you decide to visit the pharmacy for some medicine. You see two different bottles. On the front of one, it reads that this medicine has a ninety-percent chance of treating a cold effectively. However, on the other bottle, it read that it only has a ten-percent chance of not being able to treat a cold. It's the same thing, right? It's just phrased differently. However, in a research experiment carried out, far more people purchased the medicine that promised a ninety-percent success rate. Why? That's easy. Its message was more positive. Simply put, people react much better to positive messages than to negative ones.

해석
M Professor: 긍정적인 사고는 사람들이 할 수 있는 것 중에서 가장 중요한 것입니다. 긍정적인 사고는, 부정적인 사고와 반대로, 다양한 상황에 대한 사람들의 대처 방식에 극적인 영향을 미칠 수 있죠. 제가 알려 드릴 사례가 다소 흥미롭게 생각되실 수도 있을 거예요.

모두가 일기 예보를 봅니다, 그렇죠? 음, 저도 오늘 아침에 보았는데, 기상 캐스터가 오늘 맑을 확률이 50퍼센트라고 하더군요. 그 말은 물론 흐리거나 비가 내릴 확률이 50퍼센트라는 뜻입니다. 하지만 그는 구름이나 비에 대해서는 아무 말도 하지 않았어요, 그렇죠? 네, 그는 "맑다"라는 단어만 사용했습니다. 자, 오늘 일기 예보를 들은 사람이 몇 명인가요? 좋아요, 몇 사람이 있군요. 그러면 오늘 우산을 가져온 사람은 몇 명인가요? 한 명도 없군요. 예상대로예요. 기상 캐스터가 흐릴 확률이 50퍼센트라고 얘기한다면 대부분의 사람들이 우산을 가져갈 거예요. 하지만 맑을 확률이 50퍼센트라고 얘기하면 우산을 들고 올 사람이 거의 없을 거예요. 바로 긍정적인 사고가 작용한 것입니다.

또 다른 예를 들어 드리죠. 요즘은 독감이 유행하는 시기라서 여러분이 아마도 약국에 약을 사러 가야겠다고 마음먹을 수도 있을 거예요. 서로 다른 두 개의 약병이 보입니다. 한 병에는 이 약의 효과적인 감기 치료의 가능성은 90퍼센트라고 적혀 있어요. 하지만 다른 병에는 감기가 낫지 않을 가능성이 10퍼센트라고만 적혀 있어요. 같은 말이에요, 그렇죠? 표현만 다를 뿐입니다. 하지만 진행된 실험에서는 훨씬 더 많은 사람들이 90퍼센트의 성공률을 약속한 약을 구입했습니다. 왜일까요? 간단합니다. 그 메시지가 더 긍정적이었죠. 간단히 말해서 사람들은 부정적 메시지보다 긍정적 메시지에 훨씬 더 잘 반응을 합니다.

Organization

1 The professor focuses his lecture on positive thinking and how it affects the ways in which people behave.
2 He first discusses the weather forecast from earlier in the day.
3 He states that since the weatherman claimed there was a fifty-percent chance of sunny weather, no one brought umbrellas with them.
4 He next compares the labels on two medicine bottles.
5 One claims it has a ninety-percent chance of success while the other states that it only fails ten percent of the time.

Comparing

Sample Response
Script 🎧 04-22

The professor focuses his lecture on positive thinking and how it affects the ways in which people behave. He first discusses the weather forecast from earlier in the day. He states that since the weatherman had claimed there was a fifty-percent chance of sunny weather, no one brought umbrellas with them. However, he notes that on the occasions when the weatherman claims there is a fifty-percent chance of cloudy or rainy weather, then people will bring their umbrellas. While the forecast hasn't changed, people's perceptions of it have. He next compares the labels on two medicine bottles. One claims it has a ninety-percent chance of success while the other states that it only fails ten percent of the time. Although they have the same effectiveness, people most often

choose the one that advertises its success rate. The reason is that it is more positive than the other medicine.

해석

교수는 강의에서 긍정적인 사고와 그것이 사람들의 행동에 어떠한 영향을 미치는지를 주로 이야기한다. 그는 먼저 그날 오전에 나왔던 일기 예보를 논의한다. 그는 기상 캐스터가 날씨가 맑을 확률이 50퍼센트였다고 말했기 때문에 아무도 우산을 가져오지 않았다고 말한다. 하지만 기상 캐스터가 흐리거나 비올 확률이 50퍼센트라고 얘기한다면 사람들이 우산을 가져올 것이라고 말한다. 일기 예보는 바뀌지 않았지만 그에 대한 사람들의 인식이 바뀌게 된다. 그는 다음으로 두 약병에 든 라벨을 비교한다. 한 병에는 치료 가능성이 90퍼센트라고 적혀 있고 다른 병에는 치료 실패의 가능성이 10퍼센트라고 적혀 있다. 비록 약효는 동일하지만 사람들은 대부분 치료 가능성이 90퍼센트라고 적힌 약을 선택한다. 그 이유는 다른 약보다 더 긍정적인 메시지를 전달하고 있기 때문이다.

Unit 56 Psychology III

Exercise p.170

Listening
Script 🎧 04-23

W Professor: The end of the school year is coming up, and I know some of you will be graduating then. I imagine that a few of you will have graduation parties for your friends and relatives. In the process of planning your graduation party, you'll most likely engage in two types of thinking. I'm referring to divergent thinking and convergent thinking.

In the initial stages of your planning, most of your thinking will be divergent thinking. For instance, you're going to brainstorm ideas to come up with the ideal graduation party. You might think about having the party at your home, at a restaurant, at a resort, or even on a tropical island. You'll consider what kinds of foods and drinks to provide from hamburgers and chips to steak and caviar. This is what divergent thinking is all about. When you practice it, you're being as creative as possible and are coming up with a wide variety of ideas. You're interested in exploring many different possibilities, not eliminating any of them.

After you've brainstormed and come up with your ideas, it's time for convergent thinking. This is a more focused type of thinking in which you're interested in selecting one thing from multiple choices. For instance, you might choose to have the party at your home since going to a tropical island is unfeasible for most people.

You'll probably not select steak and caviar as foods either since they're expensive and not to everyone's tastes. When you narrow down the list of choices to the location, the foods and drinks, the people you're going to invite, and the time and date of the event, you've done convergent thinking.

해석

W Professor: 학년 말이 다가오고 있는데, 여러분 중 몇몇은 그때 졸업을 하게 될 것으로 알고 있어요. 여러분 중 일부는 친구들과 친지들을 위해 졸업 파티를 열 것으로 생각합니다. 졸업 파티를 계획하는 과정에서 여러분들은 아마도 두 가지 유형의 사고를 하게 될 거예요. 확산적 사고와 수렴적 사고를 말씀드리는 것입니다.

계획 초기 단계에서 여러분의 대부분의 생각은 확산적 사고가 될 거예요. 예를 들어 브레인스토밍을 해서 이상적인 졸업 파티를 떠올릴 것입니다. 집에서 파티를 하거나, 식당, 리조트, 혹은 열대의 섬에서 파티를 하는 것에 대해서도 생각해 볼 수 있죠. 햄버거와 감자튀김에서 스테이크와 캐비아에 이르기까지 어떤 음식과 음료를 제공할 것인지 생각하게 될 거예요. 이는 모두 확산적 사고에 해당됩니다. 확산적 사고를 하면 최대한 창의적이 되고 매우 다양한 아이디어들을 떠올리게 되죠. 서로 다른 다수의 가능성들을, 없애는 것이 아니라, 살펴보는 것에 관심을 갖게 됩니다.

브레인스토밍을 해서 아이디어를 떠올린 이후에는 수렴적 사고를 할 때입니다. 이는 보다 집중된 형태의 사고로, 이 경우 다양한 선택 사항 중에서 하나를 선택하는데 관심을 갖게 되죠. 예를 들어 열대의 섬에 가는 것이 대부분의 사람들에 실행이 불가능한 일이라서 여러분들은 집에서 파티를 열기로 결정할 수도 있을 거예요. 스테이크와 캐비아는 비싸며 모든 사람들의 입맛에 맞는 것은 아니기 때문에 아마 이들도 선택하지 않을 것입니다. 장소, 음식 및 음료, 초대할 사람, 그리고 행사 일자와 시간에 대한 선택 범위를 좁혔다면 여러분은 수렴적 사고를 한 것입니다.

Organization

1 The topic of the lecture is two types of thinking and how people engage in them.
2 The first kind of thinking the professor discusses is divergent thinking.
3 The professor states that it is like brainstorming and that the idea is to think of as many ideas as possible when doing it.
4 The second kind of thinking the professor discusses is convergent thinking.
5 The professor says that this involves taking choices and then selecting only one of these options.

Comparing

Sample Response
Script 🎧 04-24

The topic of the lecture is two different types of thinking and how people engage in them. The professor mentions

that they are divergent and convergent thinking. She points out that some students in the class will be graduating soon and that they may have graduation parties to celebrate. She then notes that the students will engage in both kinds of thinking when they are in the process of planning their parties. First, they need to do divergent thinking. She says that this is brainstorming and that the objective is to come up with as many ideas as possible. She gives examples such as where to have the party and what kinds of foods and drinks to serve at it. After all of the divergent thinking is done, the students will do convergent thinking. This involves taking all of the choices proposed and then selecting one for each category.

해석

강의의 주제는 서로 다른 두 가지 유형의 사고와 사람들이 이를 어떻게 하는지에 관한 것이다. 교수는 그것이 확산적 사고와 수렴적 사고라고 말한다. 그녀는 수업을 듣는 몇몇 학생들이 곧 졸업을 할 것이며 이를 기념하기 위해 졸업 파티를 할 수도 있을 것이라고 말한다. 그런 다음 그녀는 학생들이 파티를 계획하는 과정에서 두 가지 종류의 사고를 모두 하게 될 것이라고 주장한다. 먼저 학생들은 확산적 사고를 해야 한다. 그녀는 이것이 브레인스토밍이며 그 목적은 최대한 많은 아이디어를 떠올리는 것이라고 말한다. 그녀는 어디에서 파티를 해야 하는지, 어떤 종류의 음식과 음료를 제공해야 하는지와 같은 예를 든다. 모든 확산적 사고가 끝나면 학생들은 수렴적 사고를 하게 될 것이다. 이는 제안된 모든 선택 사항을 살펴보고 각각의 카테고리에서 하나를 선택하는 것이다.

Unit 57 Biology IV

Exercise ·· p.172

Listening
Script 🎧 04-25

M Professor: Let me talk for a bit about bioluminescence. It's the ability of living organisms to create their own light through various chemical processes in their bodies. Surprisingly, there are a large number of animals that can do this. Numerous marine species are bioluminescent, and so are certain types of insects and fungi. Bioluminescent organisms use this ability for several different reasons. Let me tell you about a couple of them.

First, take a look at this picture . . . It's a firefly, which is also known as a lightning bug. I'm sure many of you have seen fireflies lighting up the sky in your yard during summer. Some of you may have even caught them sometimes. Interestingly, all firefly larvae can make light, but not all adult species can. Those that do create their own light in order to find a mate. Now, uh, look at this creature . . . It's a lanternfish, which lives deep beneath the surface of the ocean. It is also bioluminescent. It creates its own light for several reasons, but one of them is also to find a mate.

Okay, uh, let's move on to another reason that organisms make their own light. Look at this picture . . . This is an anglerfish. Notice the long protrusion above its head. Well, that makes light, which attracts various creatures since it lives in the darkness of the deep sea. You'll notice that the protrusion is near its mouth. So . . . it's should be apparent that the anglerfish uses light to attract prey in order to catch and consume it. Some species of octopus are also bioluminescent. They use their light to attract prey such as plankton in order to consume it.

해석

M Professor: 잠시 생물 발광에 대한 이야기를 해 보죠. 이는 신체 내 다양한 화학적인 과정을 통해 살아 있는 생물이 스스로 빛을 내는 능력입니다. 놀랍게도 상당수의 동물들이 그렇게 할 수가 있어요. 다수의 해양 생물들이 생물 발광을 하며 일부 곤충과 균류도 그렇습니다. 생물 발광을 하는 생물들은 서로 다른 몇 가지 이유로 이러한 능력을 사용해요. 그중 두 개에 대해 말씀을 드리죠.

먼저 이 사진을 보시면… 개똥벌레라고도 알려져 있는 반딧불이입니다. 분명 여러분 중 다수는 여름에 마당에서 반딧불이가 하늘을 밝게 비추는 모습을 본 적이 있을 거예요. 심지어 여러분 중 일부는 때때로 이들을 잡기도 했을 거예요. 흥미롭게도 모든 반딧불이 애벌레는 빛을 낼 수 있지만 모든 성체가 빛을 내는 것은 아닙니다. 빛을 내는 반딧불이는 짝을 찾기 위해 그러는 것이에요. 자, 어, 이 생물을 보세요… 바늘치인데, 이들은 해수면 아래 깊은 곳에서 서식합니다. 이것 역시 생물 발광을 하죠. 몇 가지 이유로 빛을 내지만 그중 하나는 역시 짝을 찾는 것입니다.

좋아요, 어, 생물이 스스로 빛을 내는 또 다른 이유로 넘어가 보죠. 이 사진을 보시면… 아귀입니다. 머리 위에 있는 기다란 돌출부에 주목해 주세요. 음, 이것이 빛을 내는데, 아귀가 깊고 깜깜한 바다에서 살기 때문에 이러한 빛이 다양한 생물들을 유인합니다. 돌출부가 입 근처에 있는 모습을 보시게 될 거예요. 따라서… 아귀가 먹이를 잡아먹으려고 빛을 이용해 먹이를 유인한다는 점은 명백합니다. 일부 종의 문어들 또한 생물 발광을 해요. 이들은 플랑크톤과 같은 먹이를 먹기 위해 빛을 이용해서 먹이를 유인합니다.

Organization

1 The lecture is about bioluminescence and why some organisms use it.
2 The first reason that the professor mentions is to find a mate.
3 The professor uses the firefly and the lanternfish as examples.
4 The second reason that the professor mentions is to catch prey.
5 The professor uses the anglerfish and the octopus as examples.

Comparing

Sample Response

Script 🎧 04-26

The lecture is about bioluminescence and why some animals use it. Bioluminescence is the ability of an organism to create its own light. According to the professor, some marine creatures, insects, and fungi are capable of using it. He states there are various reasons why organisms use bioluminescence and then describes two of them. The first reason that he gives is that some animals use bioluminescence to attract mates. He points out that fireflies use it this way, and so does the lanternfish, which is a fish that lives deep in the ocean. The second reason that he provides is to find prey. The professor first describes the anglerfish, which has a protrusion that hangs over its mouth. This protrusion can create light, which the anglerfish uses to attract prey. He then adds that some species of octopus can also use bioluminescence when they search for food.

해석

강의는 생물 발광과 동물들이 그것을 사용하는 이유에 관한 것이다. 생물 발광은 스스로 빛을 내는 생물의 능력이다. 교수에 의하면 일부 해양 생물, 곤충, 그리고 균류가 이를 이용할 수 있다. 그는 생물들이 생물 발광을 하는 다양한 이유가 존재한다고 말한 후 그중 두 가지를 설명한다. 그가 제시한 첫 번째 이유로 일부 동물들은 짝을 유인하기 위해 생물 발광을 한다. 그는 반딧불이가 그러한 방식으로 생물 발광을 이용하며 바다 깊은 곳에 사는 물고기인 바늘치 또한 마찬가지라고 말한다. 그가 제시한 두 번째 이유는 먹이를 찾기 위해서이다. 교수는 먼저 아귀를 설명하는데, 아귀의 입 위쪽에는 돌출부가 있다. 이 돌출부가 빛을 낼 수 있으며, 아귀는 이를 이용해 먹이를 유인한다. 그리고 나서 그는 몇몇 종의 문어들 또한 먹이를 찾을 때 생물 발광을 이용할 수 있다고 덧붙인다.

Unit 58 Marketing II

Exercise p.174

Listening

Script 🎧 04-27

M Professor: Marketing is vital to businesses which are trying to sell more goods and services. Many businesses attempt various promotions to attract more customers and to entice them to make more purchases. There are a lot of different types of promotions. Right now, I'd like to talk about a couple of the more successful ones.

Flash sales are one of these types of promotions. Basically, a business announces that it's having a sale for a short period of time. It could be one day or even an hour. In many cases, the discount is fairly large. Some flash sales might be just ten or twenty percent whereas others could offer discounts of up to ninety percent in some cases. Flash sales are effective at getting customers to make purchases immediately. They are used by online stores more than by physical stores since customers can simply click on buttons to make rapid purchases online.

Another type of promotion is a lifestyle discount. This type of discount is for a certain type of person, such as a student, a veteran, or a senior citizen. I'm sure you've all been to the movie theater and showed your student ID card to save a dollar or two off the cost of your ticket. Everyone has done that before, right? Well, that was a lifestyle discount. Many restaurants have early-bird specials that offer inexpensive dinner prices to senior citizens who come before traditional dinner times. These early-bird discounts may last from two to four in the afternoon. They're not only effective at increasing sales, but people who receive these discounts typically tell others about them, which can lead to increasing numbers of customers for businesses.

해석

M Professor: 마케팅은 더 많은 상품과 서비스를 판매하려는 업체들에게 필수적인 것이에요. 많은 업체들이 다양한 프로모션으로 더 많은 고객들을 유치하고 이들로 하여금 더 많이 구입하도록 만들기 위해 노력하죠. 각기 다른 다양한 유형의 프로모션이 존재합니다. 이제 두 가지의 보다 성공적인 프로모션에 대해 이야기를 하고 싶군요.

반짝 세일이 이러한 유형의 프로모션 중 하나예요. 기본적으로 업체는 짧은 시간 동안 세일을 실시할 것이라고 안내합니다. 하루가 될 수도 있고 불과 한 시간이 될 수도 있죠. 많은 경우 할인폭이 상당히 큽니다. 몇몇 반짝 세일에서는 10퍼센트나 20퍼센트의 할인이 이루어질 수도 있지만, 일부 경우 최대 90퍼센트까지의 할인이 적용될 수도 있어요. 반짝 세일은 고객들의 즉각적인 구매를 유도하는데 효과적입니다. 이는 오프라인보다 온라인 매장에서 더 많이 사용되는데, 그 이유는 고객들이 버튼을 클릭만 하면 온라인으로 빠르게 제품을 구입할 수 있기 때문이죠.

또 다른 유형의 프로모션은 라이프스타일 할인입니다. 이러한 유형의 할인은, 예컨대 학생, 제대 군인, 혹은 노인과 같이, 특정한 유형의 사람을 대상으로 하죠. 분명 여러분 모두 영화관에 갔을 때 학생증을 보여 주고 티켓 가격에서 1달러나 2달러를 아낀 적이 있을 것입니다. 모두들 전에 그랬던 적이 있었죠, 그렇죠? 음, 그것이 라이프스타일 할인이었습니다. 많은 식당들은 전형적인 저녁 시간 전에 오는 노인들에게 저렴한 식사 가격을 제시하는 얼리버드 스페셜 메뉴를 갖추고 있어요. 이러한 얼리버드 할인은 오후 2시에서 4시까지 계속될 수도 있습니다. 이는 매출 증대에 효과적일 뿐만 아니라 이러한 할인을 받은 사람들이 보통 그에 대한 이야기를 다른 사람에게 함으로써 해당 업체를 찾는 고객의 수가 증가할 수 있습니다.

Comparing

Sample Response
Script 🎧 04-28

The professor lectures to the students about two different types of successful marketing promotions. The first example that he tells the students about is flash sales. These are sales that businesses announce that last for a short time, such as an hour or maybe a few days. The discounts could be low, but they could also be as high as ninety percent. Flash sales are good at getting people to make immediate purchases, and they are commonly used by online stores since customers only have to click on buttons to make purchases. The second example the professor gives is lifestyle discounts. He provides one example of students using their school ID cards to get discounts at movie theaters. Another example he uses is senior citizens getting early-bird discounts at restaurants when they visit establishments in order to eat before typical dinner times.

해석

교수는 학생들에게 서로 다른 두 가지 유형의 성공적인 마케팅 프로모션에 대해 강의를 한다. 그가 말하는 첫 번째 예는 반짝 세일이다. 이는 업체들이 한 시간이나 며칠과 같은 짧은 기간 동안 지속된다고 안내하는 세일이다. 할인폭이 적을 수도 있지만 90퍼센트까지 높을 수도 있다. 반짝 세일은 사람들의 즉각적인 구매를 유도하는데 효과적이며, 고객들이 버튼을 클릭만하면 구매를 할 수 있다는 점에서 온라인 매장에서 흔히 사용된다. 교수가 제시하는 두 번째 예는 라이프스타일 할인이다. 그는 학생들이 영화관에서 학생증을 보여 주고 할인을 받는 사례를 든다. 그가 말하는 또 다른 예는 전형적인 저녁 시간 시간보다 일찍 식사를 하기 위해 업체를 방문하는 노인들에게 식당이 얼리버드 할인을 제공하는 것이다.

Exercise ·· p.176

Listening

Script 🎧 04-29

W Professor: If you have ever gone into a garden and dug in the ground, then you surely came across a worm or two. Most people don't really think about worms that much, but they actually should. The reason is that worms are of great importance to their ecosystems.

One benefit that worms provide is that they can help create healthy soil. They do this in a couple of ways. First of all, worms are almost constantly on the move and are also continually eating. This means that they excrete a lot. This excretion is known as worm cast. It's high in vital nutrients, which can be utilized both by plants growing in the soil and by various organisms living in the soil. Worms also help the soil when they move. Their movement through the ground loosens the soil and creates pockets of air. By aerating the soil, worms enable nutrients to reach the surface more easily, and they also help prevent both flooding and erosion.

Another way that worms benefit their ecosystems is by serving as food sources for other animals. Birds, of course, catch and consume worms, which are excellent sources of nutrients for birds. Other animals, including frogs and lizards, commonly eat worms that they catch. Hedgehogs are another animal that may dig in the soil in order to catch and eat worms. Worms can provide a large amount of sustenance for these animals and others. So they are an important part of many food chains wherever they live.

해석

W Professor: 정원에 가서 땅을 파 본 적이 있다면 분명 한두 마리의 지렁이를 보셨을 거예요. 대부분의 사람들이 사실 지렁이에 대해 많이 생각을 하지는 않는데, 실제로는 그래야 합니다. 그 이유는 지렁이가 생태계에서 매우 중요하기 때문이에요.

지렁이가 가져다 주는 한 가지 혜택은 이들이 건강한 토양을 만드는데 도움을 준다는 점입니다. 두 가지 방법으로 그렇게 하죠. 먼저 지렁이는 항상 몸을 움직이며 계속해서 먹이를 먹습니다. 이는 그들이 배설하는 양이 많다는 뜻이에요. 이러한 배설물은 분변토라고 알려져 있습니다. 분변토에는 중요한 영양분이 많이 들어 있으며, 이는 땅속 식물과 땅속에 사는 다양한 생물 모두에게 활용될 수 있습니다. 지렁이는 또한 움직임으로서 토양에 도움을 줍니다. 이들이 땅속에서 움직이면 토양이 엉성해져서 공기층이 만들어집니다. 토양에 공기가 통하게 함으로써 지렁이는 영양분이 보다 쉽게 지표면에 도달하도록 만들며, 또한 홍수 및 침식 예방에도 도움을 줍니다.

지렁이가 생태계에 혜택을 가져다 주는 또 다른 방식은 이들이 다른 동물들의 먹이가 된다는 것이에요. 물론 새들이 지렁이를 잡아먹는데, 이는 새들에게 훌륭한 영양분을 제공해 줍니다. 개구리와 도마뱀을 포함해서 다른 동물들도 보통 자

신이 잡은 지렁이를 잡아 먹어요. 고슴도치도 지렁이를 잡아먹기 위해 땅속을 파는 동물이고요. 지렁이는 이러한 동물 및 기타 동물들에게 다량의 양분을 제공해 줄 수 있습니다. 따라서 지렁이는 어디에 살더라도 여러 먹이 사슬에서 중요한 부분을 차지합니다.

Organization

1 The professor talks to the class about worms and two of the benefits that they provide their ecosystems.
2 The first benefit that the professor covers is that worms improve the quality of the soil.
3 She mentions that worm cast and aeration of the soil are two ways that worms provide these benefits.
4 The second benefit discussed by the professor is that worms serve as food sources for many animals.
5 Animals catch and consume worms, which provide them with sustenance.

Comparing

Sample Response

Script 🎧 04-30

The professor talks to the class about worms and two of the benefits they provide their ecosystems. The first benefit she mentions is that worms improve the quality of the soil that they live in. She talks about both worm cast and aeration. Worm cast is excreted by worms, and it's very high in nutrients. Plants and animals living underground can use worm cast to get the nutrients they need. In addition, as worms tunnel through the ground, they aerate the soil. This lets nutrients rise to the surface more easily and also helps reduce flooding and erosion. The second benefit is that worms themselves are sources of food for animals. She notes that birds, frogs, lizards, and hedgehogs all eat worms and that they get a lot of sustenance from doing that. In this way, worms are an important part of various food chains wherever they live.

해석

교수는 수업에서 지렁이와 지렁이가 생태계에 제공하는 두 가지 혜택에 대해 이야기한다. 그녀가 언급한 첫 번째 혜택은 지렁이가 자신이 사는 토양의 질을 향상시킨다는 것이다. 그녀는 분변토와 통기에 대해 이야기한다. 분변토는 지렁이의 배설물로서 많은 영양분을 지니고 있다. 땅속에 사는 식물과 동물들은 분변토를 이용해 필요한 양분을 얻을 수 있다. 또한 지렁이가 땅굴을 파기 때문에 토양에 공기가 통하게 된다. 이로써 양분들이 지표면에 보다 쉽게 도달하게 되고 홍수와 침식 또한 줄어들게 된다. 두 번째 혜택은 지렁이 스스로가 동물들의 먹이가 된다는 점이다. 그녀는 새, 개구리, 도마뱀, 그리고 고슴도치 모두 지렁이를 잡아먹으며, 그렇게 해서 많은 양분을 얻어간다고 말한다. 이러한 식으로 지렁이는 어디에 서식하든지 다양한 먹이 사슬에서 중요한 부분을 차지한다.

Exercise p.178

Listening

Script 🎧 04-31

M Professor: Humans are not the only animals capable of communicating. Many animals can do it. After all, dogs bark, cats meow, cows moo, and horses whinny. Of course, there are other methods of communication that some animals use. I'd like to talk about two of the largest animals on the Earth, the sperm whale and the elephant, and tell you how they communicate at times.

Sperm whales are enormous animals capable of growing to be around sixty feet long. They often use clicks to communicate under the water. These clicks can be incredibly loud with some reaching 230 decibels, which is loud enough to burst a person's eardrums. They typically use these clicks to communicate with other sperm whales. What's interesting is that these clicks are not universal for all sperm whales. By that, uh, I mean that scientists have noticed that groups, or pods, of sperm whales use different patterns of clicks. It's almost like they have different dialects depending upon which part of the ocean they live in.

What about elephants? Well, whereas sperm whales make sounds that are incredibly loud, elephants can make sounds that are so low that the human ear cannot hear them. Elephants, however, can sense them from at least 150 miles away . . . and possibly even farther. The vibrations elephants send out travel through the ground, and elephants detect them with their feet. Scientists know how elephants transmit vibrations, but they are still unsure about what kinds of messages the creatures are sending out. They believe some of these vibrations tell elephants to gather together and others indicate that predators are nearby and that their calves need to be protected.

해석

M Professor: 인간이 커뮤니케이션을 할 수 있는 유일한 동물은 아닙니다. 많은 동물들이 커뮤니케이션을 하죠. 어쨌거나 개들은 멍멍, 고양이는 야옹, 소는 음메, 그리고 말은 히이잉거리니까요. 물론 다른 커뮤니케이션 수단을 가지고 있는 동물들도 있습니다. 지구에서 가장 커다란 두 동물인 향유고래와 코끼리, 그리고 이들이 때때로 어떻게 커뮤니케이션을 하는지에 대해 말씀을 드리죠.

향유고래는 거대한 동물로 몸길이가 약 60피트까지 자랄 수 있습니다. 이들은 종종 수중에서 클릭음을 사용해 커뮤니케이션을 해요. 이러한 클릭음은 엄청나게 커서 약 230데시벨에 이를 수도 있는데, 이는 사람의 고막을 손상시킬 정도로 큰 소리입니다. 이들은 보통 이러한 클릭음으로 다른 향유고래들과 커뮤니케이션을 합니다. 흥미로운 점은 이러한 클릭음이 모든 향유고래들에게 통하는 것은 아니라는 점이에요. 이 말은, 어, 향유고래의 무리, 혹은 떼가 서로 다른 패

턴의 클릭음을 사용한다는 점을 과학자들이 알아냈습니다. 자신이 바다의 어느 지역에 사느냐에 따라 서로 다른 사투리를 쓴다는 것과 다를 것이 없죠.

코끼리는 어떨까요? 음, 향유고래가 엄청나게 큰 소리를 내는 반면 코끼리는 너무 낮아서 인간의 귀에는 들리지 않는 소리를 낼 수 있어요. 하지만 코끼리는 적어도 150마일 떨어진 곳에서도 그 소리를 들을 수 있는데… 아마도 훨씬 더 떨어져 있어도 가능할 거예요. 코끼리가 내는 진동음은 땅속을 통과하며 코끼리는 발로 이를 감지합니다. 과학자들은 코끼리가 어떻게 진동음을 발산하는지 알고 있지만 이 동물이 발산하는 메시지가 어떤 것인지는 아직 모르고 있어요. 그들의 생각으로 이러한 진동 중 일부는 코끼리들에게 모이라고 말을 하는 것이고, 일부는 포식자가 근처에 있으니 새끼들을 보호해야 한다는 점을 알려 주는 것입니다.

Organization

1 The professor talks to the students about types of communication used by sperm whales and elephants.
2 Sperm whales communicate by making extremely loud clicks.
3 Scientists have noticed that different pods of sperm whales use different click patterns.
4 Elephants use very low vibrations to communicate.
5 They think that elephants use this method of communication to tell others to gather and to warn about danger.

Comparing

Sample Response

Script 🎧 04-32

The professor talks to the students about types of communication used by sperm whales and elephants. The first method he discusses is the clicks used by sperm whales. These clicks are so loud that they could burst a person's eardrums. The clicks that sperm whales use are not all the same though. Different groups of sperm whales use different patterns of clicks. So scientists believe that these differences are something like dialects for sperm whales. Next, the professor tells the students about elephants and a method of communication that they employ. Elephants can send very low vibrations that humans cannot hear through the ground, and other elephants detect these vibrations with their feet. Scientists are not sure exactly why elephants send these vibrations out. However, some believe that elephants use these vibrations as gathering calls. They may also send vibrations to warn of danger, especially to elephant calves.

해석

교수는 학생들에게 향유고래와 코끼리가 사용하는 커뮤니케이션 방식에 대해 이야기한다. 그가 언급한 첫 번째 방법은 향유고래가 사용하는 클릭음이다. 이 클릭음은 너무나 커서 사람의 고막을 찢을 수도 있다. 하지만 향유고래가 사용하

는 클릭음이 다 똑같은 것은 아니다. 서로 다른 향유고래 무리들은 서로 다른 패턴의 클릭음을 사용한다. 따라서 과학자들은 향유고래들에게 이러한 차이는 사투리와 같은 것이라고 생각한다. 다음으로 교수는 학생들에게 코끼리 및 코끼리가 사용하는 커뮤니케이션 방식에 대해 이야기한다. 코끼리는 인간이 들을 수 없는 매우 낮은 진동음을 땅속으로 보낼 수 있으며, 다른 코끼리들이 이러한 진동을 발로 감지하게 된다. 과학자들은 코끼리들이 정확히 왜 이러한 진동음을 내보내는지 모르고 있다. 하지만 일부는 코끼리들이 이러한 진동음을 소집 목적으로 사용한다고 생각한다. 또한 진동을 이용하여, 특히 새끼 코끼리에 대한 위험을 경고할 수도 있다.

Actual Test

Actual Test 01

Task 1

Sample Response 🎧 05-03

I'm the kind of person who enjoys watching television. The first reason is that watching TV relaxes me. When I'm resting, I don't like to do anything but sit on the sofa and watch a good television program. Watching TV takes no effort at all, and it's also an effective way to get rid of stress at the same time. Another reason is that I actually learn a lot from watching TV. Simply put, I watch many educational programs and even the news at times. Nowadays, there are so many channels and shows that are specifically geared toward learning. Since I learn better through visual methods than with textual methods, it really makes sense for me to watch television as much as possible.

해석

나는 텔레비전 시청을 좋아하는 편이다. 첫 번째 이유는 TV를 보면 마음이 편해진다. 나는 휴식을 취할 때 소파에 앉아서 좋은 TV 프로그램을 시청하는 것 외에는 아무것도 하고 싶지 않다. TV 시청은 아무런 노력을 필요로 하지 않으며 동시에 스트레스를 해소할 수 있는 효과적인 방법이기도 하다. 또 다른 이유는 실제로 TV 시청을 통해 내가 많은 것을 배우기 때문이다. 간단히 말해서 나는 많은 교육적인 프로그램과 때때로 뉴스를 시청한다. 오늘날에는 학습에 특별히 초점을 맞춘 채널과 프로그램이 매우 많다. 나는 교재로 공부하는 것보다 시각적인 방법을 통해 공부할 때 더 많이 배우기 때문에 나로서는 최대한 TV 시청을 많이 하는 편이 바람직하다.

Task 2

Reading

해석

모든 학생들이 기숙사에서 생활하게 됩니다

내년 가을 새로운 학년의 시작과 함께 모든 학생은 대학 기숙사에서 생활해야 합니다. 모든 학생들이 교내에서 생활하도록 함으로써 대학측은 지난 5년 동안 매년 그렇게 해야 했던 것과 달리 학생들의 기숙사비를 인상하지 않아도 될 것입니다. 모든 학생들이 교내에서 더 많은 시간을 보내게 될 것이라는 점 때문에 학생들은 더 많은 과외 활동에 참여할 수 있을 것입니다. 대학 당국은 학생들이 대학에서 완벽한 경험을 쌓기 위해서는 강의실 밖에서 진행되는 활동에도 참여하는 것이 중요하다고 생각합니다.

Answers, Scripts, and Translations　71

W Student: Talk about annoying. I can't believe I'm going to have to live on campus next year. I can't stand the dorms.

M Student: Well, I rather like the idea. It would be nice not to have to pay for another increase in housing fees. I've had to pay more and more every semester, and it's not easy on my wallet. Frankly, it's becoming quite a burden.

W: Okay, I can understand that. But I was living at home. That's free. I shouldn't be punished by having to live in a dormitory.

M: Yeah, but there may be exceptions to the rule. You should look into that.

W: You're right.

M: However, I do like the idea of getting everyone to participate in extracurricular activities.

W: But you don't do any activities yourself.

M: That's true, but the reason is that nobody else has been doing them. Now, since it looks like more people will be getting involved, I'll probably sign up for a couple of clubs or maybe join an intramural sports team.

W: It sounds like you're going to be busy.

해석

W Student: 짜증나는 이야기네. 내년에 교내에서 생활해야 한다니 믿기지가 않아. 나는 기숙사가 정말 싫은데.

M Student: 음, 나는 아이디어가 마음에 드는걸. 기숙사비를 또 다시 더 내야 하지 않아도 되니까 좋은 것 같아. 학기마다 점점 더 많은 돈을 내야 해서 지갑 사정이 좋지 못하거든. 솔직히 말해서 상당한 부담이 되고 있지.

W: 그래, 그건 이해할 수 있어. 하지만 난 집에서 다녔어. 공짜였다고. 내가 기숙사에서 생활하라는 처벌을 받아서는 안 되잖아.

M: 그래, 하지만 규정에 대한 예외가 있을 수 있어. 알아 봐.

W: 네 말이 맞아.

M: 그런데 모든 학생들을 과외 활동에 참여시키려는 아이디어는 마음에 들어.

W: 하지만 너는 아무런 활동을 하지 않잖아.

M: 그건 그렇지만, 그 이유는 다른 누구도 그러는 것을 보지 못했기 때문이야. 이제 보다 많은 사람이 참여하게 될 것처럼 보이기 때문에 아마 나도 두어 개의 동아리에 가입하거나 어쩌면 교내 운동부에 들어갈 수도 있을 것 같아.

W: 곧 바빠질 것 같구나.

Sample Response 🎧 05-05

According to the announcement, all students at the school have to live in on-campus dormitories starting next semester. The man supports this idea for a couple of reasons. More than anything else, he supports it because this new regulation will keep the cost of housing from going up. The man is pleased that the price of housing will be staying the same next semester. He states that he's having trouble paying the fees, which have been increasing every semester. Another thing he mentions is that he's going to participate in some extracurricular activities next semester. While the man doesn't currently do any other activities, since there will be more students doing them, he's going to join a couple of clubs with all of the new people. He says that he might even try playing on an intramural sports team as well.

해석

공지에 따르면 교내의 모든 학생들이 다음 학기부터 교내 기숙사 생활을 해야 한다. 남자는 두 가지 이유로 이러한 아이디어를 지지한다. 무엇보다 남자가 이를 지지하는 이유는 이번 새 규정으로 기숙사비가 인상되는 일이 없을 것이기 때문이다. 남자는 다음 학기에 기숙사비가 동결될 것이라는 점에 만족해 한다. 그는 매 학기마다 기숙사비가 인상되어 기숙사비를 내기가 힘들다고 말한다. 그가 언급한 또 다른 이유는 자신이 다음 학기부터 과외 활동에 참여할 것이기 때문이다. 남자는 현재 아무런 활동도 하지 않지만 이제 더 많은 학생들이 활동을 할 것이기 때문에 그도 새로운 사람들과 함께 두어 개의 동아리 활동을 할 것이다. 그는 자신이 심지어 교내 운동부에서 활동할 수도 있다고 말한다.

Task 3
Reading

해석

표본 오차

데이터를 분석하는 어떤 조사나 과학적 연구에서도 연구자들은 자신이 연구하는 자료에 관한 진정한 무작위 표본을 얻기 위해 최대한 노력한다. 하지만 연구에는 항상 오류의 요소가 존재한다. 이것을 표본 오차라고 부른다. 표본 오차는 보통 퍼센트로 표시되며 연구의 오차 가능성을 보여 준다. 연구자들은 최대한 표본 오차의 수를 줄이려고 노력한다. 일반적으로 표본 오차가 낮을수록 수행되는 조사의 정확도는 높아진다.

Listening

Script 🎧 05-06

W Professor: When reading surveys or studies, it's integral that you pay attention to the sampling error. No studies are perfect, but scientists try making them as perfect as possible. And the sampling error records the chance of error inherent in the study.

For example, I read about a scientist trying to determine the average size of the fish in a local lake. What did he do? He went out in a boat with a net, caught some fish, and measured them to determine their average size. However, his net was too big, so he couldn't catch any really small fish. Therefore, his study wasn't truly accurate, was it? He had to provide a sampling error to let readers know how accurate, or, uh, inaccurate, his research was.

In addition, it's an election year, so there are lots of political surveys nowadays. Did you notice that survey where the presumed frontrunner for president is running neck and neck with the other candidates? However, every other survey has him listed at least twelve points ahead. What happened? Well, the survey was done during the afternoon. This means that since it was a phone survey calling people's homes, the survey got answers from a disproportionate number of housewives. It wasn't a truly random sample of the population. That's why it had a larger-than-usual sampling error.

해석

W Professor: 조사나 연구 결과를 볼 때 표본 오차에 관심을 기울이는 것이 매우 중요해요. 완벽한 연구란 없지만 과학자들은 연구를 최대한 완벽하게 만들기 위해 노력합니다. 그리고 표본 오차는 연구에 내재된 오차의 확률을 기록합니다.

예를 들어 저는 인근 호수에 서식하는 물고기의 평균 크기를 알아내려고 하는 한 과학자에 관한 글을 읽었습니다. 그가 어떻게 했을까요? 그물을 가지고 배에 타서, 고기를 잡고, 그리고 이들을 측정해 평균 크기를 알아냈습니다. 하지만 그 물이 너무 커서 정말 작은 물고기는 잡지 못했어요. 따라서 그의 연구는 는 진정으로 정확한 것이 아니었습니다, 그렇죠? 그는 조사 결과를 읽는 사람들에게 자신의 연구가 얼마나 정확한지, 혹은, 어, 부정확한지 알 수 있도록 표본 오차를 제시했어야 해요.

또한 올해 선거가 있기 때문에 요즘 정치 관련 조사가 많이 이루어지고 있습니다. 당선이 유력한 대통령 후보가 상대 후보들과 접전을 펼치고 있다는 조사를 보셨나요? 하지만 다른 모든 조사에서는 그가 적어도 15포인트 정도 앞서는 것으로 나왔습니다. 어떻게 된 일일까요? 음, 그 조사는 오후에 이루어졌어요. 다시 말해 가정집에 전화하는 전화 설문 조사였기 때문에 가정 주부가 답하는 경우가 압도적으로 많았습니다. 진정한 의미에서 인구에 대한 무작위 표본이 아니었죠. 바로 이러한 점 때문에 평균 이상의 표본 오차가 나타났던 것입니다.

Sample Response 🎧 05-07

The professor describes the results of two recent surveys. The first was done by a scientist measuring the sizes of fish in a lake. The scientist used a net to capture fish and then averaged their sizes. However, the professor points out that due to the net's big size, many tiny fish escaped. This relates to the reading in that the survey had a sampling error, which is the possibility of error in the study. Since he couldn't capture any small fish, the study wasn't truly random but had a sampling error. The professor's second example is of a recent political survey whose results were different from what other polls were showing. The professor explains that it was conducted during the day, so there wasn't a random sampling because a higher-than-normal number of housewives answered. This caused the sampling error to be high, making the survey difficult to trust.

해석

교수는 최근의 두 설문 조사의 결과에 대해 설명한다. 첫 번째는 한 과학자가 어떤 호수에서 물고기의 크기를 측정해서 얻은 것이다. 과학자는 그물로 물고기를 잡은 다음 평균적인 크기를 알아냈다. 하지만 교수는 그물이 커서 작은 물고기들이 많이 달아났다고 지적한다. 이는 그러한 조사에 연구의 오차 가능성을 나타내는 표본 오차가 존재했다는 점에서 읽기 지문과 관련이 있다. 작은 물고기는 잡

지 못했기 때문에 그 연구에서는 진정한 의미의 무작위 추출이 이루어지지 않아서 표본 오차가 나타났다. 교수의 두 번째 예는 다른 여론 조사와 결과가 달랐던 최근의 선거 여론 조사에 관한 것이다. 교수는 그 조사가 낮에 이루어져서 보다 많은 수의 가정 주부들이 설문에 응했기 때문에 무작위 추출이 이루어지지 않았다고 설명한다. 이로 인해 표본 오차가 높아짐으로써 그 조사는 신뢰하기 어렵게 되었다.

Task **4**

Listening

Script 🎧 05-08

M Professor: I'm sure you all don't have any children of your own, but I'd still like to point out some aspects of how children learn. While their minds are such wonderful things, young children can sometimes become quite mistaken when trying to learn new things. In fact, sometimes they generalize too much while other times they make things too specific.

First, let's talk about how they generalize. Children are always curious to know the names of different things. You've probably heard the question, "Mommy, what's that?" hundreds of times if you've spent any time at all around children. And their parents are often quick to answer. But here's a problem. Perhaps a child sees a horse and asks what it is. The parent responds that it's a horse. The child remembers that, but the next time he sees another animal walking on all fours, he calls that animal a horse. What's happened? The child has generalized too much and assumed that any animal with four legs is a horse.

Of course, children can sometimes make words too specific. I have a personal example concerning that. I gave my daughter a doll for her third birthday. She loved that doll a lot and took it with her everywhere. One day, one of her friends visited the house and brought a doll of her own. My daughter asked what it was and was told that it was a doll. She refused to believe it since she thought that the only doll was her own. In fact, it took her months before she would actually acknowledge that anyone besides her had a doll. Talk about being too specific.

해석

M Professor: 여러분 중 자녀가 있는 분은 없을 것으로 확신하지만 아이들이 배우는 방식에 대한 몇 가지 측면을 논의하고자 해요. 머리는 정말 비상하나 어린 아이들은 새로운 것을 배우고자 할 때 가끔씩 실수를 저지를 수 있어요. 실제로 아이들은 때때로 너무 일반화하는 경우도 있고 너무 구체화하는 경우도 있습니다.

우선 아이들이 어떻게 일반화하는지 논의해 보죠. 아이들은 항상 다양한 것들의 이름을 알고 싶어 합니다. 아마도 아이와 함께 시간을 보낸 적이 있으신 분은 "엄마, 저건 뭐야?"라는 질문을 수백 번 들어보셨을 거예요. 그러면 종종 부모가 재빨리 대답해 줍니다. 그런데 문제는 다음과 같아요. 아이가 말 한 마리를 보고 그것이 무엇인지 묻습니다. 부모는 말이라고 대답해 주죠. 아이는 그것을 기억하

고 다음에 네 발로 걷는 동물을 보면 그 동물을 말이라고 부릅니다. 어떻게 된 걸까요? 아이는 지나치게 일반화를 한 나머지 네 발을 가진 동물을 모두 말이라고 생각했던 것이에요.

물론 아이들이 때때로 지나치게 단어를 구체화시킬 수도 있습니다. 저는 그와 관련해서 개인적 경험을 한 적이 있어요. 저는 제 딸의 세 번째 생일에 선물로 인형을 사 주었어요. 제 딸은 인형을 좋아해서 항상 가지고 다녔죠. 하루는 딸의 친구 한 명이 저희 집에 놀러 오면서 자기 인형을 가지고 왔어요. 제 딸은 그것이 무엇인지 물었고 그것은 인형이라는 대답을 들었죠. 딸은 자기가 가진 인형만 인형이라고 생각했기 때문에 그 말을 믿으려고 하지 않았어요. 실제로 자신 이외의 사람도 인형을 가지고 있다는 점을 인정하게 되기까지 여러 달이 걸렸습니다. 너무 구체화시킨다는 것이 바로 이런 것이죠.

Sample Response 🎧 05-09

The professor's lecture mentions that children often make mistakes when they're learning. First of all, he covers children's tendencies to generalize too much. The example that he gives is that a child sees a horse and asks what it is. When told that it's a horse, the child then assumes that all four-legged animals are horses. So the next time it sees, for example, a dog, it might call the dog a horse simply because it has four legs. Next, the professor mentions the children sometimes become too specific. He relates a story about his daughter getting a doll for her birthday. In her mind, her present was the only doll in the world. Even when she saw her friend's doll, she refused to call it that for the longest time. What happened is that she had thought the word had a very specific, rather than broad, meaning.

해석

교수는 강의에서 아이들이 학습을 할 때 종종 실수를 한다고 말한다. 첫째, 그는 아이들이 지나치게 일반화하는 경향이 있다고 말한다. 그가 든 예에서는 한 아이가 말을 보고 무엇인지 묻는다. 말이라는 답을 듣고서 아이는 네 발 달린 동물들을 모두 말이라고 생각한다. 그래서 예컨대 다음 번에 개를 볼 때도 아이는 발이 네 개라는 이유로 개를 말이라고 부를 수 있다. 다음으로, 교수는 아이들이 때때로 지나치게 구체화한다고 말한다. 그는 자신의 딸에게 생일 선물로 인형을 사 준 것에 대한 이야기를 들려 준다. 딸은 자기가 받은 선물이 세상에서 하나뿐인 인형이라고 생각했다. 심지어 친구의 인형을 보았을 때조차 오랫동안 그것을 인형이라고 부르지 않으려 했다. 그녀는 인형이라는 단어가 넓은 의미가 아니라 매우 구체적인 의미를 가지고 있다고 생각했던 것이다.

Actual Test 02

p.190

Task 1

Sample Response 🎧 05-12

In my opinion, I agree that it's important to have a friend who has interests different than my own. For one, thanks to that friend, I could become interested in various things

---

that I might have never known about. For example, last year, one of my friends got me into skiing, which is something I had never considered until I met her. This has helped me develop my other interests. Additionally, sometimes I just like to hear about something that I have no knowledge in. In fact, when my friends start talking about their interests that are different than mine, I usually just listen and try to learn from them. This helps me get both educated and entertained while I'm having a conversation.

해석

나는 나와 취미가 다른 친구를 사귀는 것이 중요하다는 의견에 찬성한다. 우선 그 친구 덕분에 나는 내가 전혀 모를 수도 있었던 여러 가지 것들에 관심을 가질 수 있을 것이다. 예를 들어 작년에 내 친구 중 한 명이 스키에 빠졌는데, 스키는 내가 그 친구를 만나기 전까지 전혀 생각도 못했던 것이었다. 이 일을 계기로 나는 여러 가지에 관심을 갖게 되었다. 또한 나는 때때로 내가 전혀 모르는 것에 대해 이야기를 듣는 것을 좋아한다. 실제로 내 친구들이 나와 다른 관심사에 대해 이야기를 시작하면 나는 보통 잘 듣고 그들로부터 배우려고 노력한다. 이로써 나는 대화를 하면서 지식과 즐거움 모두를 얻을 수 있다.

Task 2

Reading

해석

교내에서의 자전거 통행 금지

최근 교내에서 자동차 및 보행자와 관련한 자전거 사고가 여러 건 있었습니다. 몇 건의 사고는 너무 심각한 사고여서 사고를 당한 사람이 입원을 해야만 했습니다. 따라서 학교 당국은 교내에서 모든 자전거의 통행을 금지하기로 결정했습니다. 교내에서 자전거를 타는 대부분의 사람들의 난폭한 행동이 이러한 사고의 유일한 이유이기 때문에, 이들이 다른 사람들을 존중하는 법을 알게 되기까지, 교내에서의 자전거 통행이 금지됩니다. 하지만 학교측은 교내 운행 버스의 수를 늘릴 예정입니다. 버스가 많아지면 학생들은 아무런 문제없이 제때에 수업을 들을 수 있을 것입니다.

Listening

Script 🎧 05-13

M Student: I totally disagree with the school's ban on bicycles.

W Student: Well, I see their point. I know one of the pedestrians who got run over. She still hasn't recovered.

M: Yeah, but there are many responsible bicyclists out there. The number of reckless riders is really small. The school shouldn't punish most of the riders, like me, who obey safety rules and never come close to getting into accidents.

W: Perhaps you bicyclists should do a better job of policing your own. You know . . . get the ones who don't care about safety to be more considerate of others.

M: Yeah, that's an idea.

W: Anyway, the school's going to have more buses, so you'll still get to class on time.

M: I don't think so. I took a look at the new bus schedule.

W: And?

M: The buses are still only going to run once or twice an hour. This campus is really huge. There's no way everyone is going to be able to pile into them.

W: Hmm.

M: I foresee a lot of students being late to class in the future.

해석

M Student: 난 학교측의 자전거 통행 금지 결정에 결코 동의할 수 없어.

W Student: 음, 난 이해가 가. 나는 걷다가 자전거 사고를 당한 사람을 한 명 알고 있거든. 아직도 회복이 안 됐어.

M: 그래, 하지만 책임감을 갖고 자전거를 타는 사람도 많아. 난폭하게 자전거를 타는 사람은 사실 소수이지. 나처럼 안전 규칙을 잘 지키고 사고는 절대 일으킬 것 같지 않은 대부분의 자전거 이용자들을 학교측이 처벌해서는 안 돼.

W: 어쩌면 너처럼 자전거를 타는 사람들이 자체적으로 규정을 잘 따르도록 만들 수도 있겠군. 알겠지만… 안전 조치에 신경도 안 쓰는 사람들이 타인을 보다 배려하도록 만든다든지.

M: 그래, 좋은 생각이야.

W: 어쨌든, 학교측이 버스를 늘리면 수업에는 제때에 가게 될 거야.

M: 나는 그렇게 생각하지 않아. 새로운 버스 시간표를 봤거든.

W: 그랬더니?

M: 여전히 한 시간에 한두 번 정도 배차가 되고 있더라고. 우리 학교 캠퍼스는 정말 넓어. 결코 모든 학생들이 버스에 탈 수는 없을 거야.

W: 흠.

M: 앞으로 많은 학생들이 지각하는 장면을 보게 될 것 같아.

Sample Response 🎧 05-14

According to the announcement, because of the large number of recent accidents on campus involving bicycles, they are now banned from being ridden at the school. The man opposes the school's decision to ban bicycles. The first reason for this is that, according to him, there are only a small number of cyclists who ride their bikes recklessly and endanger other people. The man feels it's wrong for the school to punish the law-abiding cyclists because just a few cyclists are behaving dangerously and hurting people. Furthermore, the man doesn't believe that the increased number of buses will be enough to satisfy everyone. He points out that they will not run that often and that not everyone will be able to take them. This, he declares, will cause lots of students to be late to their classes once the policy is instituted.

해석

공지에 따르면 최근 교내에서 발생한 많은 자전거 관련 사고 때문에 교내에서의 자전거 통행이 금지되었다. 남자는 자전거 통행을 금지하는 학교 결정에 반대한다. 첫 번째 이유는, 그에 따르면, 난폭하게 자전거를 타서 다른 사람을 위험에 빠뜨리는 자전거 이용자는 소수에 불과하기 때문이다. 남자는 자전거를 위험하게 타고 다른 사람을 다치게 만드는 사람은 소수이기 때문에 학교측이 규정을 잘 따르는 자전거 이용자들까지 처벌하는 것은 잘못된 일이라고 생각한다. 뿐만 아니라 남자는 버스의 수를 늘린다고 해서 모든 학생들이 만족해 할 것이라고 생각하지 않는다. 그는 버스들이 그렇게 자주 운행되는 것은 아니며 모든 학생들이 버스를 이용하지는 못할 것이라는 점을 지적한다. 그의 주장에 따르면 해당 정책을 시행할 경우 그로 인해 많은 학생들이 지각하게 될 것이다.

Task 3

Reading

해석

동물의 가축화 가능성

지구에는 수천 종의 동물이 존재하지만 사육이 가능한 동물은 소수에 불과하다. 동물을 사육하는데 있어서 한 가지 중요한 요소는 그 종의 가축화 가능성이다. 이는 어떤 동물을 얼마나 용이하게 사육할 수 있는지를 가리킨다. 동물의 성질은 가축화 가능성을 결정하는데 중요하다. 성질이 온순한 동물은 인간에게 공격적이거나 적대적인 동물보다 훨씬 더 길들이기 쉽다. 또 다른 요소는 그 동물의 사회적 위계의 변경 가능성이다. 다시 말해서 동물이 인간을 자신의 새로운 우두머리로 인정해야 하는데, 그렇게 되면 사육하기가 용이해진다.

Listening

Script 🎧 05-15

M Professor: Why is it that some animals are more easily domesticated than others? For example, why have cows become domesticated but not, uh, lions, for example? Well, there are numerous factors involved in domesticating animals, but I want to focus on a couple of the most important right now.

One of the most crucial aspects involved is the animal's disposition. By that, I mean, how pleasant is the animal? Is it aggressive or not? Well, let me compare dogs and wolves. We've domesticated the former but not the latter. Dogs, in general, have well earned their moniker as man's best friend. Most dogs . . . not all, but most . . . have pleasant dispositions and enjoy being around humans. Wolves, on the other hand, tend to be aggressive and may often attack, and even kill, humans.

Another point to consider is how well the animal can adapt to accepting a human as its leader. Dogs are typically very willing to recognize that humans are their, uh, pack leaders, for lack of a better expression. Dogs willingly submit to human leadership. In contrast are wolves. Most wolves will not submit, which makes it virtually impossible for them to be domesticated. Some individual wolves have been domesticated, but as a species, it's all but impossible.

M Professor: 왜 어떤 동물은 다른 동물에 비해 길들이기가 쉬울까요? 예를 들어 소는 사육하기가 쉽지만, 어, 가령 사자는 그렇지 못할까요? 음, 동물의 사육과 관련된 여러 가지 요소가 존재하지만 지금은 가장 중요한 두 가지 요소에 초점을 맞추도록 하겠습니다.

가장 중요한 측면 중 하나는 동물의 성질이에요. 무슨 말인가 하면 그 동물이 얼마나 온순한지, 공격적인지 혹은 그렇지 않은지를 말씀드리는 거예요. 음, 개와 늑대를 비교해 보죠. 전자는 사육을 하지만 후자는 그렇지 않습니다. 일반적으로 개는 인간의 가장 좋은 친구라는 별명을 가지고 있어요. 대부분의 개들은… 전부는 아니지만 대부분은… 성질이 온순하고 인간 주위에 있는 것을 좋아합니다. 반면에 늑대는 공격적인 성향을 지니며 종종 인간을 공격해서 죽일 수도 있죠.

고려해야 할 또 다른 점은 그 동물이 인간을 자신의 우두머리로 얼마나 잘 받아들일 수 있는지입니다. 전형적으로 개들은 인간을, 어, 더 나은 표현이 없으니 이 표현을 쓰겠습니다만, 자신의 무리의 지도자로 기꺼이 받아들이려 해요. 기꺼이 인간 지도자에게 복종을 하죠. 늑대는 그 반대입니다. 대부분의 늑대들은 복종을 하지 않으며 사실상 이들을 사육하는 일은 불가능해요. 일부 늑대들은 사육이 되기도 했지만 종 전체로 볼 때 사육은 거의 불가능합니다.

During his lecture, the professor says some animals are easier to domesticate than others. He compares dogs and wolves to illustrate his point. According to the professor, the animal's disposition is crucial to domesticating it. He notes that dogs really are man's best friend while stating that wolves are both aggressive and hostile toward humans. The professor next points out that the animals must be willing to accept humans as their leaders before being domesticated. He notes that dogs will do this but wolves, in general, won't. These two points are related to the reading in that they describe the tameability of animals. Tameability refers to the factors involved relating to humans' abilities to domesticate animals. Ones with pleasant attitudes and those willing to let humans be their leaders may be domesticated. These are dogs. Wolves, however, don't possess these characteristics, so it's almost impossible to domesticate them.

강의에서 교수는 일부 동물이 다른 동물에 비해 사육하기가 더 쉽다고 말한다. 그는 자신의 논점을 설명하기 위해 개와 늑대를 비교한다. 교수에 따르면 동물의 성질은 사육에 있어서 매우 중요하다. 그는 개가 실제로 인간의 가장 좋은 친구라고 말하지만 늑대는 인간에게 공격적이고 적대적이라고 말한다. 다음으로 교수는 동물이 사육되기 위해서는 인간을 자신의 무리의 우두머리로 받아들여야 한다고 주장한다. 개들은 그렇게 하지만 일반적으로 늑대는 그렇지 않다고 말한다. 이 두 가지 논점은 동물의 가축화 가능성을 설명한다는 점에서 읽기 지문과 관련이 있다. 가축화 가능성은 동물을 사육할 수 있는 인간의 능력과 관련된 요소를 가리킨다. 성질이 온순한 동물과 인간을 기꺼이 자신의 우두머리로 인정하는 동물은 사육이 가능할 수 있다. 개가 여기에 해당된다. 하지만 늑대는 이런 특성들을 가지고 있지 않기 때문에 사육이 거의 불가능하다.

Task 4

Listening

Script 🎧 05-17

W Professor: That concludes my discussion on medieval painting. Let's move to the Renaissance. There were many differences between medieval and Renaissance paintings, but the biggest was in the use of perspective. In medieval paintings, the pictures were mostly two dimensional. They never used perspective. But Renaissance artists added perspective, giving their works a three-dimensional aspect. So how did they manage to add perspective to their art?

Art historians have two theories. The first is that they began using tools when creating artwork. Some artists would use mirrors when they painted. In some cases, they would reflect, say, a basket of fruit, in the mirror, and would then actually trace the lines around the reflection of the mirror. This is how many of them learned to draw perspective. Once they traced the lines, they could then transfer their work to the canvas, where they were able to give their art a more three-dimensional appearance.

Another school of thought centers on the development of oil paintings. It was only in the fifteenth century that oil paint was invented. One advantage it had over other paints was that it dried very slowly. Not only that, but oil paints are also translucent, so light is able to shine through the paint. These two factors combined to enable artists to add perspective to their paintings. How? Well, slow-drying, translucent paints gave artists enough time to create paintings with more depth. They could paint over the first coat by using different colors and shades, thereby producing works that weren't linear but were instead three-dimensional in appearance. In other words, they were able to build perspective into their paintings thanks to the paint itself.

W Professor: 중세 회화에 관한 논의는 그것으로 마무리할 게요. 르네상스로 넘어가 봅시다. 중세 회화와 르네상스 회화 간에는 많은 차이점이 존재하지만 가장 큰 차이점은 원근법의 사용에 있어요. 중세 회화 작품들은 대부분 이차원적이었습니다. 결코 원근법을 사용하지 않았죠. 하지만 르네상스 화가들은 원근법을 도입함으로써 작품을 3차원적으로 보이게 만들었어요. 그러면 어떻게 해서 작품에 원근감을 주게 되었을까요?

미술사학자들은 두 가지 이론을 제시합니다. 첫 번째는 그림을 그릴 때 도구를 사용하기 시작했다는 것이에요. 몇몇 화가들은 그림을 그릴 때 거울을 사용했을 것입니다. 어떤 경우, 가령, 과일 바구니를 거울에 비치게 해서 실제로 거울에 비친 선을 따라 그림을 그렸을 거예요. 이런 식으로 많은 화가들이 원근감을 나타내는 법을 알게 되었습니다. 선을 딴 후에는 그림을 캔버스에 옮겨 그렸는데, 이로써 작품이 보다 3차원적인 장면을 나타내게 되었어요.

또 다른 학파는 유화의 발달에 초점을 맞춥니다. 유화는 15세기에 발명되었어요. 유화의 한 가지 장점은 건조 속도가 매우 느리다는 점이었습니다. 뿐만 아니라 유화는 반투명해서 빛이 물감을 통과해 비칠 수가 있어요. 이 두 가지 요소가 합쳐짐으로써 화가들은 그림에 원근감을 더할 수 있었습니다. 어떻게요? 음, 마르는 시간이 느리고 반투명한 물감 때문에 화가들에게 보다 깊이 있는 그림을 그릴 수 있는 충분한 시간이 주어졌어요. 다른 색과 음영을 사용해 그린 첫 번째 물감 위에 다시 색을 칠함으로써 선형적인 그림이 아니라 3차원적인 그림을 그릴 수가 있었죠. 다시 말해서 바로 물감 때문에 그림에 원근감을 부여할 수가 있었습니다.

Sample Response 🎧 05-18

The professor looks into the two theories that art historians have as to how Renaissance artists were able to add perspective to their paintings while medieval artists did not. The first theory is that artists began using tools like mirrors to help them create their works. The professor points out that some artists would reflect an image in a mirror and then draw on the mirror itself to create perspective. They could then transfer their drawings to the canvas and subsequently paint over them. The second theory is that the invention of oil paints permitted perspective to be used. Due to the nature of oil paint, which dries slowly, artists had more time to work on their paintings. Before the paint dried, they could add second coats that were of different shades or colors, which then gave their paintings depth, thereby adding perspective to the paintings.

해석

교수는 어떻게 르네상스 화가들이 그림에서 원근감을 나타낼 수 있었는지와 중세 화가들은 그러지 못했는지에 관한 미술사학자들의 두 가지 이론을 살펴본다. 첫 번째 이론은 화가들이 거울과 같은 도구를 사용해 그림을 그렸다는 것이다. 교수는 일부 화가들이 어떤 이미지를 거울에 비치게 한 후 거울 위에 선을 그려 원근감을 나타냈다고 주장한다. 그런 다음에는 그림을 캔버스로 옮겨 그 위에 색칠을 할 수 있었다. 두 번째 이론은 유화의 발명으로 인해 원근법이 사용될 수 있었다는 것이다. 천천히 건조되는 유화의 특성 때문에 화가들이 그림을 완성하는 데 필요한 시간이 더 많아졌다. 물감이 마르기 전에 색조나 색깔이 다른 물감을 그 위에 한 번 더 칠함으로써 그림에 깊이가 생겼고 이로써 그림에 원근감이 더해질 수 있었다.

MEMO

MEMO

How to
Master Skills for the

Second Edition

TOEFL® iBT

SPEAKING Advanced